Library Management in 21st Century: Issues and Challenges

LIBRARY MANAGEMENT IN 21ST CENTURY

Issues and Challenges

Editors

Lallaisangzuali
Sanjeev

Ess Ess Publications
New Delhi

LIBRARY MANAGEMENT IN 21ST CENTURY
Issues and Challenges

ISBN: 978-81-7000-799-9

First Published 2016

Published by:
Ess Ess Publications
4831/24, Ansari Road,
Darya Ganj,
New Delhi-110 002.
INDIA
Phones: 23260807, 41563444
Fax: 41563334
E-mail: info@essessreference.com
www.essessreference.com

Cover Design by *Patch Creative Unit*

Printed and bound in India at Salasar Imaging Systems.

Contents

List of Contributors

Dr. Aswathy S
Sr. Scientific Assistant,
Library & Documentation Division
Liquid Propulsion Systems Centre,
Indian Space Research Organisation

Bharvey, H.C.
Assistant Librarian, K.N.K College of Horticulture
Mandsaur (M.P), India

Dr. Choudhury, Tuhina (Deb Roy)
Professional Assistant, Central Library
Assam University, Silchar-11

Das, Santanu
Librarian, Matigara Harasundar High School (H.S)
Matigara, Siliguri, West Bengal-734010

Dr. Devendra Kumar
Assistant Professor, Dept. of Library
Govt. P.G. College, Sector-39
Noida, U.P

Dr. Devi Thiyam Satyabati
Sr.Assistant Librarian (Cataloguing Head)
University of Swaziland, Swazialnd, Southern Africa

Dutta, Arpita
Library Assistant, Library,
Directorate of Distance Education
University of North Bengal, Raja Rammohunpur
Darjeeling, West Bengal- 734013

Dutta, Subhajit
Deputy Librarian, Assam Downtown University
Guwahati, Assam

Dr. Jena, Sudhir Kumar
Librarian, IIM Shillong

Dr. Jeyshankar, R.
Assistant Professor, Dept. of Lib. & Inf. Science
Alagappa university, Karaikudi- 630003

Kaur, Amandeep
Assistant Librarian, DAV University
Jalandhar, Punjab

Dr. Lallaisangzuali
Assistant Librarian
Central Library, Mizoram University
Aizawl, Mizoram- 796004

Mhonbemo Ngullie
Assistant Librarian,
Medzhiphema Campus,
Nagaland University,
Dimapur, Nagaland- 797106.

Naheem, K.T.
Professional Assistant, Central Library
Pondicherry University, Puducherry- 605014

Pal, Manoj Kumar
Professional Assistant, Central Library
Mizoram University, Aizawl- 796004

Reena Rai
Research Scholar, Dept of Lib. & Inf. Science
Kurukshetra University, Kurukshetra

Sahoo, Dipti Ranjan
IRC, Associate at TCS
Bhubaneswar

Sharma, Dhara
Junior Project Officer, Central Library
IIT Kharagpur

Dr. Sharma, Ramnivas
I/C Central Library,
Rajmata Vijayaraje Scindia Krishi Vishwa Vidyalaya
Gwalior (M.P), India

Shrivastava, Dheeraj
Technical Assistant, Rajmata Vijayaraje Scindia Krishi Vishwa Vidyalaya
Gwalior (M.P), India

Dr. Singh, A.P.
Associate Professor, Dept. of Lib. & Inf. Science
Banaras Hindu University, Varanasi – 221005

Dr. Singh, Gurdev
Librarian, Sri Guru Gobind Singh College of
Commerce Pitampura, University of Delhi. Delhi- 35

Singh, Punit Kumar
Research Scholar, Dept. of Lib. & Inf. Science
Banaras Hindu University, Varanasi – 221005

Singh, Yeshpal
Research Scholar, Dept. of Lib. & Inf. Science
Kurukshetra University, Kurukshetra

Soren, Saikat
Librarian, Ramnagar College
Depal, Purba Medinipur, West Bengal- 721453

Sujitha, I. Maria
Chief Librarian, Rajas Dental College & Hospital
Thirurajapuram, Kavalkinaru Jn.,
Thirunelveli Dist. – 627105

1
Metric Studies Through Ages: A Transition from Bibliometrics to Altmetrics

Aswathy S

ABSTRACT

The ICT propagation has made the concept of alternative metrics a reality and the need of the hour. The scholarly communication methods have shifted from print media to electronic media and various sharing and social networking sites. The evaluation of this scholarly traffic will provide the actual usage and publicity of the sources and contents of scholarly community. Various tools like altmetrics, plumX etc are provided by different service provides such as altmetrics.org, plum analytics, readermeter, scholarometer, PLoS article level metrics (ALMs) etc. It is evident from these facts that a paradigm shift has occurred in the traditional bibliometrics and other quality measures by the advent of these sites and services.

Keywords : Bibliometrics; Scientometrics; Impact Factor; Eigen Factor; Altmetrics

1. INTRODUCTION

Along with the proliferation of Information Communication Technology and increase in usage of social networking for sharing and scholarly communication, web is getting more and more personal.

The cloud technology made the storage and usage of sources and services even easier. At this juncture, it is obligatory to know if these scholarly communications is tapped, then Web Metrics Indicate Research Impact. The though "Research Dissemination is Research Impact - is now widely acceptable and these disseminations creates indicators of impact i.e. citations by measuring the following pointers like web usage, star ratings, social bookmarking, community rating, media/blog coverage and commenting activity to mention a few. Science aims to produce and communicate scientific knowledge. For science to be advanced it is not enough that fruitful ideas be originated or new experiments developed or new problems formulated or new methods instituted, but the innovations must be effectively communicated to others – something given to the common fund of knowledge. It can be said that science is a socially shared and socially validated body of knowledge. For the development of Science, only work that is effectively perceived and utilized by other scientists, then and there, matters. (Metron, 1968).

At present, techniques for measuring scholarly impact which is conventionally known as bibliometrics, are well known for measuring the scholarliness, particularly as tenure-track scholars reach beyond previously set boundaries of discipline, media, audience, and format. When Eugene Garfield the founder of ISI came up with the concept of journal impact factor in 1955, it never thought "that it would one day become the subject of widespread controversy" (Garfield, 2012). Dilemma about the scope of scholarly impact abound, even as the force to gauge such impact continues unabated or increases commencing the development of more nuanced academic specialties to the influence of blogs and social media. Along with the faculty at universities all over the world, many librarians also have stride forward to help in negotiating the landscape of both traditional impact metrics, such as h-index and journal impact factor, and emerging Web-based alternatives, sometimes called altmetrics, cybermetrics, or webometrics against the struggle to find new ways of providing evidence and substantiation of the changing scholarly value. In the new art and science of impact measurement, librarians are in a key position to take the lead in bolstering researchers' knowledge of current trends and concerns even though there is a tremendous augmentation in online venues for scholarly communication and the number of tools available for tracking online influence growing steadily.

In reality, according to Arbesman (2012), for a long period, the measurement of scientific contribution has centered on the publication, through the number of articles, the citations those articles have by other articles, or even other far more complicated metrics and most scientists are still measured by a derivative of the research article, the basic technology of scientific publishing that is well over 300 years old. The emergence of new measuring techniques and technologies can further facilitate the research process which also facilitates access to scientific results through information sharing and discussion. These circumstances solicit new management systems to facilitate scientific knowledge more accessible and useable and also demands, new measures to evaluate the reach of scientific information among professionals, specialists and also to the general public. This new science and new method of communication paved the way for new online technologies and services based on social media for quality measuring and metric concepts and CiteULike, Connotea, Mendeley, Zotero are a few among them offering the another transparent and comprehensive information on the usage and reach of scientific information (Haustein, 2011; Eysenbach, 2011; Bogers, 2008 and Li, 2011). External online tools like Wikipedia referencing of articles which is an indicator of future citations, also represent a new form of post-publication review (Evans P, 2011), a result of the filtering done by specialist authors. All these changes are stimulating the scientific community to reassess its means of communication (Fausto, 2012).

2. EARLIER RESOURCES FOR METRIC EVALUATION

Before the emergence of social networking tools, there were a few metric evaluation tools based on web and online databases. Among them a few are mentioned below including free and subscription based services.

2.1. Google Scholar Citations

Google Scholar is the scholarly search tool of the world's largest and most powerful search engine, Google. Google Scholar was developed by Anurag Acharya, an Indian-born computer scientist. It is an incredible tool allowing researchers to locate a wide array of scholarly literature on the Web, including scholarly journals, abstracts, peer reviewed articles, theses, dissertations, books, preprints, PowerPoint presentations and technical reports from universities, academic institutions, professional societies, research groups, and preprint repositories around the world. As such, it has become a gateway to accessing scholarly information on the Web. Every day more scholarly information is available online and we continue to discover new reasons to need access to this information. If Google Scholar makes more open access scholarly material accessible, the price of academic journals and databases may decrease or stabilize as they strive to compete. Thus the greater the accessibility of scholarly material, the greater is the value for researchers (Alireza Noruzi, 2005).

2.2. Web of Knowledge

Thomson Reuters Web of Knowledge SM (formerly ISI Web of Knowledge) is today's premier research platform, helping you quickly find, analyze, and share information in the sciences, social sciences, arts, and humanities. It is designed for providing access to multiple databases, cross-disciplinary research, and in-depth exploration of specialized subfields within an academic or scientific discipline. As a citation index, any cited paper will lead to any other literature (book, academic journal, proceedings, etc.) which currently, or in the past, cites this work. In addition, literature which shows the greatest impact in a field covered by Web of Science, or more than one discipline, can be selectively obtained. For example, a paper's influence can be determined by linking to all the papers that have cited it. In this way, current trends, patterns, and emerging fields of research can be assessed. Web of Science has indexing coverage from the year 1900 to the present (Thomson Reuters 2010). It is a set of multidisciplinary databases that can be used to find journal articles. It is part of the Web of Knowledge, which includes: Science, Social Sciences, Arts and Humanities Citation Indexes; Journal Citation Reports, Impact Factors, citation data and journal ranking; Essential Science Indicators which is a tool for ranking scientists, institutions, countries and journals; Current Contents which is a connect Set up subject searches and save them as e-mail alerts; ISI Proceedings such as index to the published literature of conferences, symposia and seminars and BIOSIS Previews including Journal citations from Biological Abstracts

2.3. Scopus

Scopus is an abstract and indexing database with full-text links that is produced by the Elsevier Co. The name, Scopus, was inspired by the bird, Hamerkop (Scopus umbretta), which reportedly has excellent navigation skills (Burnham, J.F, 2006). Scopus, officially named SciVerse Scopus, owned by Elsevier is a bibliographic database containing abstracts and citations for academic journal articles. A study from 2008 compares PubMed, Scopus, Web of Science, and Google Scholar and concludes PubMed and Google Scholar are accessed for free, Scopus offers about 20% more coverage than Web of Science, whereas Google Scholar offers results of inconsistent accuracy (Falagas, M. E. et al, 2007). Evaluating ease of use and coverage of Scopus and the Web of Science, a study from 2006 concludes that "Scopus is easy to navigate, even for the novice user. The ability to search both forward and backward from a particular citation would be very helpful to the researcher. The multidisciplinary aspect allows the researcher to easily search outside of his discipline" and "One advantage of WOS over Scopus is the depth of coverage, with the full WOS database going back to 1945 and Scopus going back to 1966. However, Scopus and WOS complement each other as neither resource is all inclusive" (Burnham, J.F, 2006).

2.4. Pubmed

First released in 1996, PubMed is a free database providing references and abstracts on life sciences and biomedical topics of the MEDLINE database and it is maintained by the United States National Library of Medicine (NLM) at the National Institutes of Health as part of the Entrez information retrieval system.

Fig. 1. Pubmed search interface

Pubmed provides access to older references from the print version of Index Medicus back to 1951 and earlier; references to some journals before they were indexed in Index Medicus and MEDLINE, for instance Science, BMJ, and Annals of Surgery; very recent entries to records for an article before it is indexed with Medical Subject Headings (MeSH) and added to MEDLINE; and a collection of books available full-text and other subsets of NLM records.

2.5. Scimago Journal Rank

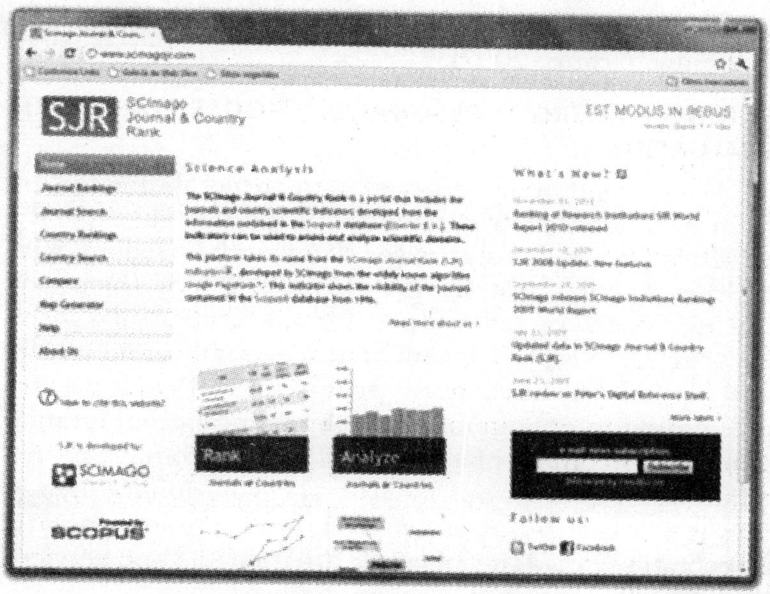

Fig. 2. SJR search interface

SCImago is a joint venture of the Universities of Granada, Extremadura, and Carlos III (Madrid) with Consejo Superior de Investigaciones (Spanish National Research Council). It is dedicated to information analysis, representation, and retrieval using visualisation techniques. Dedicated to information analysis, representation and retrieval by means of visualisation techniques, SCImago group and its measures like SCImago Journal & Country Rank is a portal that includes the journals and country scientific indicators developed from the information contained in the Scopus database. These indicators can be used to assess and analyze scientific domains. The SCImago Journal Rank (SJR) indicator, which has been developed by the SCImago Research Group headed by Professor Felix de Moya, and launched in December 2007, is a size-independent, web-based metric aimed at measuring the current "average prestige per paper" of journals. This indicator shows the visibility of the journals contained in the Scopus database (SCImago Group, 2007).

3. NEWLY EMERGED RESOURCES / TOOLS FOR METRIC EVALUATION

As mentioned earlier, it is the need of time to shift from traditional metric evaluations to alternative metrics which is offered by various social network based analysis techniques and tools. In view of Taylor (2013), the period during which we relied upon formal citation of article-by-article as a measurement of usage, quality, and impact will appear to have been primitive and now we are attempting to enlarge our view by using formal citation of articles in online platforms will be seen to have been a small step forward, but far from a revolutionary step in how we measure, appraise and understand scholarly impact in society. The following are the tools and services based on the social networking tools.

3.1. Altmetrics.org

As defined by Preim (2010), altmetrics is the creation and study of new metrics based on social web or analyzing and informing scholarship. Altmetrics, or alternative or article level metrics, are so called which differentiates them from bibliometrics and the decade's old systems of counting publications and citations and also from webometrics which is the measurement of web page rank or influence by analyzing links between pages on the web (Wiang, 2013). In line with the opinion of Priem (2012), there are a number of new kinds of data that are being collected about scholarly works, such as article page views, document saves or bookmarks, PDF downloads, tags, likes or shares on social networks, saves to reference managers, comments or posts on blogs, each reflecting in a different dimension of influence.

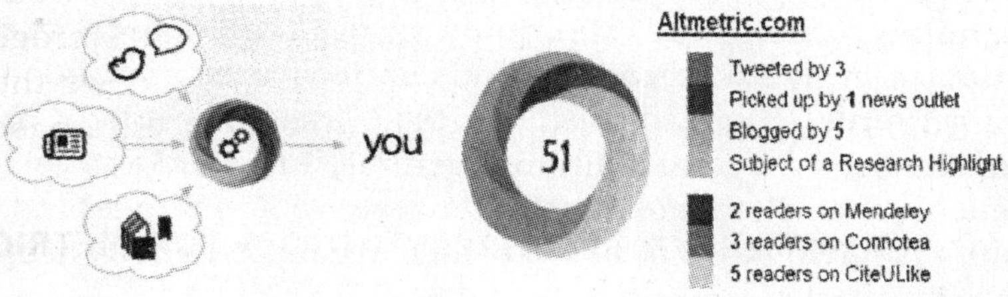

Fig. 3. An Altmetric Index

These various metrics, collectively called altmetrics, have been the subject of extensive study over the past few years and show modest correlation to the traditional citation-based metrics, but also reveal new types of impact i.e. impact on the non-publishing consumers of research and also impact of non-journal forms of academic output such as code, datasets, or simply individual bits of data or figures too small for a traditional publication (Priem, 2012). This free Web site is cofounded by prominent figures in the world of bibliometrics, such as Jason Priem and Heather Piwowar and maintains links to new online tools for calculating impact.

3.2. Impact Story

Formerly known as Total Impact, Impactstory being funded by the Alfred P. Sloan Foundation, a nonprofit corporate, is an open-source, web-based tool that helps researchers explore and share the diverse impacts of all their research products from traditional ones to emerging products like blog posts, datasets, and software. By helping researchers tell data-driven stories about their impacts, we're helping to build a new scholarly reward system that values and encourages web-native scholarship. While Impact Story is designed to support URL-based publishing through the aggregation of online altmetrics, users can create collections of materials through online identifiers, such as Google Scholar Profiles, DOIs, and PubMed IDs and the Impact Story uses more than a dozen APIs to search for metrics on these collected items, with sources ranging from popular social media to scholarly tools like Mendeley and PLoS, which are subsequently assigned in various impact categories, such as generally/highly "saved," "cited," "recommended," or "discussed." In nontraditional venues, Impact Story is a resource which is most useful for researchers publishing, but it is having the limitation of lack of comprehensiveness in tracing web impact.

3.3. PLoSArticle Level metrics

Public Library of Science or PLoS which is available for free online is the first proposer about the transparency and comprehensiveness of information usage and reach of articles which entire academic community have access and also assess the value which is termed as 'Article-Level Metics" again which is different from journal-level measures of research quality. This Open Access journal and repository has materialized as the leading open access journal repository, owing to its high traditional impact factors. PLoS also offers an alternative to traditional impact in the form of Article Level Metrics, which tracks the influence of individual PLoS articles, from number of times downloaded to mentions in social media and blogs and also tracks internal article metrics, including comments, notes, and ratings. Even though, this resource represents an important new avenue for metrics, which future publishers will likely replicate, at present only PLoS articles benefit from its metrics, which is also a valuable resource for impact.

3.4. Publish or Perish

The phrase "Publish or perish" is coined to express the pressure in academia to rapidly and continuously publish research papers to sustain in the field. Publish or Perish is a software program by Harzing, A.W. which retrieves and analyzes academic citations using Google Scholar and provides the following statistics such as total number of papers, total number of citations, average number of citations per paper, average number of citations per author, average number of papers per author, average number of citations per year, Hirsch's h-index and related parameters, Egghe's g-index, the contemporary h-index, the age-weighted citation rate, two variations of individual h-indices and an analysis of the number of authors per paper.

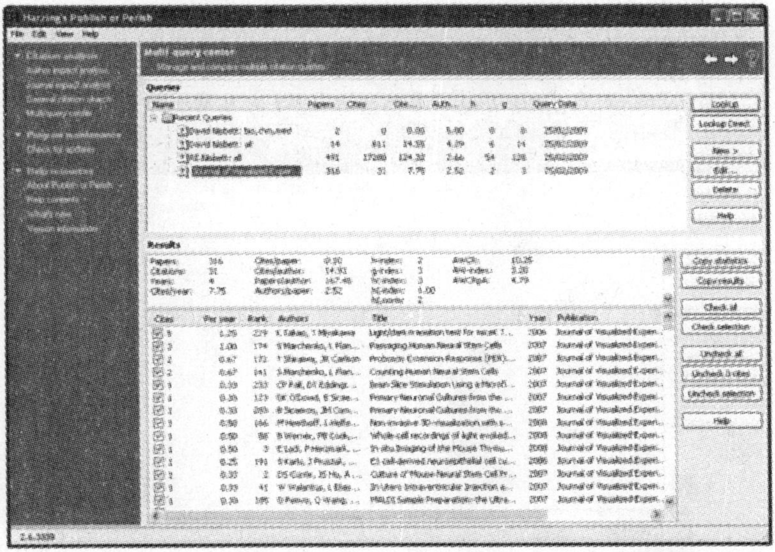

Fig. 4. Publish or perish

Publish or Perish is a valuable programme that combats many of the problems of interpreting Google Scholar outputs and allows academics to easily check their own or others' performance and presents academic outputs quickly and computes excellent citation statistics about each author's work, including an overall 'times cited' score and times cited per year since publication. It also has the limitation of Google Scholar of limiting the results to first thousand entries.

3.5. Scholarometer

Scholarometer is a social tool for scholarly services developed at Indiana University, with the dual aim of exploring the crowd sourcing approach for disciplinary annotations and cross-disciplinary impact metrics (Hoang D T; Kaur J and Menczer F, 2010). It is a browser extension which provides an interface of Google Scholar; which does not have the limitations of server based citation analysis tools which occurs between the user and Google Scholar.

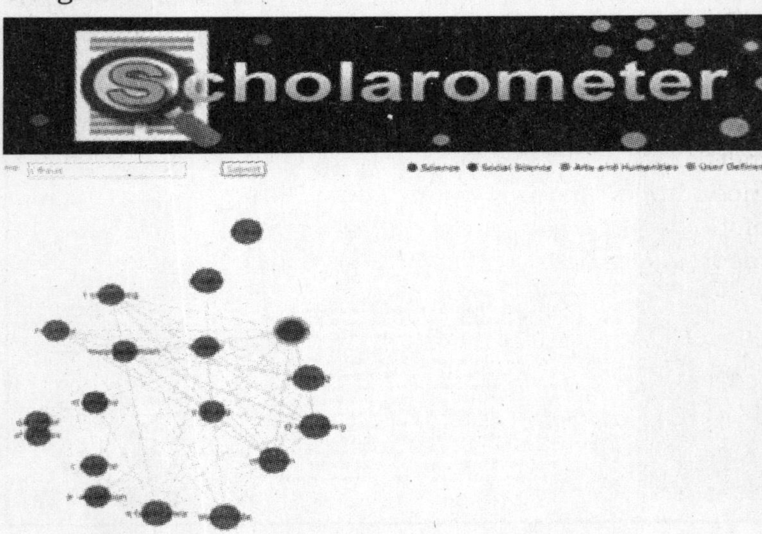

Fig. 5. Scholarometer map

Since scholarometer is not an application, such as Publish or Perish, it is platform independent and runs on every system that supports the Firefox or the Chrome browser but still, Scholarometer uses Google Scholar, which provides the most comprehensive source of citation data across the sciences and social sciences. Scholarometer provides the following facilities like empowers non-experts to submit complex queries and maintains their history, allows filtering, sorting, deleting and live search to compute error free impact measures, enables users to export individual or bulk bibliographic data, social application with tagging functionality, interactive visualization, computes the new universal h-index, provides established impact measures and careful interpretation of impact measures

3.6. Eigenfactor.org

Eigen factor rates the importance of a scientific journal. Here, journals are related according to the number of incoming citations, with citations from highly-ranked journals weighted to make a larger contribution to the Eigen factor than those from poorly-ranked journals similar to Google's page rank algorithm and this approach is considered to be more robust than the impact factor metric; which is calculation purely based on counts of incoming citations without considering the significance of the same. This metrics are strongly correlated for medical journals.

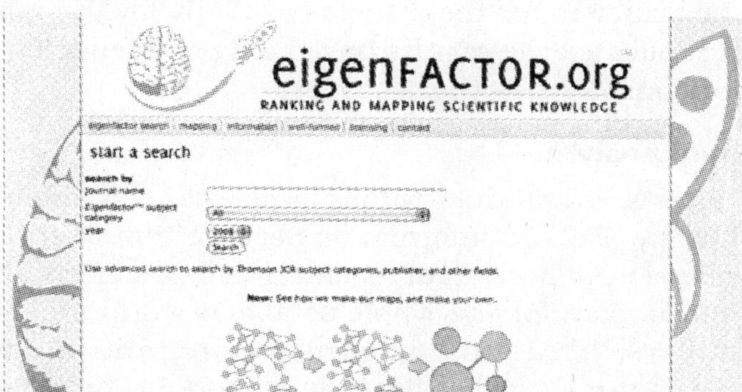

Fig. 6. Eigenfactor

To resolve the issues on impact factor, Eigenfactor™ Metrics has developed as a complement to impact factor and other measures based on direct citation counts. Scholarly citations form a vast network of links among papers and journals, and we can use the full structure of the network to evaluate the importance of citations from various sources. At the freely available Web site http://www.eigenfactor.org, the Eigenfactor Metrics for scholarly journals, computed using citation data from the Thomson Reuters Journal Citation Reports (JCR) are provided. (Bergstrom, Carl T and Jevin D, West 2008).

3.7. ReaderMeter

ReaderMeter is a tool based on the impact of the processed data from Mendley which is also free created by Dario Taraborelli of the Wikimedia Foundation and it distincts with traditional bibliometric tools in the focus on readership, not citation. Based on authors' names compiled and processed through the Mendeley the site provides the measures of impact which highlights information such as an author's "HR-Index," "GR-Index," "Total Bookmarks," and "Top Publications by Readership." It discovers areas of real-time impact which are not visible to traditional citation-based measurements and the readership data is made available via the Mendeley API. But the criticism for these tools is mainly for the reason that it replicates the results based only on Mendeley and are not considering other sources.

3.8. Plum Analytics

PlumX is a product of Plum Analytics wholly-owned subsidiary of EBSCO Information Services that distributes a more absolute portrait of research and questions about research impact for the whole scholarly world including researchers, librarians, administrators, and funders. Plum Analytics was co-founded in 2011 by Andrea Michalek and Mike Buschman which is a self-funded startup, who had worked together in leadership roles at

Serials Solutions on the creation and launch of Summon, the next generation discovery tool for libraries. PlumX is a database based on Library Journal emerged in 2013, congregates metrics across five categories including usage, mentions, captures, social media and citations and is termed as artifacts which in deep is more than just the journal articles that a researcher authors. Articles, blog posts, book chapters, books, cases, clinical trials, conference papers, datasets, figures, grants, interviews, letters, media, patents, posters, presentations, source code, theses / dissertations, videos, and webpages etc are included in these artifacts. Plum Analytics collects the information which is presented in a variety of ways including data visualizations, dashboards, and widgets and synthesizes the metrics data for custom analysis for each institution and for publishers.

4. PEER NETWORKS FOR SCHOLARLY COMMUNICATION

There exist various peer networks and services which shares the communications and scholarly content among the scientists and researchers. These platforms basically working on social networking concepts do tremendous transactions among the peers which is measurable. Academia.edu is free and online sharing platform which encourages the visibility of the research and provides impact metrics similar to those offered by many blogs, and include profile views, document views, and country-based page traffic. VIVO is a free, downloadable semantic Web application designed and developed by Cornell University, to facilitate research collaboration both within and between institutions and also invites institutions to upload data related to faculty profiles, which it crawls in order to draw meaningful connections between researchers. A recent startup and a free service, Mendeley combines social network with a citation manager which can create a research portal which is comprehensive in nature. Social Science Research

Network (SSRN) is an online article repository with three key features such as a database of more than 400,000 abstracts, a large electronic paper collection, and 20 specialized subject networks through which registered users can promote their work and connect to free abstracts and articles

Other Medias and blogs used for sharing include Citation Culture, Jason Priem's Website and Scholarly Kitchen. OII toolkit for the impact of digitised scholarly resources., Elsevier Bibliometrics Research Program (EBRP) , ACM Web Science Conference, ASIST SIGMETRICS and International Society for Scientometrics and Informetrics (ISSI) etc hosts

5. CONCLUSION

Since the process of science evaluating is slow, we need more instant ways of evaluating scientific output. Even though the process of categorization of the directions and research is intricate, but is valuable. Scientists must be evaluated for hiring and promotion, and informed decisions need to be made about how to distribute research funding which goes beyond the level of individuals. It is often important to evaluate the team research of scientists including laboratories, departments, centers, and institutions. Similarly, funding organizations and agencies need to evaluate the output from various initiatives and funding mechanisms. Alternative metrics and other measures serve as a merger between the traditional bibliometrics and the newly emerged alternative metrics. With these new tools and services, sharing through the new social sharing sites such as twitter, face book, wall posts, research highlights, blogs etc are also measurable.

With the increase in the technology improvement, the public interest in science information also got a wide exposure. The emerging new technologies in communication technology and internet based tools leads to a novel resource which improves the scholarly communication, promotion and assessment and also it allows methods to acquire, store, preserve and manipulate the vast amount of data to facilitate the research activities. The contents which were restricted to specialists are now available to extensive spectators with the improvement in the method of accessing, preserving, discussing and sharing methods (Molloy, 2011 and Schofield, 2009). At this juncture, need for a new method measuring and evaluating mechanism arises to reach the scientific information which is to have a strong relation to the new online technologies and services based in social media. Social networking and sharing tools like social bookmarks and online reference managers, blogs, twitter, linked in and others proposes new alternative, transparent and more comprehensive information about the vigorous interest, usage and reach of scientific publications. Till now the academic institutions, development agencies and corporations in the field of planning and managing the development and outlaying the policies of Science and Technology were relying the traditional methodologies and instruments like Bibliometric and Scientometric tools which helps in decision making in identification and promotion of new areas of research, and many other issues in strengthening and growth of S&T activities. These tools provide the figures and gauges which helps to generate measures of published scientific research output and their impact.

REFERENCES

1. Arbesman, S. (2012). *New ways to measure sciencee.* Retrieved 2014, from Social dimension wired science blogs: http://www.wired.com/wiredscience/2012
2. Berfstrom, C. (2007). Eigenfactor measuring the value and prestige of scholarly journals. *College and Research Libraries News*, *68* (5), 314.
3. Bogers, T. & van den Bosch, A. (2008). Recommending scientific articles using CiteULike. *ACM Conference on*

Recommender Systems (pp. 287-290). New York: ACM.

4. Burnham, J.F. (2006). Scopus database: a review. *Biomedical digital libraries , 1,* 3.
5. Evans, P & Krauthammer, M. (2011). Exploring the use of social media to measure journal article impact. *AMIA Annual Symposium Proceedings* (pp. 374-378). AMIA.
6. Eysenbach, G. (2011). Can tweets predict citations? Metrics of social impact based on twitter and correlation with traditional metrics of scientific impact. *Journal of Medical Internet Research , 13* (4).
7. Falagas, M.E...[et al.]. (2007). Comparison of PubMed, Scopus, Web of Science and Google Scholar: strengths and weakness. *THE FASEB Journal , 22* (2), 338-342.
8. Fausto, S ...[et al.]. (2012). Research blogging: indexing and registering the change in science 2.0. *PLoS ONE , 7* (12).
9. Garfield, E. (2012). Journal impact factor: a brief overview. *Canadian Medical Association Journal , 161* (8), 979-80.
10. Hamaker, C. & Spry, B. (2005). Google Scholar. *Serials , 18* (1), 70-72.
11. Haustein, S & Siebenlist,c T. (2011). Applying social bookmarking data to evaluate journal usage. *Journal of Informetrics , 5* (3), 446-457.
12. Hoang, D.T; Kaur, J & Menczer, F. (2010). Crowdsourcing scholarly data. *Web Science Conference: extending the frontiers of society online.*
13. Li, X; Thelwal, M & Giustini, D.i. (2012). Validating online reference managers for scholarly impact measurements. *Scientometrics , 91*, 461-471.
14. Molloy, J.C. (2011). The open knowledge foundation: open data means better science. *PLoS Biology , 9* (12).
15. Mtron, R. K. (1968). The Matthew effect in science. *Science , 159,* 56-63.
16. Nouruzi, A. (2005). Web impact factors for Iranian Universities. *Webology , 2* (1).
17. Priem, Jason ...[et al.]. (2010). *Altmetrics: a manifesto* (Vol. 10).
18. Priem, Jason; Groth, Paul & Dairo Taraborelli. (2012). Altmetrics in the wild: using social media to explore scholalrly impact. *ACM Web Science Conference.* New York: ACM.

19. Priem, Jason; Groth, Paul & Taraboreli, Dairo. (2012). Altmetrics collection. *PLoS ONE* , *7* (11).

20. Schofield, P.N. (2009). Postpublication sharing of data and tools. *Nature* , *10,* 171-173.

21. SCImago Group. (2012). *from SJR-SCImago Journal and Country Rank.* Retrieved 2014, from http://www.scimajor.com

22. Scopus. (2012). *from Journal metrics research analytics redefined.* Retrieved 2014, from http://www.journalmetrics.com/about-scopus.php

23. Taylor, M. (2013). Exploring the boundaries: how altmetrics can expand our vision of scholalry communication and social impact. *Information Standards Quarterly* , *25* (2), 27-32.

24. Wang, Xianwen; Zhi Wang and Shenmeng Xu. (2013). Tracing scientist's research trends realtimely. *Scientometrics, 95* (2), 717-729.

2

Journal of "Vegetable Science": A Bibliometric Study

H.C.Bharvey
Ramnivas Sharma
Dheeraj Shrivastava

ABSTRACT

This paper present the finding of a bibliometric study of journal of "Vegetable Science" for the period of 2008-2012. A Total 355 articles from 11 issues carrying 3883 citation were analyzed and 699 author contributed articles during the five year. In this study cleanly show that collaborative contribution was half of the single author contribution. Moreover, it was found that India is leading contributed nation i.e.384 articles.

Keywords : Bibliometrics, Scientometric, Vegetable Science, Authorship Pattern etc.

1. INTRODUCTION

Bibliometrics is the application of quantitative techniques to analyze the volume, the movement, the frequency and the characteristics, etc of published documents and the related activities. Alan Pritchard was first to use the word "Bibliometrics" in an article "Statistical Bibliography or Bibliometrics" published in the 1969 issue of the "Journal of Documentation". He defines Bibliometrics as "the application of mathematical and statistical methods to books and other media of communication." In a later article, Pritchard explained Bibliometrics as the "metrology of the information transfer process and its purpose is analysis and control of the process". Bibliometrics is a set of methods used to study or measure texts and information (Wikipedia, 2011).

The present study has been undertaken in order to know the nature and content of articles in the journal of "Vegetable Science" during the period of 2008-2012.

2. HISTORY OF THE VEGETABLE SCIENCE JOURNAL

The first issue of the journal "Vegetable Science" was published in early 1974 and continued every six month since that year. The aim of this journal is to providing information on Vegetable crop for the welfare of human society. The society has developed a strict system for the review of manuscript and discourages the publication of manuscripts based on the one year data, Relation to field-related problem, harvesting, shipping and final consumption, together with scientific input about vegetable provide growers extension specialist industry field personnel marketing personnel post harvesting storage physiologist engineers transportation specialist mission and basic scientist and government administrator and legislator with a forum experts views ideas concepts research finding and marketing friends we have published more than 75 issues till now.

3. OBJECTIVES OF THE STUDY

The study analysis the academic and scholarly communication of journal of "Vegetable Science" from 2008 to 2012 with application of bibliometric indicators. The objectives of the study are as follows:

- To study the year-wise distribution of articles;
- To study the issue-wise distribution of articles;
- To study the frequently used keyword in the articles;
- To study the authorship pattern of articles;

- To find out the author's degree of collaboration;
- To find out the ranking of author's by publication of articles;
- To study the distribution of articles by institution wise;
- To study the geographical distribution of articles;
- To study the distribution of articles by country;
- To study the citation of articles by year and issue wise; and
- To study the length of articles.
- To study the types of articles.

4. METHODOLOGY

The study analysis the academic and scholarly communication of journal of "Vegetable Science" from 2008 to 2012. Keeping the objectives of the study in mind, a total number of 355 articles published during the stated period were downloaded from the archives of the open access sources journal. The citation affixed at the end of each articles were photocopied for analysis. Concurrently, content pages of all articles were also photocopied for the sake of examining the authorship pattern, length of articles and geographical distribution of contributing authors. The collected data were fed into MS excel worksheet to process the gathered for further analysis. The table and graphs were generated in accordance with the objective of the study. The study employed required bibliometric measures to test the validity of the finding.

5. ANALYSIS OF DATA

5.1. Distribution of articles-Year-wise

Table 1, show the distribution of articles by year. It is observed that a total number of 355 articles were published in Vegetable Science from 2008 to 2012. The number of articles publisher per year has consistently witnessed an up-and-down trend during this period. Although the year 2009 showed highest number of 115(32.39%) articles contribution and number of 58(16.33%) articles contribution in 2012.

Table 1. Distribution of Articles Year-wise

Year	*Vol. No.*	*No. of Issues*	*Total Articles*	*Percentage*
2008	35	2	62	17.46
2009	36	3	115	32.39
2010	37	2	56	15.77
2011	38	2	64	18.05
2012	39	2	58	16.33
Total	**11**	**355**	**100**	

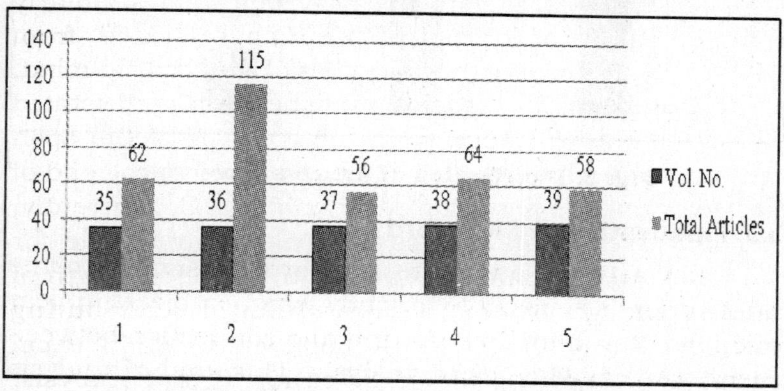

Fig. 1. Distribution of Articles Year-wise

5.2. Distribution of articles-Issue-wise

Table 2, show that the distribution of articles by issue during the period of five year (2008-2012).The researcher found that the volume 36 issue is highest number of articles 115 published, followed by volume 38 issue 64 articles, volume 35 issue 62 articles, volume 39 58 articles and volume 37 issue is lowest 56 articles published.

Table 2. Distribution of Articles Issue-wise

Issue	*Volume*					*Total*
	35	36	37	38	39	
1	31	37	28	31	28	155
2	31	35	28	33	30	157
3	-	43	-	-	-	43
Total	62	115	56	64	58	355

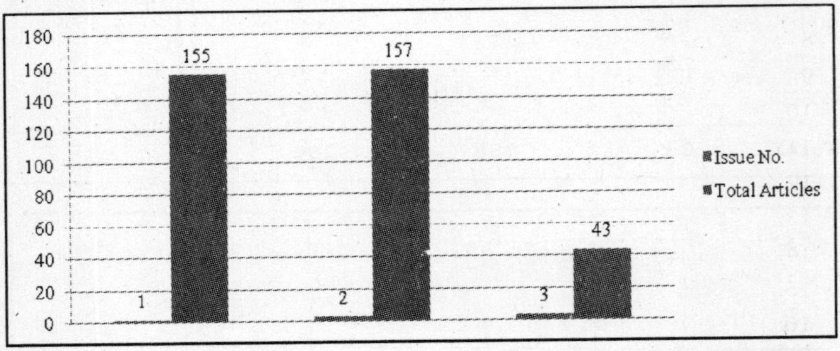

Fig. 2. Distribution of Articles Issue-wise

5.3. Frequently Used Keyword

If you have adequate keywords assigned to the publication it is possible to study which subjects appear often in the publication of a unit and connection between them, a so called co-word analysis. This kind of analysis is easier to make if the reference contain term from a controlled vocabulary like MeSH (Medical Subject Heading). Table 3, shows the word Combining Ability used 12 times. During 2008 to 2012 as it is word Yield used 10 times and Capsicum, Heterosis & Okra are used 5 times.

Table 3. Frequently used key word in Articles

S.No.	*Keywords*	*Total*	*Rank*
1.	Combining Ability	12	I
2.	Yield	10	II
3.	Capsicum	5	III
4.	Heterosis	5	III
5.	Okra	5	III
6.	Tomato	4	IV
7.	Cucumber	3	V
8.	Line x Tester	3	V
9.	Onion	3	V
10.	Pea	3	V
11.	Bottle gourd	2	VI
12.	GCA	2	VI
13.	Genetic divergence	2	VI
14.	Pochonia Chlamydosporia	2	VI
15.	SCA	2	VI
16.	99 keywords with 1 articles each	99	VII
	Total	162	

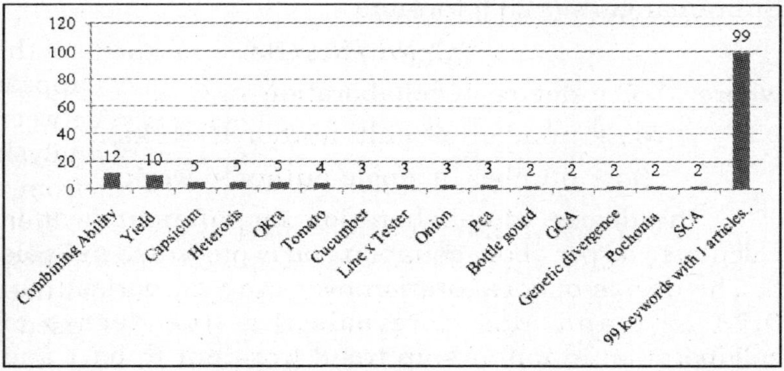

Fig. 3. Frequently used key word in Articles

5.4. Authorship Pattern

Authorship pattern of the articles is presented in the Table 4. The study reveals that a total of 355 authors have contributed the 355 articles leaving the frequencies of authors. That the highest number of articles, i.e. 281are by three & above authors. Single and Two authored contributions number 6 and 68 of the total contribution. It is observed that still the contribution by 3 and above author dominating the field.

Table 4. Authorship pattern

Year	*No. of Authors*			*Total*
	1	*2*	*3 & Above*	
2008	2	10	50	62
2009	-	21	94	115
2010	-	13	43	56
2011	4	15	45	64
2012	-	9	49	58
Total	6	68	281	355
Percentage	1.69	19.15	79.15	99.99

5.5. Degree of author's Collaboration

Table 5, show the degree of collaboration of authors in journal of "Vegetable Science". It was calculated using Subramanian's (1983) formula;

$$C=Nm/Nm+Ns$$

where C = degree of collaboration

Nm = number of multi-authored works

Ns = number of single-authored work

The degree of collaboration for different year is calculated as per above equation and is presented in Table 5. The degree of collaboration over the year varies from 0.93 to 1 and also it reveals that the degree of collaboration in authorship trend work out to be 1 and above. Thus the degree of collaboration gives a picture of extent of collaborations among the authors. The average has been arrived at 1.

Table 5. Degree of Author Collaboration

Year	*Ns*	*Nm*	*C*
2008	2	60	0.96
2009	-	115	1
2010	-	56	1
2011	4	60	0.93
2012	-	58	1

5.6. Ranking of Authors

A total number of 699 authors contributed to 355 articles published in journal of "Vegetable Science" during 2008 to 2012. The ranking of most prolific authors in according to their number of contribution to in journal of "Vegetable Science" is pointed in Table 6. It is found Mathura Rai has contributed a more number of articles (30 articles), Followed by A B Rai (29 articles), A K Singh (20 articles), Major Singh (13 articles), B Singh (11 articles), Rajesh Kumar (11 articles), S. P. Singh (11 articles), and rest of others authors.

Table 6. Ranking of Authors by Number of Publication

S.No.	*Name of the Author*	*Total*	*Rank*
1.	Mathura Rai	30	I
2.	A B Rai	29	II
3.	A K Singh	20	III
4.	Major Singh	13	IV
5.	B Singh	11	V
6.	Rajesh Kumar	11	V
7.	S P Singh	11	V
8.	K P Singh	10	VI
9.	K G Shinde	9	VII
10.	Sanjeet Kumar	9	VII
11.	40 articles by 5 authors(5*8)	40	VIII
12.	21 articles by 3 authors(3*7)	21	IX
13.	30 Articles by 5 authors(5*6)	30	X
14.	45 Articles by 9 authors(9*5)	45	XI
15.	52 articles by 13 authors(13*4)	52	XII

16.	132 articles by 44 authors(44*3)	132	XIII
17.	236 articles by 118 authors(118*2)	236	XIV
18.	536 articles by 1 author(536*1)	536	XV
	Total	**1245**	

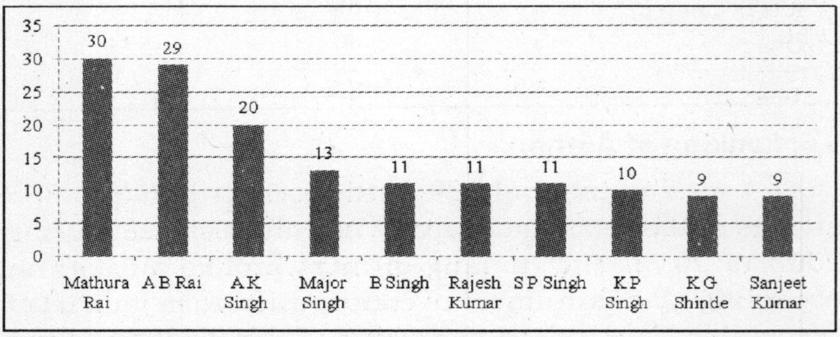

Fig. 4. Ranking of Authors by Number of Publication (Top 10)

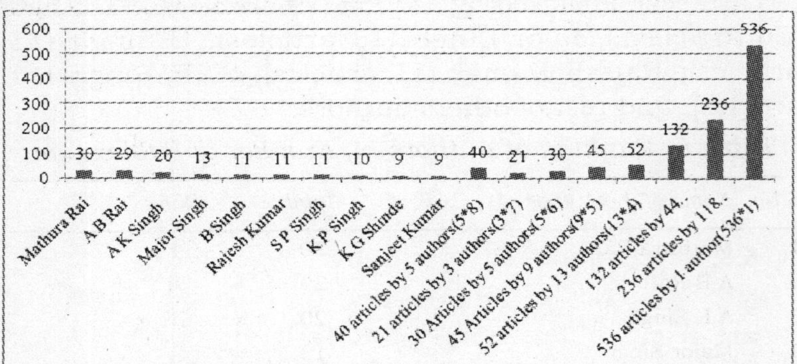

Fig. 5. Ranking of Authors by Number of Publication

5.7. Distribution of Articles Institution wise

Data pertaining to the contribution made by researcher from various field, scientist etc. in India (Table 7) showed that 355 contributions have been made by from various institution. 48.45% contribution of these had come from the Universities followed by 15.21% from colleges, 27.32% from Research and Development Centres and 9.02% from others i.e. Professionals, Scientists and researcher etc.

Table 7. Distribution of Articles Institution wise

Type of Institution	*2008*	*2009*	*2010*	*2011*	*2012*	*Total*	*%*
University	24	61	25	30	32	172	48.45
College	15	16	6	9	8	54	15.21
R & D Centres	20	29	18	17	13	97	27.32
Others	3	9	7	8	5	32	9.02
Total	62	115	56	64	58	355	100

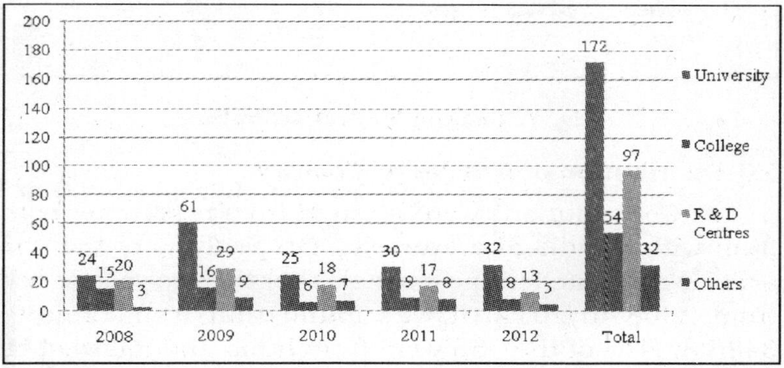

Fig. 6. Distribution of Articles Institution wise

5.8. Geographical Distribution

The Table 8 showed that most of the contributions are from Indian with 348 (98.02%) articles and only 7(1.98%) articles from rest of the countries.

Table 8. Geographical Distribution

Geographical Area	*2008*	*2009*	*2010*	*2011*	*2012*	*Total*	*%*
INDIA	57	113	56	64	58	348	98.02
FOREIGN	5	2	-	-	-	7	1.98
Total	62	115	56	64	58	355	100

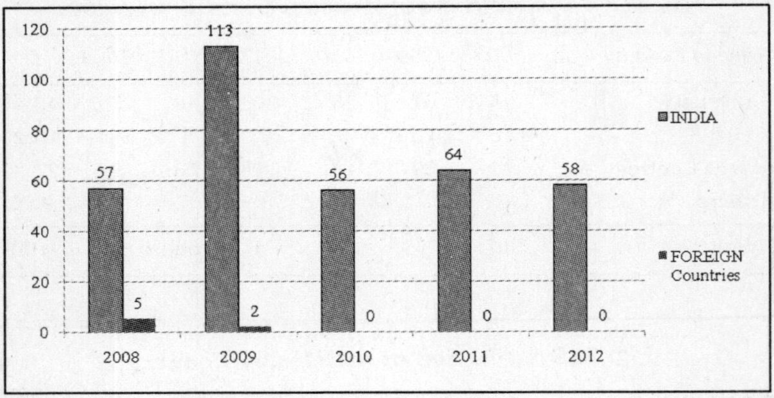

Fig. 7. Geographical Distribution

5.9. Distribution of Articles by Country

Contributions were received from researcher both from within India and overseas. On analysis of the 355 articles published in the journals over the five year period from 2008 to 2012. It was found that from table 9: 348(98.04%) of the 355 were from India and followed by Srinagar (J & K) 2 (0.56%), Aizawl 2(0.56%), Meghalaya, Sri Lanka and Belgium countries contributed one articles.

Table 9. Distribution of Articles by Country

Country	*No. of Articles*	*Cumulative No. of Articles*	*%*
India	348	348	98.02
Srinagar (J & K)	2	350	0.56
Aizawl	2	352	0.56
Meghalaya	1	353	0.28
Sri Lanka	1	354	0.28
Belgium	1	355	0.28

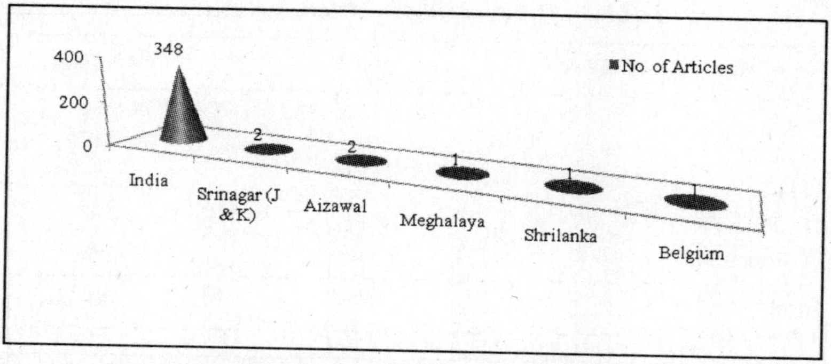

Fig. 8. Distribution of Articles by Country

5.10. Citation of Articles-Year and Issue wise

Table 10, indicates the total citation of every issue and year and it shows that the highest citation references 1197 in 2009, followed by 688 citation in 2008,757 citation in 2010,630 citation in 2012 and 611 citation in 2011.

Table 10. Citation of Articles –Year and Issue wise

Issue	*Year*				
	2008	*2009*	*2010*	*2011*	*2012*
1	348	389	385	331	332
2	340	430	372	280	298
3	-	378	-	-	-
Total	688	1197	757	611	630

5.11. Length of Articles (Pages)

Table 11, indicated the length of articles of pages. Out of total 355 articles 336 of the articles are between 1-5 pages, 12 of the articles between 6-10 and 4 of the articles 11-15, 2 of the articles between 16-20 and only one articles published above 21 page during period 2008-2012.

Table 11. Length of Articles (Pages)

No. of Pages per Articles	No. of Articles	Percentage
1-5	336	94.64
6-10	12	3.40
11-15	4	1.12
16-20	2	0.56
21 and Above	1	0.28
Total	355	100

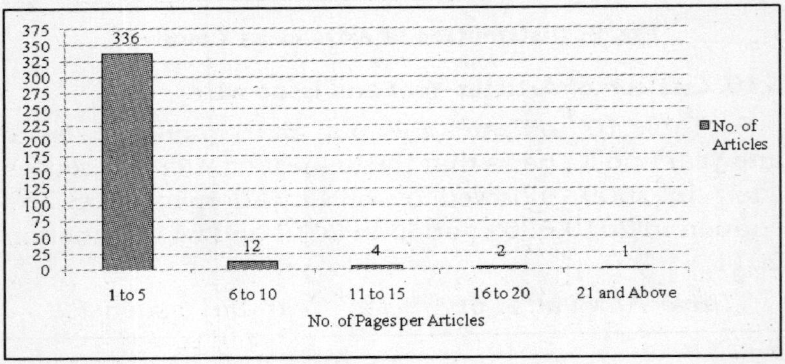

Fig. 9. Length of Articles (Pages)

5.12. Articles type-wise

Table12 indicates articles type the total articles 355 in during year 2008 to 2012, year 2008 in 35 research, 25 short communication and 2 review articles total 62 articles, year 2009 in 54 research articles, 59 short communication and 2 review articles total 115 articles, year 2010 in 32 research articles, 22 short communication and 2 review articles total 56 articles, year 2011 25 research, 32 short communication and 1 review articles total 64 articles, year 2012 in 25 research articles, 32 short communication and 1 review articles published.

Table 12. Articles type-wise

Year	Review articles	Research articles	Short Communication	Total
2008	2	35	25	62
2009	2	54	59	115
2010	2	32	22	56
2011	1	26	37	64
2012	1	25	32	58
Total	8	172	175	355

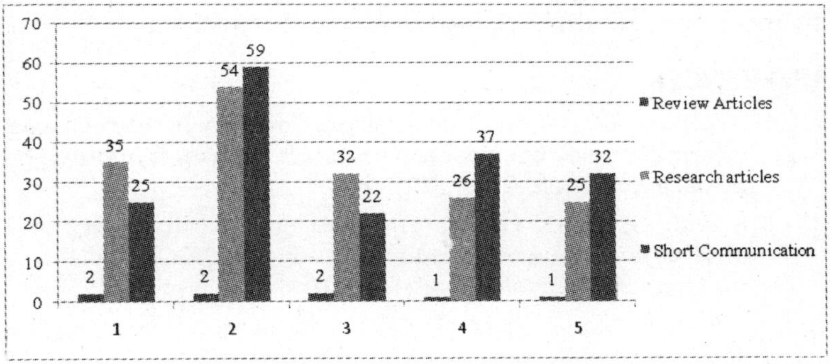

Fig. 10. Articles type-wise

6. SUMMARY OF FINDING

The number of articles published in journal of "Vegetable Science" on an average per year and issue has consistently an up and down during the period of 2008 to 2012. The issue of year 2009 each year is highest number of articles, 115 published. The keyword "yield" was used 10 times than other words. There is complete domination of single author contribution during the stated period. The degree of collaboration in Vegetable Science ranged from 0.27 to 0.47 during the publication phase under study. The author Mathura Rai, A B Rai was found that to the leading contributor with a maximum contribution of 30 articles, followed by A K Singh (20 articles), Major Singh (13 articles). In regards to country productivity, India topped the table and followed by Belgeum, Aizawl, Meghalaya, Sri Lanka and Srinagar.

7. CONCLUSION

Journal of "Vegetable Science" has successfully completed 39 year of publication. It has got global recognition in the field vegetables Science and is steadily growing to be a very promising journal in the area of the same .The scholarly content of this journal is fairly cited. However, new editorial policy and good reviewer of this journal can bring good quality of output and also it can be increase the impact factor in the future.

REFERENCES

1. Buttlern, L. (1999). Information Sources in library and information science doctoral research. *Library & Information Science Research*, 21(2), 227-245.
2. Kumar, P. S. G. (1998). Doctoral studies in library and information science in India: a study. *DESIDOC Bulletin of Information Technology*, 18(1), 5-9.
3. Kumar, S. and Kumar, S. (2005). Bibliometric study of the Journal of Oilseeds Research since (1993-2001). *SRELS Journal of Information Management*, 42(3), 305-334.
4. शर्मा, रामनिवास (2007). "ग्रंथालय विज्ञान" पत्रिका का ग्रंथमिति अध्ययन. *ग्रंथालय विज्ञान*, 38(1–2).
5. Sharma, Ramnivas and others (2012). A New Concept of Indian Doctoral Dissertations. *Granthalaya Vigyan*, 43, 26-35.
6. Sharma, Ramnivas (2012). Bibliometric and Citation Analysis of Ph.D. Theses in Library and Information Science 2001 to 2008. (*Ph.d. Thesis*) Gwalior: Jiwaji University.
7. Sharma, Ramnivas and Others (2012). Bibliometric Monitoring of Research Performance in the Hindi in Jiwaji University, Gwalior (1971-1990). *Research Discourse*, 2(2), 237-241.
8. Sharma, Ramnivas and others (2012). Electronic Thesis and Dissertations: Better Concept for Present to Future. UGC–Sponsored 2 Days National Conference on "Redesigning Libraries & Information Centers In Digital Era"(RLICDE) 26th & 27th December 2012, Organized by Department of Library,

A.V. Education Society's, Degloor College, Degloor (M.S.)

9. Sharma, Ramnivas and Sharma, Arvind (2013). Bibliometric Monitoring of Research Performance in the Library and Information Science in Uttar Pradesh Universities (2001-2008). *Journal of Library Metamorphosis,* 1(1), 32-43

10. Sharma, Ramnivas and Bharvey, Harish C. (2013). Bibliometric Study of M.Sc. Theses submitted in K.N.K. College of Horticulture, Mandsaur, RVSKVV, Gwalior (M.P.) during 2008-2012. *Journal of Information Technology and Library Science,* 1(1), 43-56.

11. Sharma, Ramnivas and others (2014). Bibliometric Monitoring of Research Performance in the field of Dairy Science with special reference to Krishiprabha. In Stanley Madan Kumar and others. Information Access in Digital Libraries. New Indian Publishing Agency, New Delhi.

12. Sharma, Ramnivas and others (2014). Monitoring of Research Performance in the Library and Information Science in Uttar Pradesh and Rajasthan Universities: A Bibliometric Study. UGC Sponsored National Seminar on Best Practices in the College Libraries, 21st Nov. 2014. Organized by The Department of Library, Shri Guru Buddhiswami Mahavidyalaya, Purna (MS).

13. Sharma, Ramnivas and others (2015). A New Concept of Indian Doctoral Dissertations: with special reference to Krishiprabha. Bilingual International Conference on Information Technology: yesterday, today and tomorrow, Feb. 19-21, 2015. Defence Scientific Information & Documentation Centre (DESIDOC), DRDO, Metcalfe House Delhi.

14. Sharma, Ramnivas and others (2015). Descriptive study of M.Sc. thesis in Fruit Science. Bilingual International Conference on Information Technology: yesterday, today and tomorrow, Feb. 19-21, 2015. Defence Scientific Information & Documentation Centre (DESIDOC), DRDO, Metcalfe House Delhi.

15. Sharma, Ramnivas and Bharvey, Harish C. (2015). Study of M.Sc. Theses in Floriculture and Landscape Architecture Department at K. N. K. College of Horticulture Mandsaur, (M.P.). National Conference on Contrivance of Academic Libraries in Digital Era (NCCALDE-2015) on February 6-7, 2015 (Fri-Sat) at Vikram University, Ujjain, Madhya Pradesh.

16. Wikipedia (2011): *http://en.wikipedia. org/wiki/Bibliometrics*

3

Position of Websites of Universities in South India by Alexa Inlinks: A Webometric Point of View

R. Jeyshankar
I. Maria Sujitha

ABSTRACT

Context: Metric studies like librametrics, bibliometrics, scientometrics, informetrics and webometrics are well known. Newer concepts and methods are being developed in the Metric study in Library and Information Science. One such newest method of studying the inlinks of the university is 'Sites Linking In' or Inlinks of Alexa, the Web Information Company.

Materials and Methods: The study was designed by collecting the number of inlinks of websites of universities for the four states viz, Tamil Nadu, Andhra Pradesh, Karnataka and Kerala.

Statistical Analysis Used: The data collected by providing the website of the university in the 'Sites Linking In' column in the website of Alexa, the outcome was explored to rank the website by MS Office Excel and through SPSS to find Cross Tabulation, Mean, Descriptive Statistics, and one way ANOVA were calculated.

Result: In Tamil Nadu, 5 universities namely AMET University, Bharath University, SASTRA University, Saveetha University and

Tamil Nadu Physical Education and Sports University were ranked with above 1000 Alexa Inlinks. In Andhra Pradesh, 5 universities such as Jawaharlal Nehru Technological University - Kakinada, Kakatiya University, Mahatma Gandhi University, Sri Padmavati Mahila Vishwavidyalayam and Sri Venkateswara Veterinary University were ranked with above 1000 Alexa Inlinks. In Karnataka, 6 universities were ranked with above 1000 Alexa Inlinks. They are Indian Institute of Science and Manipal Academy of Higher Education, Jawaharlal Nehru Centre for Advanced Scientific Research and National Institute of Mental Health and Neuro Sciences, Gulbarga University and Karnataka Veterinary, Animal and Fisheries Sciences University. In Kerala, no university is ranked with more than 1000 Alexa Inlinks.

Moreover, there is significant difference between the Types of Universities with their Inlinks is prevailing.

Conclusion: State Government Universities need to concentrate on their website issues in order to get more inlinks from other such websites.

Keywords: Webometrics, Alexa Sites Linking In, Websites

INTRODUCTION

The great technological revolution that brought in vast amount of and nearly unlimited accessibility of information, the user and his/her ability to shift through the vast sea of information will be the primary research focus in the twenty-first century. Information and knowledge present powerful tools for the advancement of personal and communal life; knowledge of their positive use is imperative. The websites of higher education plays a major role in communicating the world by providing useful and current information. The interdisciplinary nature of the field of Library and Information Science has caused some of the issues related to information science to be directed at related fields: technology for those involved in computer science and information systems and administration for people engaged in management and organization.

Webometrics : The term webometrics is a coinage from two modern English words, "web" and "metric". The word web is a short form of WWW. The study of the quantitative aspects of the construction and use of information resources, structures and technologies on the WWW drawing on Bibliometrics and Informetrics approaches.

The term webometrics was first coined by Almind and Ingwersen in the year 1997. It is further expanded as "the study of web-based content with primarily quantitative methods for social science research goals using techniques that are not specific to one field of study" (Thelwall, 2009), which emphasises the development of applied methods for use in the wider social sciences. The purpose of this definition was to help publicise appropriate methods outside of the information science discipline rather than to replace the original definition within information science. Similar scientific fields are Bibliometrics, Informetrics, Scientometrics, Virtual ethnography, and Web mining.

The idea of applying bibliometric techniques to the web was proposed by Almind and Ingwersen, (1997) According to them WIF should be defined as the ratio of links made to a website, to the number of pages at the website. Ingwersen distinguished between:

- The External link WIF, the ratio of external links to the number of pages.
- The internal or Self WIF, the ratio of internal links within the site to number of pages.
- The Revised WIF, the ratio of inlinks to the target site, to the number of pages at the site.

In links from outside represent more effort to point to target pages, and thus contain more valuable information. However, it is not always easy to separate self links from inlinks (Li, 2003).

REVIEW OF LITERATURE

Web links studies have been conducted by the

scholars and information professionals all over the world from its introduction by Thelwall. Web link research in webometrics research started with Larson, Rousseau, and Almind and Ingweson. They are highlighted their research with the citation counts thus by focused on Web Impact Factor. Several studies by Ramesh Babu, R., Jeyshankar and Rao P. N. (2010), Rousseau (1997), Shukla and Tripathi (2009), Islam and Alam (2011) and Lee and Park (2012) on subsequently been carried out with many of them focusing on the Academic institutions like colleges and universities.

Thelwall (2003) introduced two web link count metrics to complement the existing Web Impact Factor. The first is provisionally cast as an indicator of the average degree of online informal scholarly communication and information use by the academics in a given university. The second has a similar construction but focuses on the degree of web interconnection in terms of both inlinks and outlinks. The latter metric is based upon a more elaborate mechanism than raw link counts: totaling the minimum number of links between universities over all distinct pairs in the chosen set that include the given institution.

Jose, Isidro and **Jose (2006)** conducted a longitudinal study of the evolution and the state of 738 websites in two different points in time (1997 and 2004). It tries to establish the rate of growth and decay of the Web and all the web elements. To this end, the structure and the contents of these websites are extracted through a crawler and compared at the two different moments in time. The main results confirm a growth of web contents and elements in the web, although there is also a high degree of web content decay. The results suggest that in the seven year period covered by this study the web is characterised by both strong dynamism and instability.

Didegah and **Goltaji (2010)** the Islamic world universities' link analysis and web impact factor was carried out by this study. By the Parameters like Size, Visibility, Richness and Scholarliness, the sample universities were selected from the top universities listed by www.webometrics.info. The search strategy of Altavista advanced search was used to obtain linkages and calculated Web Impact Factor and Revised Web Impact Factor. The internal links or self links had played vital role in the universities ranking had been found out. When omitting the self-links, the result of some universities websites ranking went negatively. It was revealed that there was a strong correlation between the Universities World Rank and Web Impact Factor of such universities.

Erfanmanesh and **Didegah (2011)** attempted to rank the websites of Iranian research institutions according to their total links, percentage of Iranian and foreign users and number of pages viewed by per user and were compared with one another. The study had used Alexa Internet to collect data. The study employed Correspondence Analysis and grouped the institutions into three sections. The institutions which had largest number of links framed the first group. The language barrier was shown and it was found that foreign users were deprive of visiting such institutions. The webmasters were asked to improve the website qualities in the cyberspace. Institutions administrators were asked to advertise their services to their audiences through the websites.

On the basis of six criteria **Didegah** and **Erfanmanesh (2010)** evaluate Malaysian websites. Traffic rank, Average number of Pages viewed, Time spent on site per user, Number of links received from other websites and Percentage of Malaysian and Foreign users were the attributes by which the study had been conducted. The findings of the study revealed that no particular university was well performed in all but, each had its benefits and advantages. The study suggested that the web designers' attention on services of the website was in order to earn more user satisfaction and also to gain more links from other such websites. Connectivity and ranking played important role in attracting foreign visitors to the website.

DATA COLLECTION AND ANALYSIS

Sites linking from other websites are called Inlinks. It is a feature of Alexa, the web information company which mean number of websites connected to a certain website, which shows its popularity. The data were collected were analysed with the help of Excel and SPSS package and discussed in the light of Statistics.

Table I : Distributions of Types of Universities in South India

Sl. No	Types	Tamil Nadu		Andhra Pradesh		Karnataka		Kerala		Total	
		n	%	n	%	n	%	n	%	n	%
1	State	19	13.19	32	22.22	22	15.28	11	7.64	84	58.33
2	Central	4	2.78	4	2.78	3	2.08	2	1.39	13	9.03
3	Private	25	17.36	6	4.17	15	10.42	1	0.69	47	32.64
	Total	48	33.33	42	29.17	40	27.78	14	9.72	144	100.00

The data was collected from Alexa websites for the universities in south India such as Tamil Nadu, Andhra Pradesh, Karnataka and Kerala in August 2012. There are 48 (33.33%) universities in the State of Tamil Nadu, 42 (29.17%) universities belong to the State of Andhra Pradesh, 40 (27.78%) universities belong to the State of Karnataka and 14 (9.72%) universities belong to the State of Kerala. In other words as grouped by the nature of management, there are 84 (58.33%) universities are owned by State government, 13 (9.03%) universities are owned by central government and the remaining 47 (32.64%) universities are owned by private sectors which outline the part of this study.

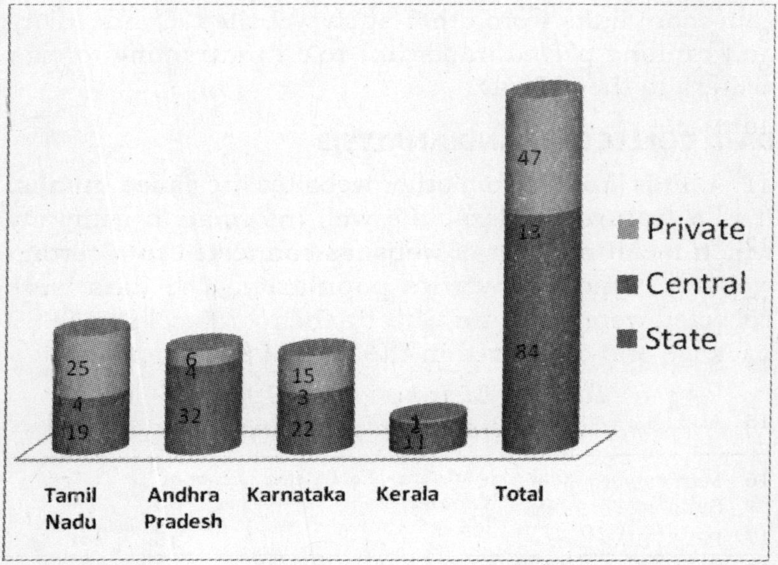

Fig. 1. Types of Universities in South India

Tables II to V provides the Universities with their URL, Type and the Inlinks which is retrieved from the Alexa website. The universities were positioned in Descending Order on the basis of the inlinks or 'Sites linking in' of Alexa.

Table 2. Inlinks Retrieved from Alexa of Websites of Universities in Tamil Nadu

S. No.	*Name of the University*	*URL*	*Type*	*Sites linking in*
1	AMET University	*www.ametuniv.ac.in*	Private	2711
2	Bharath University	*www.bharathuniv.com*	Private	2711
3	SASTRA University	*www.sastra.edu*	Private	2103
4	Tamil Nadu Physical Education and Sports University	*www.tnpesu.org*	State	2038
5	Saveetha University	*www.saveetha.com*	Private	1388
6	Indian Maritime University	*www.imu.edu.in*	Central	887

7	Kalasalingam University	*www.kalasalingam.ac.in*	Private	797
8	Amrita University	*www.amrita.edu*	Private	762
9	Central University of Tamil Nadu	*www.cutn.ac.in*	Central	697
10	Mother Teresa Women's University	*www.motherteresa womenuniv.ac.in*	State	671
11	Avinashilingam University	*www.avinuty.ac.in*	Central	584
12	Periyar Maniammai University	*www.pmu.edu*	Private	577
13	Vel Tech Technical University	*www.veltechuniv.edu.in*	Private	514
14	Sri Ramachandra University	*www.sriramachandra. edu.in*	Private	420
15	Alagappa University	*www.alagappa university.ac.in*	State	378
16	Manonmaniam Sundaranar University	*www.msuniv.ac.in*	State	339
17	PRIST University	*www.prist.ac.in*	Private	334
18	Karpagam University	*www.karpagamuniv.com*	Private	320
19	S.R.M University	*www.srmuniv.ac.in*	Private	300
20	St. Peter's University	*www.stpeters university.org*	Private	293
21	Tamil Nadu Veterinary and Animal Sciences University	*www.tanuvas.tn.nic.in*	State	269
22	Vinayaka Missions University	*www.vinayaka mission.com*	Private	199
23	Dr.M.G.R. University	*www.drmgrdu.ac.in*	Private	189
24	Tamil Nadu Dr. M.G.R. Medical University	*www.tnmgrmu.ac.in*	State	188
25	Sathyabama University	*www.sathyabama university.ac.in*	Private	173
26	Chettinad University	*www.chettinadhealth city.com*	Private	160
27	Meenakshi University	*www.maher.ac.in*	Private	158
28	Tamil Nadu Dr. Ambedkar Law University	*www.tndalu.ac.in*	State	153
29	Annamalai University	*www.annamalai university.ac.in*	State	141
30	Periyar University	*www.periyar university.ac.in*	State	138

31	Anna University	*www.annauniv.edu*	State	136
32	Bharathiar University	*www.b-u.ac.in*	State	132
33	Hindustan University	*www.hindustanuniv.ac.in*	Private	131
34	Tamil University	*www.tamiluniversity.ac.in*	State	129
35	Gandhigram Rural Institute	*www.ruraluniv.ac.in*	Central	129
36	Tamil Nadu Agricultural University	*www.tnau.ac.in*	State	125
37	Karunya University	*www.karunya.edu*	Private	115
38	Thiruvalluvar University	*www.thiruvalluvar university.ac.in*	State	94
39	Noorul Islam University	*www.niuniv.com*	Private	93
40	Tamil Nadu Open University	*www.tnou.ac.in*	State	92
41	University of Madras	*www.unom.ac.in*	State	92
42	VIT University	*www.vit.ac.in*	Private	87
43	Tamil Nadu Teacher Education University	*www.tnteu.in*	State	85
44	SCSVMV University	*www.kanchiuniv.ac.in*	Private	79
45	B.S. Abdur Rahman University	*www.bsauniv.ac.in*	Private	68
46	Bharathidasan University	*www.bdu.ac.in*	State	60
47	Vels University	*www.velsuniv.ac.in*	Private	47
48	Madurai Kamaraj University	*www.mkuniversity.org*	State	43

Table II shows the Inlinks retrieved from Alexa of Websites of Universities in Tamil Nadu. From the table it is seen that AMET University, Bharath University, SASTRA University, Tamil Nadu Physical Education and Sports University and Saveetha University are high in their links and are ranked at the top. Thiruvalluvar University, Noorul Islam University, Tamil Nadu Open University, University of Madras, VIT University and Tamil Nadu Teacher Education University, SCSVMV University, B.S. Abdur Rahman University, Bharathidasan University, Vels University and Madurai Kamaraj University are ranked last with less number of inlinks.

Table 3. Inlinks Retrieved from Alexa of Websites of Universities in Andhra Pradesh

S. No	*Name of the University*	*URL*	*Type*	*Sites linking in*
1	Jawaharlal Nehru Technological University Kakinada	*www.jntuk.edu.in*	State	5631
2	Sri Venkateswara Veterinary University	*www.svvu.edu.in*	State	2094
3	Kakatiya University	*www.kakatiya.ac.in*	State	2094
4	Sri Padmavati Mahila Vishwavidyalayam	*www.sriramachandra.edu.in*	State	1209
5	Mahatma Gandhi University	*www.mguniversity.ac.in*	State	1066
6	NALSAR University of Law	*www.nalsarlawuniv.ac.in*	State	505
7	Sri Venkateswara Vedic University	*www.svvedic university.org*	State	460
8	Sri Sathya Sai University	*www.sssihl.edu.in*	Private	440
9	GITAM University	*www.gitam.edu*	Private	438
10	Jawaharlal Nehru Technological University Anantpur	*www.jntuanantapur.org*	State	388
11	The English & Foreign Languages University	*www.efluniversity.ac.in*	Central	384
12	Dr. B.R. Ambedkar Open University	*www.braou.ac.in*	State	353
13	Rayalaseema University	*www.rayalaseema university.ac.in*	State	325
14	Acharya Nagarjuna University	*www.nagarjuna university.ac.in*	State	301
15	ICFAI Foundation for Higher Education	*www.ifheindia.org*	Private	255
16	International Institute of Information Technology	*www.iiit.ac.in*	Private	243
17	Vikram Simhapuri University	*www.simhapuriuniv.ac.in*	State	230
18	Sri Krishnadevaraya University	*www.skuniversity.org*	State	225
19	Jawaharlal Nehru Technological University (Hyderabad)	*www.jntuh.ac.in*	State	211

20	Telangana University	*www.telangana university.ac.in*	State	183
21	Rashtriya Sanskrit Vidyapeeth (University)	*www.rsvidyapeetha. ac.in*	Central	176
22	Palamuru University	*www.palamuru university.ac.in*	State	173
23	Sri Venkateswara Institute of Medical Sciences	*www.svimstpt.ap. nic.in*	State	163
24	Rajiv Gandhi University of Knowledge Technology	*www.rgukt.in*	State	147
25	Dr. Y.S.R. Horticulural Univerity	*www.drysrhu.edu.in*	State	133
26	Osmania University	*www.osmania.ac.in*	State	125
27	Andhra University	*www.andhra university.info*	State	120
28	NTR University of Health Sciences	*www.ntruhs.ap.nic.in*	State	114
29	Dr.B.R.Ambedkar University	*www.dbrau.ac.in*	State	109
30	Krishna University	*www.krishna university.ac.in*	State	87
31	Satavahana University	*www.satavahana. ac.in*	State	86
32	Sri Venkateswara University	*www.svuniversity.in*	State	85
33	Maulana Azad National Urdu University	*www.manuu.ac.in*	Central	83
34	A.P University of law	*www.apulvisakha.org*	State	82
35	Dravidian University	*www.dravidian university.ac.in*	State	70
36	Yogi Vemana University	*www.yogivemana univ.ac.in*	State	68
37	Potti Sreeramulu Telugu University	*www.telugu university.ac.in*	State	49
38	Vignan University	*www.vignan university.org*	Private	46
39	University of Hyderabad	*www.uohyd.ac.in*	Central	37
40	Jawaharlal Nehru Architecture and Fine Arts University	*www.jnafau.ac.in*	State	33
41	Adi Kavi Nannaya University	*www.nannaya university.info*	State	25
42	K L University	*www.kluniversity.in*	Private	20

Table III describes the Inlinks retrieved from Alexa of Websites of Universities in Andhra Pradesh. From the table, it is seen that Jawaharlal Nehru Technological University Kakinada, Sri Venkateswara Veterinary University, Kakatiya University, Sri Padmavati Mahila Vishwavidyalayam, Mahatma Gandhi University, and NALSAR University of Law are high inlinking websites. Krishna University, Satavahana University, Sri Venkateswara University, Maulana Azad National Urdu University, A.P University of law, Dravidian University, Yogi Vemana University, Potti Sreeramulu Telugu University, Vignan University, University of Hyderabad, Jawaharlal Nehru Architecture, Fine Arts University, Adi Kavi Nannaya University and K L University is ranked last with less number of inlinks.

Table 4. Inlinks Retrieved from Alexa of Websites of Universities in Karnataka

S. No.	*Name of the University*	*URL*	*Type*	*Sites linking in*
1	Jawaharlal Nehru Centre for Advanced Scientific Research	*www.jncasr.ac.in*	Private	8259
2	Indian Institute of Science	*www.iisc.ernet.in*	Central	4315
3	Gulbarga University	*www.gulbarga university.kar.nic.in*	State	3336
4	Karnataka Veterinary Animal and Fisheries Sciences University	*www.kvafsu.kar. nic.in*	State	3336
5	National Institute of Mental Health and Neuro Sciences	*www.nimhans.kar. nic.in*	Private	3336
6	Manipal Academy of Higher Education	*www.manipal.edu*	Central	1673
7	Visvesvaraya Technological University	*www.vtu.ac.in*	State	689
8	National Law School of India University	*www.nls.ac.in*	State	506
9	University of Mysore	*www.uni-mysore.ac.in*	State	421
10	Rajiv Gandhi University of Health Sciences	*www.rguhs.ac.in*	State	362

11	International Institute of Information Technology	*www.iiitb.ac.in*	Private	361
12	Karnataka State Open University	*www.ksoumysore.edu.in*	State	354
13	Christ University	*www.christuniversity.in*	Private	349
14	Alliance University	*www.alliance.edu.in*	Private	233
15	Mangalore University	*www.mangaloreuniversity.ac.in*	State	220
16	Karnatak University	*www.kud.ac.in*	State	195
17	University of Agricultural Sciences, Dharwad	*www.uasd.edu*	State	187
18	University of Agricultural Sciences, Bangalore	*www.uasbangalore.edu.in*	State	169
19	Swami Vivekananda Yoga Anusandhana Samsthana	*www.svyasa.org*	Private	155
20	Bangalore University	*www.bangaloreuniversity.ac.in*	State	151
21	K L E University	*www.kleuniversity.edu.in*	Private	151
22	Kuvempu University	*www.kuvempu.ac.in*	State	132
23	Azim Premji University	*www.azimpremjiuniversity.edu.in*	Private	125
24	Jagadguru Sri Shivarathreeshwara University	*www.jssuni.edu.in*	Private	109
25	Jain University	*www.jainuniversity.ac.in*	Private	104
26	Kannada University	*www.kannadauniversity.org*	State	91
27	NITTE University	*www.nitte.edu.in*	Private	89
28	Tumkur University	*www.tumkuruniversity.in*	State	80
29	B.L.D.E. University	*www.bldeuniversity.org*	Private	80
30	Rani Channamma University	*www.rcub.ac.in*	State	69
31	Yenepoya University	*www.yenepoya.edu.in*	Private	68
32	Central University of Karnataka	*www.cuk.ac.in*	Central	67
33	Karnataka State Law University	*www.kslu.ac.in*	State	66

34	Sri Siddhartha University	*www.sahe.in*	Private	46
35	Karnataka State Women's University	*www.kswu.ac.in*	State	43
36	Sri Devraj Urs University	*www.sduu.ac.in*	Private	30
37	Davanagere University	*www.davangere university.ac.in*	State	17
38	Karnataka Sanskrit University	*www.ksu.ac.in*	State	12
39	Vijayanagara Sri Krishnadevaraya University	*www.vskub.org*	State	12
40	KSGH Music and Performing Arts University	*www.musicuniversity. ac.in*	State	2

Table IV reveals the Inlinks retrieved from Alexa of Websites of Universities in Karnataka. It is understood from the table that Jawaharlal Nehru Centre for Advanced Scientific Research, Indian Institute of Science, Gulbarga University, Karnataka Veterinary Animal and Fisheries Sciences University, National Institute of Mental Health and Neuro Sciences, Manipal Academy of Higher Education ranked at top with high inlinks. Visvesvaraya Technological University, Kannada University, NITTE University, Tumkur University, B.L.D.E. University, Rani Channamma University, Yenepoya University, Central University of Karnataka, Karnataka State Law University, Sri Siddhartha University, Karnataka State Women's University, Sri Devraj Urs University, Davanagere University, Karnataka Sanskrit University, Vijayanagara Sri Krishnadevaraya University, KSGH Music and Performing Arts University have less than 100 inlinks and they are universities are low ranked accordingly .

Table 5. Inlinks Retrieved from Alexa of Websites of Universities in Kerala

S. No.	*Name of the University*	*URL*	*Type*	*Sites linking in*
1	Kerala University of Fisheries and Ocean Studies	*www.kufos.ac.in*	State	843

2	Sree Sankaracharya University of Sanskrit	*www.ssus.ac.in*	State	571
3	University of Calicut	*www.universityof calicut.info*	State	454
4	Kerala Kalamandalam	*www.kalaman dalam.org*	Private	400
5	National University of Advanced Legal Studies	*www.nuals.ac.in*	State	332
6	Kannur University	*www.kannur university.ac.in*	State	302
7	Mahatma Gandhi University	*www.mgu.ac.in*	State	154
8	Indian Institute of Space Science and Technology	*www.iist.ac.in*	Central	122
9	Cochin University of Science & Technology	*www.cusat.ac.in*	State	99
10	University of Kerala	*www.ideku.net*	State	94
11	Kerala University of Health Sciences	*www.kuhs.ac.in*	State	89
12	Kerala Agricultural University	*www.kau.edu*	State	60
13	Kerala Veterinary and Animal Sciences University	*www.kvasu.ac.in*	State	35
14	Central University of Kerala	*www.cukerala.ac.in*	Central	32

Table V exhibits the Inlinks retrieved from Alexa of Websites of Universities in Kerala. It is revealed from the table that Cochin University of Science & Technology, Kerala, University of Kerala, Kerala University of Health Sciences, Kerala Agricultural University, Kerala Veterinary and Animal Sciences University and Central University of Kerala have less than 100 inlinks and they are ranked accordingly.

STATISTICAL ANALYSIS

H_0: There is no significant difference in the Mean Score between the Types of Universities.

H_1: There is significant difference in the Mean Score between the Types of Universities.

Table 6. Classification of Alexa Inlinks of Websites Vs State Vs Types of Universities

S. No	*Alexa Inlinks*	*Tamil Nadu*				*Andhra Pradesh*				*Karnataka*				*Kerala*			
		CU	*PU*	*SGU*	*Total*	*CU*	*PU*	*SGU*	*Total*	*CU*	*PU*	*SGU*	*Total*	*CU*	*PU*	*SGU*	*Total*
1	Below 100	0 (0.0)	5 (10.4)	6 (12.5)	11 (22.9)	2 (4.8)	2 (4.8)	9 (21.4)	13 (31.0)	1 (2.5)	5 (12.5)	9 (22.5)	15 (37.5)	1 (7.1)	0 (0.0)	5 (35.7)	6 (42.9)
2	100 - 200	1 (0.2)	7 (14.6)	8 (16.7)	16 (33.3)	1 (2.4)	0 (0.0)	9 (21.4)	10 (23.8)	0 (0.0)	5 (12.5)	5 (12.5)	10 (25.0)	1 (7.1)	0 (0.0)	1 (7.1)	2 (14.3)
3	201 - 400	0 (0.0)	4 (8.3)	3 (6.3)	7 (14. 6)	1 (2.4)	2 (4.8)	7 (16.7)	10 (23.8)	0 (0.0)	3 (7.5)	3 (7.5)	6 (15.0)	0 (0.0)	1 (7.1)	2 (14.3)	3 (21.4)
4	401 - 1000	3 (0.6)	5 (10.4)	1 (2.1)	9 (18.8)	0 (0.0)	2 (4.8)	2 (4.8)	4 (9.5)	0 (0.0)	0 (0.0)	3 (7.5)	3 (7.5)	0 (0.0)	0 (0.0)	3 (21.4)	3 (21.4)
5	Above 1000	0 (0.0)	4 (8.3)	1 (2.1)	5 (10.4)	0 (0.0)	0 (0.0)	5 (11.9)	5 (11.9)	2 (5.0)	2 (5.0)	2 (5.0)	6 (15.0)	0 (0.0)	0 (0.0)	0 (0.0)	0 (0.0)
	Total	4 (0.8)	25 (52.1)	19 (39.6)	48 (100.0)	4 (9.5)	6 (14.3)	32 (76.2)	42 (100.0)	3 (7.5)	15 (37.5)	22 (55.0)	40 (100.0)	2 (14.3)	1 (7.1)	11 (78.6)	14 (100.0)

CU – Central University; PU – Private University; SGU – State Government University

Table VI represents the Classification of Alexa Inlinks of websites vs. State vs. Type of university. The following are the major findings derived from the table.

In Tamil Nadu, 5 universities are ranked with above 1000 Alexa Inlinks. Out of five universities, 4 universities are Private (AMET University, Bharath University, SASTRA University and Saveetha University) and 1 university belongs to State Government (Tamil Nadu Physical Education and Sports University).

In Andhra Pradesh, 5 universities are ranked with above 1000 Alexa Inlinks. All these 5 universities belong to State Government (Jawaharlal Nehru Technological University - Kakinada, Kakatiya University, Mahatma Gandhi University, Sri Padmavati Mahila Vishwavidyalayam and Sri Venkateswara Veterinary University).

In Karnataka, 6 universities are ranked with above 1000 Alexa Inlinks. Out of the six universities, 2 universities belong to Central Government (Indian Institute of Science and Manipal Academy of Higher Education), 2 universities are private (Jawaharlal Nehru Centre for Advanced Scientific Research and National Institute of Mental Health and Neuro Sciences) and 2 universities belong to Central University (Gulbarga University and Karnataka Veterinary, Animal and Fisheries Sciences University).

In Kerala, no university is ranked with above 1000 Alexa Inlinks.

The Descriptive Table provides statistics on Mean, Std Deviation and 95% confidence intervals for the Dependent Variable 'Sites linking in' and each type of universities such as Central University, Private University and Central University as well as when all groups are combined (Total). It is obvious that State University has highest mean inlinks and the State University has low in number.

Table 7. Descriptive

Sites linking in	*N*	*Mean*	*Std. Deviation*	*Std. Error*	*95% Confidence Interval for Mean*		*Minimum*	*Maximum*
					Lower Bound	*Upper Bound*		
Central University	13	706.62	1181.967	327.819	-7.64	1420.87	32	4315
Private University	47	639.70	1358.029	198.089	240.97	1038.43	20	8259
State University	84	425.36	846.443	92.355	241.67	609.05	2	5631
Total	144	520.71	1067.462	88.955	344.87	696.55	2	8259

Table 8. Test of Homogeneity of Variances

Levene Statistic	*df1*	*df2*	*Sig.*
1.692	2	141	.188

The significance value 0.188 is greater than 0.05, specifies the groups we compare have the assumption of homogeneity of variance is met.

Table 9. ANOVA

Sites linking in	*Sum of Squares*	*df*	*Mean Square*	*F*	*Sig.*
Between Groups	1878511.558	2	939255.779	.822	.442
Within Groups	1.611E8	141	1142314.597		
Total	1.629E8	143			

The p-value in the ANOVA table is .442 which is greater than 0.05 specifies the statistically significant difference in the mean score of Inlinks of Central University, Private University and State University.

Table 10. Turkey HSD Multiple Comparison between Types of Universities

(I) Type	*(J) Type*	*Mean Difference (I-J)*	*Std. Sig.*	*Error*	*95% Confidence Interval Lower Bound*	*Upper Bound*
Central Uni.	Private Uni.	66.913	334.925	.978	-726.43	860.26
	State Uni.	281.258	318.543	.652	-473.28	1035.80
Private Uni.	Central Uni.	-66.913	334.925	.978	-860.26	726.43
	State Uni.	214.345	194.688	.515	-246.82	675.51
State Uni.	Central Uni.	-281.258	318.543	.652	-1035.80	473.28
	Private Uni.	-214.345	194.688	.515	-675.51	246.82

The table of Turkey Multiple Comparison Test between the groups portrays statistically significant difference between the central university and private university, state government university (p-value .978, .652) respectively. It is also seen the statistically significant difference between the Private university and state government university (p-value is .515) which is greater than 0.05.

From the analysis it is inferred that all the Means are reliably different from any of the other Means. So our Null Hypothesis is rejected and there is inequality of number of inlinks is existing between the types of university.

CONCLUSION

The recent years have witnessed the emergence of webometrics or cybermetrics (Jeyshankar, Ramesh Babu and Gopalakrishnan, 2009). The websites are playing important role in the webometric study which consists of web domain, sites and web pages. This study emphasized on the inlinks of Alexa for each websites of universities in the four states. With the result of the analysis, it can be inferred that the central university inlinks are highest among the three, the private university is in between central and state government university and the state government university scores the last portion are revealed from our analysis. So it is suggested to the universities under state government need to attract more links by the services and update of the news and galleries.

REFERENCE

1. Alexa Internet (2008), "Alexa history", available at: www.alexa.com. (Accessed on 5th August 2012).
2. Almind, Tomas C. and Ingwersen, Peter (1997). "Informetric analyses on the World Wide Web: Methodological approaches to 'webometrics'". *Journal of Documentation,* 53 (4): 404-426.
3. Didegah, Fereshteh and Erfanmanesh, Mohammad Amin (2010). The study of Malaysian Public Universities' performance on the World Wide Web. *Library Hi Tech News,* (3):7-11.
4. Didegah, Fereshteh and Goltaji, Marzieh (2010). Link analysis and impact of top universities of Islamic world on the World Wide Web. *Library Hi Tech News,* (8):12-16.
5. Erfanmanesh, Mohammadamin and Didegah, Fereshteh

(2011). Visibility and impact of Iranian research institutions on the web. *Library Hi Tech News,* (1): 4-9.

6. Islam, M.A., and Alam, M.S. (2011). Webometric study of private universities in Bangladesh. *Malaysian Journal of Library & Information Science,* 16(2):115 126.

7. Jeyshankar, R. and Ramesh Babu, B. (2009). Websites of universities in Tamil Nadu: a webometric study. *Annals of Library and Information Studies,* 56(2):69-79.

8. Jeyshankar, R. Ramesh Babu, B and Gopalakrishnan, S. (2009). Basic frame work of webometric study: A study. *KELPRO Bulletin,* 13(1), 41-48.

9. Jose, Luis Ortega, Isidro, F. Aguillo and Joss, Antonio Prieto (2006). Longitudinal Study of Contents and Elements in the Scientific Web environment. *Journal of Information Science,* 32(4):344-351.

10. Lee, Moosung and Park, H.W. (2012). Exploring the web visibility of world-class universities. *Scientometrics,* 90(4):201-218.

11. Ramesh Babu, R., Jeyshankar and Rao P. N. (2010). Websites of Central Universities in India: A Webometric Analysis. *DESIDOC Journal of Library & Information Technology,* 30(4):33-43.

12. Ramesh Babu, R., Jeyshankar and Rao P. N. (2010). Websites of Central Universities in India: A Webometric Analysis. *DESIDOC Journal of Library & Information Technology,* 30(4):33-43.

13. Rousseau, Ronald (1997). Sitations: an exploratory study. *Cybermetrics,* 1(1):1. Available at: http://www.cindoc.csic.es/ cybermetrics/ articles/v1i1p1.html (Accessed on 5th October 2012).

14. Shukla, Akhandanand and Tripathi, Aditya (2009). Webometric Analysis of Institutes of National Importance in India. *IASLIC Bulletin,* 54 (3):165-180.

15. Thelwall, Mike and Wilkinson, David (2003). Three Target Document Range Metrics for University Websites. *Journal of the American Society for Information Science and Technology,* 54(6):489-496.

16. Wilkinson, David, Thelwall, Mike, and Li, Xuemei (2003). Exploiting Hyperlinks to Study Academic Web Use. *Social Science Computer Review,* 21(3):340-351.

4

Bibliometric Mapping of the Published Literature in the journal *Data Mining and Knowledge Discovery*, 2005-2014

Santanu Das

ABSTRACT

Data Mining and Knowledge Discovery is an International journal published by the Springer USA. A total of 358 publications from 57 issues of the journal were published during 2005 to 2014. It has outstanding contribution in the dissemination of Data Mining and Knowledge Discovery research on global platform as it publishes both in print and electronic format. A bibliometric analysis of contributions published in the journal Data Mining and Knowledge Discovery from 2005 to 2014 has been presented in this paper. Attempt has been made to study all 57 issues of this journal on the basis of different parameters, viz., author productivity, extent of authors' collaboration, authors' institutional affiliation, authors' geographic affiliation, type of publication, number of citations used per article and year-wise distribution of papers. An attempt has been made to determine the recent trends of data mining and knowledge discovery research through the present study.

Keywords: Single journal study; Bibliometrics; *Data* Mining and Knowledge Discovery, Publication analysis

1. INTRODUCTION

Scholarly journals remain the prominent and certified means of sharing recent research finding and asserting new ideas between and among academia (Tomney and Burton, 1998), building scientific communities and supplying a useable indexed archive of thought, communicating information (Campanario, 1996 and Enger, 2009). Academic journals are also the vehicles by which rewards like recognition, salaries, prestige, priority and funding are given, and they also build a collective knowledge base (Campanario, 1996). They also serve as the indicators of literature growth in any field of knowledge (Thanuskodi, 2012) and to map this growth of literature, the use of bibliometric techniques has become a norm in library and information science (LIS) research internationally for evaluation and analysis purposes. Alan Pritchard first introduced the term bibliometrics in 1969 and defined it as "the branch of information theory which attempts to analyze quantitatively the properties and, behaviour of recorded knowledge existing in the form of books, periodicals, etc". Initially, bibliometric study was a simple statistical method of counting to evaluate and quantify the growth of a subject. Bibliometric techniques are now being used for a variety of purposes like determination of various scientific indicators, evaluation of scientific output, selection of journals for the libraries, forecasting the research potential of a particular field and so on (Ramakrishnana & Babu, 2007).

The journal *Data Mining and Knowledge Discovery* provides an international forum for the publication of theory, techniques and practice for extracting information from large databases. It was first published in the year 1997 by Springer United States of America. It publishes original technical papers in both the research and practice of data mining and knowledge discovery, surveys and tutorials of important areas and techniques, and detailed descriptions of significant applications. Topics of interest include statistics, databases, pattern recognition and learning, data visualization, uncertainty modeling, data warehousing and OLAP, optimization, and high performance computing. The journal basically features theoretical, experimental and applied papers. Theoretical papers report a significant conceptual advance in the design of algorithms or other processes for some data mining and knowledge discovery task. Experimental papers detail a test of one or more theoretical ideas in a laboratory or natural setting. Application papers cover successful application of some already established technique to a significant real world problem involving Data Mining and Knowledge Discovery. According to the Journal Citation Report (JCR) of 2014, the Impact Factor (IF) of the journal is 1.987.

In this paper an attempt has been made to identify the publication growth and collaboration research on data mining and knowledge discovery through bibliometric mapping of the published literature in the journal *Data Mining and Knowledge Discovery* during the period 2005-2014.

2. LITERATURE REVIEW

Single journals have been the focus of many bibliometric and scientometric studies. A number of contributors have conducted bibliometric analysis of the literature of different subject domain in different countries around the globe. The Journal of Research in Music Education (JRME) was analysed by Ebie in the year 2002. He analysed the subject coverage of the journal to ascertain the active and poorly research areas of study in music. Ebie analysed 819 articles in volumes published between 1953 and 2002. The study reported a lack of contributions on choral or vocal music, string or orchestral groups and non-performance music education at elementary and secondary levels. Hazarika, Goswami and Das (2003) studied articles published in the journal Indian Forester. The results indicated that the number of articles published ranged from a low of 114 in 1992 to a high of 156 in 1996. The main contributors were affiliated to research institutes (51.3%) especially from the Indian Council of Forestry Research and Education; the number of foreign contributions is very small at about 2%; the percentage of multi-authored works was about 64.5%; the most popular area of research was silviculture (30.6%). Narang (2004) analysed 737 articles published in *Indian Journal of Pure and applied Mathematics* published during 1998-2002 and found that contributions are increasing in successive volumes, journal articles are the most cited items and Delhi University was the top contributors during the period of study. McElwee and Atherton (2005) undertook a bibliometric study on the International Journal of Entrepreneurship and Innovation (IJEI), to determine the publication trends and pattern of research in the field of entrepreneurship. A total of 70 articles published between 1999 and 2003 were analysed. From this analysis, the theoretical, methodology trends and themes were determined. Maheswarana, Sathish Kumar and Sridharan (2008) analyzed the *Journal of Structural Engineering* to study the main areas and topics that were the focus of the published papers during twelve years of the journal. A total of twelve year period from 1993 to 2005 was covered. The authors came up with the findings that the most popular subject was concrete composites & materials and Reinforced concrete structure. Most of the contributions were from Indian academics and the most prolific academic institution was Indian Institute of Technology, Kanpur. The literature of D-Lib Magazine was studied by Park (2010) covering thirteen years and the data were collected by examining issues from July 1995 to May/June 2008. The findings showed that two and more authors' contribution was the highest with a ratio of 57%; most of the authors had a single contribution; the proportion of the male authors was much higher with a ratio of 74%; authors from the United States contributed 70% of the articles and the average number of references was 15.

3. OBJECTIVES

In this analysis, the research publication trends in data mining and knowledge discovery as reflected through the journal *Data Mining and Knowledge Discovery are* studied. The present study has been designed with the following objectives:

- To examine the growth data mining and knowledge discovery research during 2005-2014;
- To study the main areas and topics those were the focus of the published papers during the ten years of the journal;
- To determine the pattern of authorship;
- To determine the degree of collaboration in data mining and knowledge discovery research;
- To determine the frequency and mean number of references cited by researchers in the field of data mining and knowledge discovery research
- To identify the most prolific institutions and prolific authors;
- To identify and analyse the country-wise contribution of research output in the field of data mining and knowledge discovery,
- To recognise the highly cited articles published from 2005 onwards.

4. METHODOLOGY

For the purpose of the present study, *Data Mining and Knowledge Discovery* has been selected as the source journal. Fifty Seven issues of Nineteen volumes from 2005 to 2014 (vol. 10-28) have been selected for the study.

The relevant papers for the study have been downloaded from the Springer database. The 358 papers selected for present study were entered into a Microsoft Excel spread sheet which identified variable such as author, author's affiliation, country of origin, year of publication, number of references etc. It should be noted that editorials, short Communications, notes, book review are excluded from the study. Finally, all relevant data were sorted, tabulated and assimilated in a logical order for analytical purpose.

5. ANALYSIS AND DISCUSSIONS

5.1. Year and Volume wise Distribution of Articles

Table 1 gives the year-wise distribution of articles in the said period of the journal. On the whole, from 19 volumes and 57 issues of the journal under study, the total number of papers published is 358. The number of articles varies from year to year and as per the observations, out of total 358 articles the maximum contribution of 49 articles (13.69%) was seen in the year 2014. The least contribution of 9 articles (2.51%) was made in the year 2005.

Table 1. Year, Volume & Issue-wise Distribution of Articles

Year	*Vol.*	*Issue-wise no. of contribution*					*Total*
		1	*2*	*3*	*4*	*5*	
2005	10	2	3	4	-	-	9 (2.51)
2005	11	4	5	5	-	-	14 (3.91)
2006	12	6	8	-	-	-	14 (3.91)
2006	13	5	6	5	-	-	16 (4.47)
2007	14	6	3	4	-	-	13 (3.63)
2007	15	7	6	4	-	-	17 (4.75)
2008	16	5	4	4	-	-	13 (3.63)
2008	17	8	8	5	-	-	21 (5.86)
2009	18	5	5	6	-	-	16 (4.47)
2009	19	5	8	5	-	-	18 (5.03)
2010	20	6	5	6	-	-	17 (4.75)

2010	21	7	8	7	-	-	22 (6.14)
2011	22	10	7	-	-	-	17 (4.75)
2011	23	5	5	5	-	-	15 (4.19)
2012	24	10	6	8	-	-	24 (6.71)
2012	25	5	9	9	-	-	23 (6.42)
2013	26	7	6	6	-	-	19 (5.31)
2013	27	7	4	10	-	-	21 (5.87)
2014	28	8	8	8	8	17	49 (13.69)
G. Total	118 (32.96)	114 (31.84)	101 (28.22)	8 (2.23)	17 (4.75)	358 (100)	

Note: Numeric in parentheses represents percentage.

5.2. Authorship pattern of the contributions

Table 2 gives a detailed overview of authorship pattern of papers published from 2005 (vol.10) to 2014 (vol. 28). It can be seen from the Table that papers with more than 3 authors, 122 articles (34.08%) occupied the first position, followed by papers with two authors, 107 articles (29.89%). More than Five author papers took the last place that is 14 articles (3.91%). It can be seen that authors tend towards collective writing and research work is very much group oriented.

Table 2. Year wise authorship pattern

Year	*Number of Authors*						*Total*
	Single	*Two*	*Three*	*Four*	*Five*	*More than Five*	
2005	2	8	7	4	2	-	23
2006	1	7	13	6	2	1	30
2007	3	12	6	5	2	2	30
2008	2	8	13	6	2	3	34
2009	3	12	8	8	3	-	34
2010	4	7	9	12	3	4	39
2011	3	8	10	6	4	1	32
2012	5	16	15	6	3	2	47
2013	2	13	18	5	2	-	40
2014	4	16	23	4	1	1	49
Total	29 (8.1)	107 (29.89)	122 (34.08)	62 (17.32)	24 (6.7)	14 (3.91)	358 (100)

Note: Numeric in parentheses represents percentage.

5.3. Degree of Collaboration

In order to determine the degree of collaboration in quantitative terms, the formula suggested by Subramanyam has been used (1982). The formula is given below:

Degree of collaboration $C = N_m/(N_m+N_s)$

- C = Degree of collaboration
- N_m = Number of Multiple authors
- N_s = Number of Single authors

Table 3 displays the trend in patterns of single and joint authorship in the journal *Data Mining and Knowledge Discovery* during 2005-14. The degree of collaboration ranges from 0.86 to 0.97. The highest degree of collaboration was seen in the year 2006 (0.97). The average degree of collaboration is 0.92 during the period under study.

Table 3. Year wise Degree of Collaboration

Year	*Single Authored Papers (N_s)*	*Multi Authored Papers (N_m)*	*Degree of Collaboration (C)*
2005	2	21	0.91
2006	1	29	0.97
2007	3	27	0.9
2008	2	32	0.94
2009	3	31	0.91
2010	4	35	0.86
2011	3	29	0.91
2012	5	42	0.89
2013	2	38	0.95
2014	4	45	0.92
Total	29	329	0.92

5.4. Distribution of References

Table 4 shows the number of citations, total number of references, and average number of references per article. A Total of 13093 references are distributed amongst 57 journal issues having 358 articles. It is observed that the number of references per year varies from year to year. The year 2014 has the highest number of references per article and the year 2005 has the lowest number of references per article.

Table 4. Year wise distribution of Reference

Year	*Number of Papers*	*Number of References*	*Average no. of References per Paper*
2005	23	547	23.78
2006	30	996	33.2
2007	30	1132	37.73
2008	34	1098	32.29
2009	34	965	28.38
2010	39	1237	31.72
2011	32	1166	36.44
2012	47	1992	42.38
2013	40	1752	43.8
2014	49	2208	45.06
Total	358	13093	36.57

5.5. Subject areas of the articles

Table 5 gives the discipline-wise distribution of papers, which shows that the subject Web mining constituted the highest number of articles, i.e., 61 (17.04%) followed by the subject Data visualization with 44 articles (12.3%). Interactive Information Retrieval occupied the third place with 42 articles (11.73%). Other broad subject fields include Cluster analysis, Sequential pattern mining, Algorithm Analysis and Problem Complexity, Artificial Intelligence etc.

Table 5. Broad Subject Areas Covered by Articles

Sl. No.	Subject Areas	No. of Articles	Percentage (%)
1	Web mining	61	17.04
2	Data visualization	44	12.3
3	Interactive Information Retrieval	42	11.73
4	Cluster analysis	34	9.49
5	Sequential pattern mining	31	8.66
6	Algorithm Analysis and Problem Complexity	27	7.54
7	Artificial Intelligence	23	6.42
8	Computing Methodologies	23	6.42
9	Probability and Statistics in Data Mining	22	6.15
10	Decompounding	18	5.03
11	Others	33	9.22
	Total	358	100

5.6. Distribution by Nature of Research

The nature of research in the publications is grouped as theoretical, experimental, general review, application based etc., as per the classification adopted by the Springer database. Table 6 shows that 27.09% of the articles are experimental in nature, 15.64% are theoretical, 14.52% are application based and 13.69% are both theoretical and experimental based. Experimental articles in data mining and knowledge discovery seem to be popular among the contributions.

Table 6. Distribution of articles by nature of research

Sl. No.	Nature of Research	No. of Articles	Percentage (%)
1	Theoretical	56	15.64
2	Theoretical and Experimental	49	13.69
3	Experimental	97	27.09
4	Applications	52	14.52
5	Applications and Theoretical	29	8.1
6	Applications and Experimental	36	10.06
7	General-Review	22	6.15
8	Others	17	4.75
	Total	358	100

5.7. Most Productive Institution

Table 7 presents the most prolific institution, which produces the most number of authors, which contributed papers to the journal under study. It is found that University of Minnesota, USA has contributed most number of papers. This centre has produced 28 papers during the period of study, followed by University of Antwerp, Belgium with 25 articles. Other prolific institutions include Tsinghua University, Wayne State University, Saarland University etc.

Table 7. Top 10 most productive Institution

Sl. No.	*Name of the Institution*	*Country*	*No. of Article*
1	University of Minnesota	United States of America	28
2	University of Antwerp	Belgium	25
3	Tsinghua University	China	22
4	Wayne State University	United States of America	18
5	Saarland University	Germany	14
6	University of Trento	Italy	11
7	University of Illinois at Urbana-Champaign	United States of America	11
8	Simon Fraser University	Canada	8
9	Karlsruhe Institute of Technology	Germany	8
10	University of Cordoba	Spain	7

5.8. Most Prolific Author

Table 8 presents the data on the contribution of prolific authors. On the whole, a total of 1102 authors contributed 358 papers over a period of ten years during 2005-2014. The most prolific author is Nikolaj Tatti of University of Antwerp who contributed 23 papers, followed by George Karypis with 17 papers, Jilles Vreeken and Lizhu Zhou 14 papers each and Chandan K. Reddy with 12 papers.

Table 8. Top 10 most productive Author

Ra-nk	Name	Institutional Affiliation	Country	No. of Article
1	Nikolaj Tatti	University of Antwerp	Belgium	23
2	George Karypis	University of Minnesota	United States of America	17
3	Jilles Vreeken	Saarland University	Germany	14
4	Lizhu Zhou	Tsinghua University	China	14
5	Chandan K. Reddy	Wayne State University	United States of America	12
6	Alessandro Moschitti	University of Trento	Italy	10
7	Jie Tang	Tsinghua University	China	9
8	Ming Ji	University of Illinois at Urbana-Champaign	United States of America	9
9	Achim Rettinger	Karlsruhe Institute of Technology	Germany	8
10	Michael Brydon	Simon Fraser University	Canada	8

5.9. Geographical Distribution of articles

On the whole 1072 authors belonging to 64 countries contributed a total of 358 papers. Table 9 shows that the country wise distribution of the articles and reveals that 19.27% of the total articles were contributed by the authors from USA, followed by China (10.61%), Belgium (7.26%) and Germany (6.99 %) respectively.

Table 9. Country wise distribution of articles

Sl. No.	Country	No. of Articles	Percentage (%)
1	United States of America	69	19.27
2	China	38	10.61
3	Belgium	26	7.26
4	Germany	25	6.99
5	United Kingdom	12	3.35
6	Spain	11	3.07
7	Italy	10	2.79
8	3 countries with 9 articles	27	7.54

9	4 countries with 7 articles	28	7.82
10	7 countries with 5 articles	35	9.78
11	11 countries with 3 articles	33	9.22
12	12 countries with 2 articles	24	6.71
13	20 countries with 1 article	20	5.59
	Total	358	100

5.10. Highly cited articles

Table 10 showcases the highly cited papers which were published during the period of study. For this particular analysis, the data was collected through *Google Scholar.* Out of 358 papers, 342 papers got at least one citation. A paper by Ying Zhao et al., published in the year 2005, received highest numbers of citation (437).

Table 10. Top 10 Highly cited papers (According to Google Scholar)

Ra-nk	*Title of the Article*	*Author*	*Year*	*No. of Citations*
1	Hierarchical clustering algorithms for document datasets	Ying Zhao et al.	2005	437
2	Computing LTS Regression for Large Data Sets	Peter J. Rousseeuw & Katrien Van Driessen	2006	332
3	Ordinal, Continuous and Heterogeneous *k*-Anonymity Through Microaggregation	Josep Domingo Ferrer and Vicenç Torra	2005	289
4	Finding frequent patterns in a large sparse graph	Michihiro Kuramochi and George Karypis	2005	230
5	Automatic Subspace Clustering of High Dimensional Data	Rakesh Agarwal et al.	2005	189
6	GenMax: An Efficient Algorithm for Mining Maximal Frequent Itemsets	Karam Gouda and Mohammed J. Zaki	2005	160
7	A systematic approach to the assessment of fuzzy association rules	Didier Dubois et al.	2006	160

8	Fast Distributed Outlier Detection in Mixed Attribute Data Sets	Matthew Eric Otey et al.	2006	146
9	Manifold elastic net: a unified framework for sparse dimension reduction	Tianyi Zhou et al.	2011	143
10	Accurate Prediction of Protein Disordered Regions by Mining Protein Structure Data	Jianlin Cheng et al.	2005	141

Note: As on 28.04.2015

5.11. Special Issues

Special issues of the journal are brought out to present a collection of papers that focus on a single topic or theme. Table 11 identifies the special issues published in the *Data Mining and Knowledge Discovery* for the period of study. There have been a total of 15 special issues for the period of study. The special issues have focused on topics that are of significant interest to computer science professionals. It can be noticed that special issues on current topics of readers' interest such as Data Mining with Matrices, Intelligent Interactive Data Visualization etc. have been brought out.

Table 11. Special issues published during 2005-2014

Sl. No.	*Year*	*Vol. No.*	*Issue No.*	*Topic*
1	2008	17	1	Selected Papers from ECML PKDD 2008
2	2008	17	2	Special Issue on Utility-Based Data Mining
3	2009	19	2	Selected Papers from ECML PKDD 2009
4	2010	20	2	Outlier Detection
5	2010	20	3	Impacting Patient Care by Mining Medical Data
6	2010	21	1	Global Modeling Using Local Patterns
7	2010	21	2	Selected Papers from ECML PKDD 2010
8	2011	22	3	Data Mining with Matrices
9	2012	24	2	Data Mining for Sustainability
10	2012	24	3	A Decade of Mining the Web

11	2012	25	2	Selected Papers from ECML PKDD 2011
12	2012	25	3	Data Mining Technologies for Computational Social Science
13	2013	27	1	Intelligent Interactive Data Visualization
14	2013	27	3	ECML PKDD 2013 and ECML PKDD 2012
15	2014	28	5-6	ECML PKDD 2014

6. CONCLUSION

When a single journal is studied bibliometrically, it creates a portrait of the journal, provides an insight that is beyond the superficial. It helps to indicate the quality, maturity and productivity of the journal. It informs about the research orientation that the journal supports to disseminate and its influence on author's choice as a channel to communicate or retrieve information for their research needs. It helps indicate the importance or significance of the journal in a field and somehow reflects the activity of research in the field. The journal *Data Mining and Knowledge Discovery* is a prominent journal in the data mining and knowledge discovery field. Though the number of articles published each year shows variations, the increasing number of citations per year shows that data mining and knowledge discovery research workers are seeking a greater platform for their work. The analysis shows that there have been statistically significant changes in the types of article and in the numbers of references per article. Contributions to the journal are more from the American authors. It is further concluded that the field of research, covering web mining technologies, has produced greater output in the form of research papers, indicating enhanced interest of researchers and authors in data mining and knowledge discovery research.

REFERENCE

1. Campanario, J. M. (1996). The competition for journal space among referees, editors and other authors ad its influence on journals impact factors. *Journal of the America Society*

for Information Science, 47(3), 184-192.

2. Ebie, B. (2002). Characteristics of 50 years of research samples found in the "Journal of Research in Music Education". *Journal of Research in Music Education, 50*(4), 280-291.

3. Enger, K. B. (2009). Using citation analysis to develop core book collections in academic libraries. *Library and Information Science Research , 31*(2), 107-112.

4. Hazarika, T., Goswami, K., & Das, P. (2003). Bibliometric analysis of Indian Forester: (1991-2000). *IASLIC Bulletin, 48*(4), 213-223.

5. Maheswaran, S., Sathish Kumar, R. D., & Sridharan, K. (2008). Research publication trends in structural engineering based on Journal of Structural Engineering. *Annals of library and Information studies, 55*(1), 17-26.

6. McElwee, G., & Atherton, A. (2005). Publication trends and patterns in entrepreneurship: The case of The International Journal of Entrepreneurship and Innovation. *Journal of Small Business and Enterprise Development, 12*(1), 92-103.

7. Narang, A. (2004). Indian Journal of Pure and Applied Mathematics: A Bibliometric Study. *Annals of library and Information studies, 51*(1), 28-38.

8. Park, T. K. (2010). D-Lib Magazine: Its first thirteen years.. *D-Lib Magazine, 16*(1/2). Retrieved on July 19, 2014, from http://www.dlib.org/dlib/january10/park/01park.html

9. Pritchard, A. (1969). 'Statistical Bibliography or Bibliometrics?. *Journal of Documentation, 25*(4), 348-349.

10. Ramakrishnana, J., & Babu, B. R. (2007). Literature on hepatitis (1984-2003): A bibliometric analysis. *Annals of library and Information studies, 54*(4), 195-200.

11. Subramanyam, K. (1983). Bibliometric studies of research collaboration: A review. *Journal of Information Science, 6*(1), 33-38.

12. Thanuskodi, S. (2012). Bibliometric Analysis of Indian Journal of Agricultural Research. *International journal of information dissemination and technology, 2*(3), 170-175.

13. Tomney, H.C., & Burton, P.F. (1998). Electronic journals: a case study of usage and attitudes among academics. *Journal of Information Science, 24*(6), 1-10.

5

Performance Measurement and Metrics (PMM) Journal (2005- 2014): A Bibliometric Analysis

Naheem K.T.

ABSTRACT

This chapter presents results of bibliometric analysis of 145 articles which were published during the period 2005-2014 (Ten Years), in the Performance Measurement and Metrics (PMM) journal of Emerald. The purpose of the study is to explore the publication trends of the scholarly journal Performance Measurement and Metrics (PMM), and highlight its various important aspects like year-wise distribution, authorship pattern & author productivity, most prolific authors, degree of collaboration, average number of citations and geographical distribution of articles. The results indicate that out of 145 articles, only 74(51%) are multi authored and rest 71 (49%) by single authored. The average number of authors per article is 1.92 and the average productivity per author is 0.52. The average degree of collaboration is found 0.51 per cent.

Keywords: Bibliometric analysis, Performance measurement, Authorship pattern, Author productivity, Degree of Collaboration.

INTRODUCTION

Bibliometric is an emerging thrust area of research in different branches of human knowledge since its inception (Singh & Chander, 2014). It is still acting as a core area of research in LIS domain. The term was coined by Alan Pritchard in a paper published in 1969, titled *Statistical Bibliography or Bibliometrics?(* Pritchard, 1969). It is an application of statistical and mathematical methods to bibliographical studies. It can be defined as the study and measurement of the publication patterns of all forms of written communication and their authorship (Potter, 1981). Bibliometrics has emerged as handy tool to study collection evaluation and building, ranking of journals, identification of core literature, to know the structure of literature, to know the prolific authors to observe the obsolesce of literature, to study user behavior and forecast their further needs (Satija, 2004 & Singh & Chander, 2014).

A bibliometric study of the articles published in journals shows the status of advancement and research in a subject field. Several studies have been conducted using bibliomteric techniques on individual journals in different subject fields including Library and Information Science. So far, there has not been conducted such studies on the "*Performance Measurement and Metrics*" journal of Emerald. So the present study is taken up by the authors.

SOURCE JOURNAL

The study based on *Performance Measurement and Metrics* (PMM) is a leading quarterly double-blind refereed, online international journal of Emerald, charting new qualitative and quantitative developments and techniques for measurement and metrics in the field of Library and Information Science (LIS). It provides an international forum for cross-discipline information professionals, whether practitioners or academics. The journal publishes conceptual papers, empirical research, literature reviews, practical case studies and book reviews three times a year.

Performance Measurement and Metrics (PMM) is abstracted and indexed in *Current Abstracts; Current Awareness Abstracts; Education Full Text; Emerald Management Reviews; INSPEC; Library, Information Science and Technology Abstracts; Library Literature and Information Science Full Text; OmniFile Full Text Mega; OmniFile Full Text Select; Scopus; zetoc* (Emeraldinsight, 2015).

RELATED STUDIES

Single journals have been the focus of many bibliometric and scientometric studies. A number of contributors have conducted bibliometric analysis of library and information science literature in different parts of globe and still it is relatively new and valuable area of research LIS domain. Some of the notable recent studies on LIS journals, which are formed background of the present study, are:

Singh, K. P. et al., (2011) analyzed "DESIDOC Bulletin of Information Technology" for a period of ten years (1992-2002). This study reveals that total 145 articles were published in the 60 issues of the journal. Out of the 145 publications 97 (66.90%) articles published by single author. The study also reveals that 128 items (88.28%) were contributed from India and rest 17 items (11.72%) were contributed from rest of the countries.

Gurjeet Kaur Rattan et.al. (2012) carried out a study on "Malaysian Journal of Library and Information Science" during the period (2007-2011). The results show that out of 100 articles, single authors contributed 27 (27%) articles while the rest 73 (73%) articles are contributed by joint authors. It has been revealed that most of the contributors are from Malaysia. The study shows that about 62.54% of citations are from periodicals.

Swain, C. et.al. (2013) examine the scholarly communications in "Library Review (LR) from 2007 to 2011. The study finds that single authored articles occupy the prominent position indicating the supremacy of solo research in LR. The degree of collaboration in the publications of this journal is found to be 0.36. It is evident that LR has accommodated over 22 citations per article during the publication phase from 2007 to 2011. In regard to country productivity, the UK leads the table, followed by the USA and Nigeria.

Nelson, E. (2013) examined "Journal of Information and Knowledge Management (IIJIKM)" over a four year period of 2010-2013. This study revealed the absence of international collaboration among authors published in the journal. Majority of the authors prefer multiple authorship rather than single authorship.

Mamdapur, G.N. et.al (2013) studied "College & Research Libraries journal" during the period of 1997-2011 revealed Singie authored articles are found to be the highest followed by two and three authored articles. The average degree of collaboration in College & Research Libraries is 0.57. The average author per article is 1.88 for 479 articles. USA has topped the list of ranking of country productivity with 93.24 per cent contributions followed by Canada and China.

Thavamani, Kotti (2014) carried out a bibliometric study of "Malaysian Journal of Library and Information Science" showed that the journal has an average number of authors per paper is 2.06. The highest number of author productivity i.e., 72 (12.522%). Majority 180 (64.516%) of the total contributions represent collaborative research. The average degree of collaboration has been arrived at .64 during the study period.

Tella et.al (2014) examined "*African Journal of Library, Archives and Information Science* (AJLAIS)" for the period between 2000 and 2012. The results of the study reveal that a total of 218 articles were published in the 13-year period, with 21 (9.63 per cent) articles being the highest total in the year 2002. The study showed that the majority of the articles, i.e. 126 (57.8 per cent), were published by single authors. Volume 19 in 2009 had the highest number of citations with a total of 451 (12.4 per cent).

Pandita, Ramesh (2014) carried out a study on "DESIDOC Journal of Library and Information Technology" during the period 2003-2012. A maximum of 147 articles contributed in the journal are on two author pattern, followed by 139 articles as single author. On average 6.20 articles were published by the journal in each issue during the period of investigation with total references 5063, thereby making average 13.83 references each article.

Mulla, K. R.; Dhanamjaya, M. (2014) carried out a Bibliometric analysis "SRELS Journal of Information Management (SRELS-JIM)" during periods of 2000 to 2009. Overall average number of authors per article is 1.66 and average productivity per author is 0.60; majorities 544(79.30%) of articles are published by Indian contributors followed by USA and alternative contributors.

Singh, K.P. Chander, Harish (2014) explored the publication trends of the scholarly journal "*Library Management*" during the period 2006-2012. The results indicate that the majority of the contributions by single authors and most cited documents are journal articles.

OBJECTIVES OF THE STUDY

The following are the objectives of the present study

1. To map year-wise distribution of articles
2. To examine the authorship pattern of the contributions
3. To study author productivity and single and multi authored papers by year

4. To determine degree of collaboration; and
5. To identify the most prolific authors
6. To find the average number of citations per volume; and
7. To examine the geographical distribution of articles.

METHODOLOGY

The data for the present study is collected from the publisher website (*http://emeraldgrouppublishing.com/*) of the journal *"Performance Measurement and Metrics"* covering the period from 2005 to 2014 (Ten Years). A total of 145 articles with necessary details covering information about year –wise distribution of articles, author productivity, authorship pattern by single and multi authored articles by year, degree of collaboration, most prolific authors, average number of citations and geographical distribution of articles were noted down for the present study. Further the collected data were exported into Microsoft Excel, and the same has been verified and taken for the purpose of the study. The collected data was analysed with the Statistical tools such as frequency distribution and percentage analysis and Bibliometric indicators such as Authorship pattern, Citation count; Degree of collaboration, etc to find out the possible solutions for the desired objectives of the present the study. The authorship pattern has been analysed by using K Subramanyam's degree of collaboration in quantitative terms. Average author per paper and productivity per author have been calculated using formula given by Yoshikane et al. Following section discusses the analysis of the data collected and presented under different table headings as per the objectives of the study.

DATA ANALYSIS AND FINDINGS

Year-Wise Distribution of Articles

Table 1 depicts the number of articles published from 2005 to 2014 in the source journal PMM. A total of 145 articles were published during the study period (2005 -2014), out of which the highest number of 22 (15.17 per cent) articles are published in the years 2010, followed by 19 (13.10 per cent) articles in the year 2012 and 16 (11.03 per cent) articles in the year 2009 and so on. The lowest number of articles are published in the years 2005. And in the volumes 7, 8 and 15, equal numbers of articles are published as 13 in each year's viz., 2006, 2007 and 2014. It is found that this journal have an average of 14.5 articles per issue. The number of papers published each year is nearly consistent.

Table 1. Year-wise Distribution of Articles

Year	*Volume*	*No. of issues*	*No. of Articles*	*Percentage*
2005	6	3	8	5.52
2006	7	3	13	8.97
2007	8	3	13	8.97
2008	9	3	14	9.66
2009	10	3	16	11.03
2010	11	3	22	15.17
2011	12	3	13	8.97
2012	13	3	19	13.10
2013	14	3	14	9.66
2014	15	3	13	8.97
10 Years	10 Vols	30	145	100

Authorship Pattern

Table 2 shows the authorship pattern of the journal articles. Single authored articles are top in the list having 71 (48.97 per cent) followed by the two authored articles 37 (25.52 per cent), three authored articles 24 (16.55 per cent), four authored articles 7 (4.83 per cent), and so on during the ten years. It is evidenced that multi authored articles i.e 74 (51 per cent) have only a minor advantage over single authored articles 71 (49 percent) during the period 2005-2014.

Table 2. Distribution of Articles by Authorship

Year	*No. of articles*	*Authorship Value*							*Occurrence of authors*
		One	*Two*	*Three*	*Four*	*Five*	*Six*	*Seven*	
2005	8	5	1	1	1	0	0	0	14
2006	13	7	2	2	1	0	1	0	27
2007	13	6	3	3	1	0	0	0	25
2008	14	8	2	3	1	0	0	0	25
2009	16	7	4	5	0	0	0	0	30
2010	22	9	6	5	1	0	1	0	45
2011	13	7	3	2	0	1	0	0	24
2012	19	9	7	1	1	0	1	0	36
2013	14	6	6	0	1	1	0	0	27
2014	13	7	3	2	0	0	0	1	26
Total	145	71	37	24	7	2	3	1	279
%age	48.97	25.52	16.55	4.83	1.38	2.07	0.69	100.00	

AUTHOR PRODUCTIVITY

Table 3 depicts the data pertaining to author productivity and average author per paper. The Average Author Per Paper (AAPP) and Productivity Per Author is calculated using the formula given by Yoshikane et al (Yoshikane et al, 2009). The formula is mathematically represented as below:

Average Author Per Paper = No. of Authors/No. of Papers

Productivity Per Author = No. of Papers/No. of Authors

It is revealed from the Table 3, that the average number of authors per article is 1.92 for 145 articles published during the period 2005-2014. It is also clear from above Table 3 that for the years 2007 & 2008 and

2009 & 2011 equal average number of authors per article is recorded i.e., 1.69 and 2.17 respectively. The average productivity per author for the period 2005-2014 is 0.52. The years 2000 & 2003, 2002 & 2004 and 2009 & 2011 have recorded equal productivity per author i.e., 0.59, 0.54 and 0.46 respectively.

Table 3. Author Productivity

Year	*Total No. of Papers*	*Total No. of Authors*	*AAPP*	*Productivity per author*
2005	8	24	1.75	0.57
2006	13	27	2.08	0.48
2007	13	25	1.92	0.52
2008	14	25	1.79	0.56
2009	16	30	1.88	0.53
2010	22	45	2.05	0.49
2011	13	24	1.85	0.54
2012	19	36	1.89	0.53
2013	14	27	1.93	0.52
2014	13	26	2.00	0.50
Total	145	279	1.92	0.52

Single and Multi Authored Papers by Year

Table 4 shows the single and multi authored papers. This reveals that there is only a slight advantage of multi authored i.e., 74 (51 per cent) research among the contributions over the single authored articles i.e., 71 (49 per cent). The highest number of multi authored articles i.e., 13 (17.57 per cent) are published in the year 2010 and lowest is in the year 2005 i.e., 3 (4.05 per cent). With regard to the single authored articles, same highest number i.e., 9 (12.68 per cent) articles are found in the years 2009 and 2012. The lowest number in this group is 5 (7.04 per cent) found in the year 2005. This reveals that there has been a positive movement towards the collaborative research among the authors.

Table 4. Single and Multi Authored Papers by Year

Year	Single Authored Articles	%	Multi Authored Articles	%	Total
2005	5	7.04	3	4.05	8
2006	7	9.86	6	8.11	13
2007	6	8.45	7	9.46	13
2008	8	11.27	6	8.11	14
2009	7	9.86	9	12.16	16
2010	9	12.68	13	17.57	22
2011	7	9.86	6	8.11	13
2012	9	12.68	10	13.51	19
2013	6	8.45	8	10.81	14
2014	7	9.86	6	8.11	13
Total	71	100	74	100	145
%age	49		51		100

DEGREE OF AUTHOR'S COLLABORATION

The degree of collaboration among authors who published in the sourse journal "PMM" was determined using the formula proposed by Subramanyam (Subramanyam, 1983), C = Nm / (Nm+Ns) where, C = Degree of collaboration; Nm = number of multi authored works; Ns = Number of single authored works.

In the present study NM = 74, NS = 71, C = 74/ 71+145, C = 0.51

The results of the analysis are presented below in Table 4 revealed that the value of the higher Degree of Collaboration (DC) was 0.59 for the year 2010 followed by 0.57 for the year 2013. The Degree of Collaboration is almost constant during the period covered (i.e., 2005-2014) for the present study.

As a result, the degree of author collaboration in the *Performance Measurement and Metrics* (PMM) journal is 0.51 per cent, which is clearly indicates the improving trend of collaborative research in LIS domain.

Table 4. Degree of Collaboration by Year (Subramanyam's Formula)

Year	Single (Ns)	Multi (Nm)	Total (Nm+Ns)	Degree of Collaboration (DC)
2005	5	3	8	0.38
2006	7	6	13	0.46
2007	6	7	13	0.54
2008	8	6	14	0.43
2009	7	9	16	0.56
2010	9	13	22	0.59
2011	7	6	13	0.46
2012	9	10	19	0.53
2013	6	8	14	0.57
2014	7	6	13	0.46
Total	71	74	145	0.51

PROLIFIC AUTHORS AND THEIR CONTRIBUTIONS DURING 2005-2014

Ranking of authors by number of Articles is given in Table 5. It is found that the leading author is Kyrillidou, M. with 8 articles followed by Chiranov, M. and Poll, R. with 6 articles each. Broady-Preston, J. and Streatfield, D. shared the third position with 4 articles each. There are 6 authors contributing 3 articles each followed by 17 authors contributing 2 articles each and 131 authors contributing 1 articles each during the period 2005-2014.

Table 5. Ranking of authors by no. of Articles

Sl.No	Name	Number of Articles	Rank
1	Kyrillidou, M.	8	1
2	Chiranov, M.	6	2
3	Poll, R.	6	2
4	Broady-Preston, J.	4	3
5	Streatfield, D.	4	3
6	Creaser, C.	3	4

7	Cook, C.	3	4
8	Nagata, H.	3	4
9	Pors, N.O.	3	4
10	Thompson, B.	3	4
11	Voorbij, H.	3	4
12	17 authors contributing 2 each	34	-
13	131 authors contributing 1 each	131	-

DISTRIBUTIONS OF CITATIONS (VOLUME WISE)

For the period under study of the journal PMM, (2005-2014), Table 6 reveals that 10 Volumes have 538 citations appended to the 145 articles. Out of total 538 citations vol.9 (2009) has highest numbers i.e. 116 (21.56 percent) followed by vol.7 (2006) with 113(21.00 per cent) and vol.15 (2014) has the lowest numbers of citations i.e. 2 (0.37 per cent). It worth mentioning here that, though highest number of papers (i.e., 22) are published in the vol. 11 (2010), it hasn't received maximum number of citations. The average number of citations per paper is almost 4. This shows that authors are depending different sources for writing papers.

Table 6. Distributions of Citations (Volume wise)

Year	*Vol. no*	*No. of contributions*	*No. of Citations*	*%*	*Av. No. of Citation/Paper*
2005	6	8	54	10.04	7
2006	7	13	113	21.00	9
2007	8	13	63	11.71	5
2008	9	14	116	21.56	8
2009	10	16	65	12.08	4
2010	11	22	68	12.64	3
2011	12	13	31	5.76	2
2012	13	19	14	2.6	1
2013	14	14	12	2.23	1
2014	15	13	2	0.37	0
	Total	145	538	100	4

GEOGRAPHICAL DISTRIBUTIONS

Geographical distribution of contributions of the source journal PMM, during the study period is given in the Table 7, revealed that majority of the contributors are from UK with 32 (22.7 percent) followed by USA with 29 (20 percent). It is worth mentioning that, the journal attracted authors from 36 countries of different continents. The contributions from India during the study period are only 2 (1.38 per cent).

Table 7. Geographical Distributions

Rank	*Name of the Country*	*No. of Articles*	*Percentage*
1	UK	32	22.07
2	USA	29	20.00
3	Germany	7	4.83
4	Bangladesh	6	4.14
4	Romania	5	3.45
4	Neterlamnds	5	3.45
4	Italy	5	3.45
4	Australia	5	3.45
5	Denmark	4	2.76
6	Southa Africa	3	2.07
6	New Zealand	3	2.07
6	Iran	3	2.07
6	Greece	3	2.07
6	Croatia	3	2.07
7	UAE	2	1.38
7	Spain	2	1.38
7	Portugal	2	1.38
7	Lithuania	2	1.38
7	Latvia	2	1.38
7	Japan	2	1.38
7	India	2	1.38
7	Hungary	2	1.38
7	Canada	2	1.38
7	Bulgria	2	1.38
8	Viatnam	1	0.69
8	South Korea	1	0.69

8	Quatar	1	0.69
8	Poland	1	0.69
8	Pakistan	1	0.69
8	Oman	1	0.69
8	Nigeria	1	0.69
8	Malaysia	1	0.69
8	Malawi	1	0.69
8	Finland	1	0.69
8	Estonia	1	0.69
8	Botswana	1	0.69
Total		145	100

CONCLUSION

This bibliometric study examines the articles published in the Performance Measurement and Metrics journal of Emerald. Various important aspects like growth of contributions by year and volume, authorship patterns, author productivity, single and multi authored papers by year, most prolific contributors, degree of collaboration average number of citations and geographical distribution of articles were examined. There have been 145 articles contributed by 279 authors were identified in last ten years which coming under the preview of the analysis. The highest number of articles 22 (15.17 per cent) were published in the year 2010. Out of the total 145 articles, 74 (51 per cent) articles have been written by multi authors and rest 71 (49 per cent) are single authored. Average Authors per Paper (AAPP), which shows that the average number of authors per the entire article is 1.92. The degree of author collaboration in the PMM journal is 0.51 per cent, which is clearly indicates the improving trend of collaborative research in LIS domain. Further the journal attracted authors from various countries from different parts of the world; this shows the value and popularity of the journal in LIS fraternity.

REFERENCES

1. Emeraldinsight (2015), *Performance Measurement and Metrics,* available at: http://emeraldgrouppublishing.com/products/journals/journals.htm?id=pmm (accessed 7 April 2015).
2. Gurjeet Kaur, R., & Kamini, G. (2012). Bibliometric Analysis of Malaysian Journal of Library and Information Science: 2007-2011. *International Journal Of Information Dissemination & Technology, 2*(4), 307.
3. Mamdapur, G. N., Rajgoli, I. U., & Mamdapur, A. G. (2013). Scientometric Analysis of Contributions to the Journal College and Research Libraries (1997-2011). *Library Philosophy & Practice,* 1-16.
4. Mulla, K. R., & Dhanamjaya, M. (2014). The SRELS Journal of Information Management (2000-2009): A Bibliometric Study. *International Journal Of Information Dissemination & Technology, 4*(2), 110.
5. Nelson, E. (2013). An Analysis of a Nigerian Library and Information Science Journal: A Bibliometric Study. *Library Philosophy & Practice,* 1-12.
6. Pandita, R. (2014). DESIDOC Journal of Library and Information Technology (DJLIT): A Bibliometric Study (2003-12). *Library Philosophy & Practice,* 1-16.
7. Potter, W. G. (1981). Introduction to Bibliometrics. *Library trends, 30*(1), 5-7.
8. Pritchard, A. (1969). Statistical bibliography or bibliometrics?. *Journal of documentation,*(25), 348-349.
9. Singh, K., & Chander, H. (2014). Publication trends in library and information scienceA bibliometric analysis of Library Management journal. *Library Management, 35*(3), 134. doi:10.1108/LM-05-2013-0039.
10. Singh, K. P., Jain, A., & Babbar, P. (2011). DESIDOC Bulletin of Information Technology: A Bibliometric Study. *SRELS Journal Of Information Management, 48*(1), 57-68.
11. Subramanayam, K. (1983), Bibliometric studies of research in collaboration: A review, *Journal of Information Science,* 6(1): 33-38.
12. Swain, C., Swain, D. K., & Rautaray, B. (2013). Bibliometric analysis of Library Review from 2007 to 2011. *Library Review, 62*(8/9), 602-618. doi:10.1108/LR-02-2013-0012

13. Tella, A., & Olabooye, A. A. (2014). Bibliometric analysis of African Journal Of Library, Archives and Information Science from 2000-2012. *Library Review, 63*(4/5), 305-323. doi:10.1108/LR-07-2013-0094

14. Thavamani, K. (2014). Authorship Patterns and Collaborative Research in Malaysian Journal of Library and Information Science, 1996 - 2012. *Library Philosophy & Practice*, 2-19.

15. Yoshikane, F et al (2009), An analysis of the connection between researchers' productivity and their co-authors' past contributions, including the importance in collaboration networks, *Scientometrics*, 79(2):435-449.

6

Cloud Computing: An Overview and Its Impact on Libraries

Dhara Sharma
Dipti Ranjan Sahoo

ABSTRACT

The application of information and communication technology in libraries increasing day by day and the modern libraries are converting towards paperless or virtual libraries. The cloud computing is a new technology model and it is becoming popular in the every field. In libraries it provides a common platform for all and facilitates to information storage and sharing on a single efficient system that saves the cost and time. Cloud computing technology came up as a boon for libraries and is offering various opportunities for libraries to connect their services with clouds. This paper overviews the basic concept of newly develop area known as cloud computing and its applications in libraries. Libraries have also started adopting this technology as cost effective tool which involves delivering hosted service over the web. This paper also tries to give clear idea that how cloud technology help libraries to provide a better service to the library community make librarians to think on using it for designing and providing different services with modern infrastructure and technology.

Keywords : Cloud computing, Cloud computing Types, Cloud Deployment Models & Cloud based library services

1. INTRODUCTION

Today we are living in the age of information. Information technology plays a very vital role in collecting, storing, organizing, processing & analyzing of information. However, with the introduction of new technologies, the scenario has totally changed as today the information can be made available 24x7, crossing all the geographical boundaries. The mission of the libraries is to provide information services to patrons. In order to deliver the fast services, the libraries are now adopting new technologies. However, with the fast technological developments, users' information requirements are becoming more and more personalized so libraries are entering into a new era of using newer technology, i.e., cloud computing which offers user centred personalised services, leading to greater satisfaction among users.

Cloud computing represents one of the most important technology trends of our time The cloud computing is the new technological trends and it will change the way of use computer and the internet. Cloud computing portends a major change in how we store information and run application. Instead of running programs and data on an individual desktop computer, everything is hosted in the "cloud" that is a nebulous assemblage of computers and servers accessed via the internet. Cloud computing can access all application and documents from anywhere in the world and making it easier for group members in different locations to collaborate. Every day we make use of computing and information resources through a web browser powered by some distant and diffuse infrastructure. It provides the user to use various applications without installation of that application in their own computer to access their personal files or official documents and capable of bringing together collection of documents and resources stored in various personal computers, personal server and other equipment in to one place and putting them on the cloud for the use of the user community. Cloud computing is so named because the information being accessed is found in the "clouds", and does not require a user to be in a specific place to gain access to it. Cloud Computing is one of the hottest and value added term in the field of Computing and Libraries.

2. CLOUD COMPUTING

As we explained above cloud computing here are some more simple words and the paragraphs to understand efficiently cloud computing.

- We see Cloud Computing as a computing model, not a technology. In this model "customers" plug into the "cloud" to access IT resources which are priced and provided "on-demand". Essentially, IT resources are rented and shared among multiple tenants much as office space, apartments, or storage spaces are used by tenants. Delivered over an Internet connection, the "cloud" replaces the company data center or server providing the same service. Thus, Cloud Computing is simply IT services sold and delivered over the Internet.
- The "Cloud" element of cloud computing can be seen as an acronym that stands for C- Computing resources L- that is location independent, O-accessed via online means, U-used as an utility and D- on demand availability. It is a new technology which is an improvement of distributed computing, parallel computing and grid computing. The basic principle of cloud computing is making tasks distributed among large number of computers but not in local computers or remote servers. This is a dynamic model, based on pay-per-use (subscription) or scalable system in which configuration of resources (hardware, platform/services) can be graded to suit the needs of the users for optimum utilisation of resources. In simple words, it is a

subscription-based or pay-per-use real time service over the internet.

- Cloud computing can be understood as a way to use off-site computer processing power to replace content creation and servers that were traditionally hosted onsite. In layman's terms this means "using Web services for our computing needs" (Kroski, 2009). Cloud computer allows content creation to be made "when data and software applications reside on and are drawn from the network rather than locally on any one workstation". By utilizing online applications, users can create and save their files online, share content (often for free!), work collaboratively with others or create entire services that can all be accessed online without need of having the programs on their own computer. These online services can reduce the need for expensive software, hardware, and even advanced technical knowledge from library staff since cloud computing services are often streamlined to be very user-friendly.
- Different definitions given by different people:-

According to *Kroski*, "Cloud computing means web services for out computing needs which could include using software application, storing data, accessing computing power or using a platform to build applications".

According to *Berkely*, "Cloud Computing refers to both the applications delivered as services over the Internet and the hardware and systems software in the data centers that provide those services."

U.S. National institute of standards and technology (NIST) defines, "cloud computing is a model for enabling convenient, on-demand network access to a shared pool of configurable computing resources (e.g. networks, servers, storage, application and services) that can be rapidly provisioned and released with minimal management effort or service provider interaction.

According to *Wikipedia* "Cloud computing, or in simpler shorthand just "the cloud", also focuses on maximizing the effectiveness of the shared resources. Cloud resources are usually not only shared by multiple users but are also dynamically reallocated per demand."

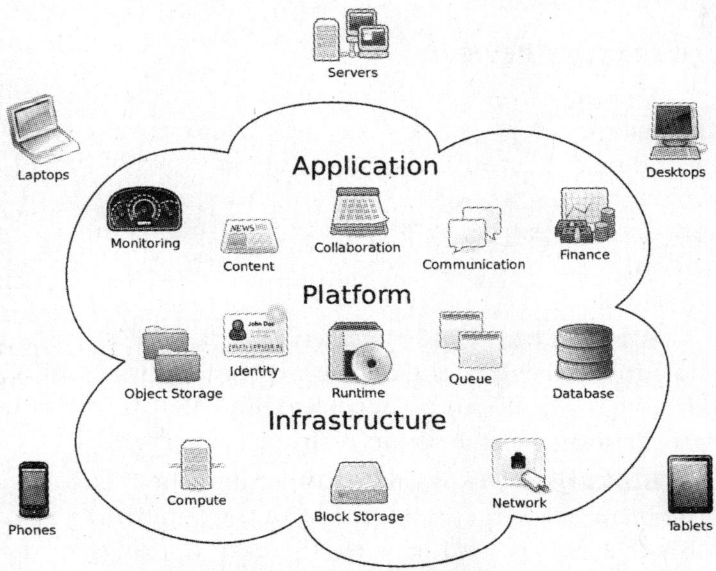

Cloud Computing

In cloud computing, the word *cloud* (also phrased as "the cloud") is used as a metaphor for "*the Internet*," so the phrase *cloud computing* means "a type of Internet-based computing," where different services — such as servers, storage and applications — are delivered to an organization's computers and devices through the Internet/Or " It is a phrase that is being used today to describe the act of storing, accessing, and sharing data, applications, and computing power in cyberspace". In simple term Cloud Computing is a technology that basically using virtual servers as infrastructure and that have been made available to the third parties via the internet. With the use of cloud computing, anyone can gain access at any time through any device, via the Internet to data and files which you have uploaded, or to software applications which you need to use for personal or professional use. Today the phrase 'cloud computing' is being used more and more in business. It is important for any professional to understand what it is all about.

3. LITERATURE REVIEW

Review of related literature is conducted to enable the researcher to get a clear understanding about the specific field of study. Considerable amount of literature is available regarding cloud computing. A review of the literature shows that "cloud computing is not a new concept. Various studies were conducted on cloud computing.

Stroh, et al. (2009) stated that "Cloud Computing is nothing more than the collection of computing software and services that can be accessed via the Internet rather than residing on a desktop or internal server.

Blokdijk & Menken (2009) stated that "The origins of the term "Cloud" can be traced to the concealing nature of this technology's framework; the system works for users yet they really have no idea the inherent complexities that the system utilizes. The "means of communication between client and cloud have been termed middleware and depend very much on formation of images of virtual machines"

Andrew (2012) represented as cloud symbol. Usually, "cloud services are based on the Internet which are accessed, transported & used over the Internet in user`s web browsers.

Mavodza (2013) stated that "libraries have stepped and are increasingly stepping into the realm of digital librarianship as well as platforms that extend IT's existing capabilities, and this extensively depends on using the cloud".

Berry & Reisman (2012) stated that "Demand for cloud computing services in India is growing along with supply and Indian firms in numerous industries are adopting cloud services"

Liu & Cai (2013) asserts that "driven by this new technology trend and the benefits of cloud computing, an increasing number of libraries are shifting their key applications and services to the cloud".

Lingling Han and Lijie Wang (2011) investigated the possibility of using cloud computing in digital libraries, and provided a design model for a platform for digital library in the cloud platform. The model has four layers: infrastructure, data, management, and service.

Erik Mitchell (2010) studied and evaluated changing from current IT infrastructure to cloud computing in libraries. It was found that cloud services allow better server sharing and service delivery.

Goldner expressed the view with regard to cloud computing, how cloud computing is differed from the other computing and its advantages to libraries in three basic areas: Technology, data and community.

Srivastava presented the vision of cloud computing with various commercially cloud services available on the Infrastructure as-a-Service (IaaS) and found that cloud computing is changing the way towards hardware and software for on demand capacity fulfillment and development of web applications to make business decisions.

Sasikala argued the concept of cloud computing from the perspectives of diverse technologists, services and models available, cloud standards, cloud in government, enterprises and higher education, along with opportunities, challenges and implications on the basis past, present and future situation.

Jordan expressed that cloud computing technology are clubbing with libraries services and web scale services are developing on the web in order to present the library services when and where required the users by example of Online Computer Library Center (OCLC) services.

Wang examined the trends of cloud computing on the basis of extant information systems literature, industry reports and practical experience reflections and also pointed out the significance of cloud computing and its implications for practitioner and academics.

Khan provided the concept of cloud computing and also highlighted that how libraries can be benefited using cloud computing technology.

4. TYPES OF CLOUD COMPUTING SERVICES

The following are types of cloud computing:-

Software as a Service (SaaS)

Software package such as CRM or CAD/CAM can be accessed under cloud computing scheme. Here a customer upon registration is allowed to use software accessible through net and use it for his or her business process. The related data and work may be stored on local machines or with the service providers. SaaS services may be available on rental basis or on per use basis.

Platform as a Service (PaaS)

Cloud vendors are companies that offer cloud computing services and products. One of the services that they provide is called PaaS. Under this a computing platform such as operating system is provided to a customer or end user on a monthly rental basis. Some of the major cloud computing vendor is Amazon, Microsoft, and Google etc.

Infrastructure as a Service (IaaS)

The cloud computing vendors offer infrastructure as a service. One may avail hardware services such as processors, memory, networks etc. on agreed basis for specific duration and price. (Ogwu & Lawal, 2013)

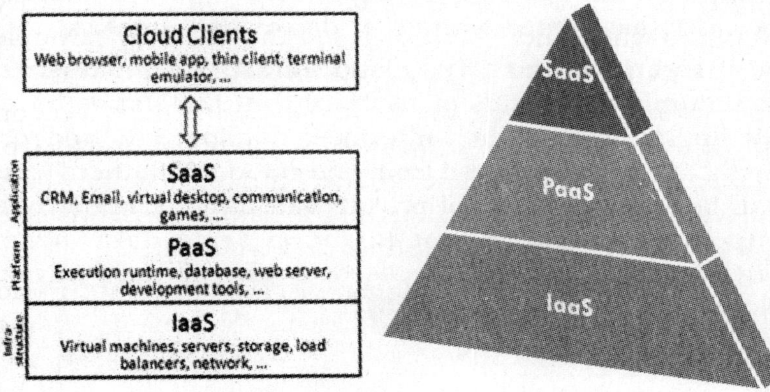

Cloud Computing Layers

5. CLOUD DEPLOYMENT MODELS

Deploying cloud computing can differ depending on requirements, and the following four deployment models that have been identified, each with specific characteristics that support the needs of the services and users of the clouds in particular ways.

Private Cloud : The cloud infrastructure has been deployed, and is maintained and operated for a specific organization. The Operation may be in-house or with a third party on the premises.

Community Cloud : The cloud infrastructure is shared among a number of organizations with similar interests and requirements. This may help limit the capital expenditure costs for its establishment as the costs are shared among the organizations. The operation may be in-house or with a third party on the premises.

Public Cloud : The cloud infrastructure is available to the public on a commercial basis by a cloud service provider.

This enables a consumer to develop and deploy a service in the cloud with very little financial outlay compared to the capital expenditure requirements normally associated with other deployment options.

Hybrid Cloud : The cloud infrastructure consists of a number of clouds of any type, but the clouds have the ability through their interfaces to allow data and/or applications to be moved from one cloud to another. This can be a combination of private and public clouds that support the requirement to retain some data in an organization, and also the need to offer services in the cloud. **(Ogwu & Lawal, 2013)**

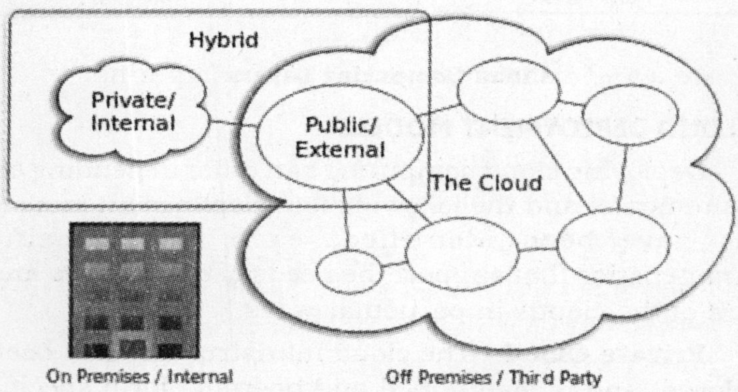

Cloud Computing Types

6. ESSENTIAL CHARACTERISTICS

The following are characteristics of cloud computing:

- Self-Healing
- Multi-tenancy
- Linearly Scalable
- Service-oriented
- SLA Driven
- Virtualized

- Flexible (Ogwu & Lawal, 2013)

7. BENEFITS AND LIMITATIONS OF CLOUD COMPUTING

Here are some advantages of cloud computing:-

- Cost Efficiency
- Easy on Installation and Maintenance
- Increased Storage
- Highly Automated
- Flexibility
- Better Mobility
- Shared Resources
- Back up and Restoration
- Environmentally Friendly Cloud

Here are some disadvantages of cloud computing:-

- Data security and privacy
- Network connectivity and bandwidth
- Dependence on outside agencies
- Limited flexibility
- Knowledge and integration Service Unavailability due to Power Outage
- Long Term Stability of Service Provider (Joshi & Prajapati, 2013)

8. APPLICATIONS OF CLOUD COMPUTING IN LIBRARIES

The application of technologies in libraries increasing day by day and the modern libraries are converting towards paper less or virtual libraries. Cloud computing offers many interesting possibilities for libraries that may help to reduce technology cost and increase capacity reliability, and performance for some type of automation activities. Most of us are very much acquainted with fast computing power being delivered from systems that we can see and touch.

Cloud computing is a completely new in technology and it is known as 3rd revolution after PC and Internet. It has large potential for libraries. Libraries may put more and more content into the cloud. In this technological era, libraries are improved constantly by adopting many new IT technologies.

Libraries are shifting their services with the attachment of cloud and networking with the facilities to access these services anywhere and anytime. In the libraries, the following possible areas were identified where cloud computing services and applications (Cloud based library services) may be applied:

Automation : In the field of library automation there are several commercial suppliers already offering various adaption's of their products which make the use of the cloud possible to a lesser or greater extent. For example vendors such as Ex-Libris, OSS Labs are offering this service on the cloud. Automation in libraries is being undertaken on locally hosted servers using different types of commercial and open source integrated library management software and managed either by internal IT or library staff.

Digital Library Services : In the libraries cloud computing is used to build a digital library and to automate housekeeping operations using third party services. Digital libraries or institutional repositories have become part of modern libraries owing to changing format of information. A proof-of-concept application comprising typical digital library services was developed and deployed in the cloud environment and evaluated for scalability when the demand for more data and services increases. Existing digital library systems could be migrated and deployed into the cloud. The DSpace Foundation and Fedora Commons have developed a new service named DuraSpace to serve academic libraries, universities and other organizations in providing perpetual access to digital content.

Office application : Web based office solutions are new alternatives to creating documents, spreadsheets and presentations that make a departure from traditional installed office software like Microsoft office, Open office and Word perfect. The primary difference is that they are Web Based or on servers at different locations across the Internet. Google Docs, Microsoft office online, cloud-convas.com, write.com etc are the web-based office application suite available on the internet may be used in the libraries to undertake office operations, which also allows storing and sharing of resources with other colleagues, who can remotely work on the documents irrespective of their geographical location. However, Microsoft recently released an updated set of Office web Apps, accessible to individual users from their SkyDrive accounts which currently come with 7 free gigabytes of storage.

Storage and back up : Storing data on the cloud is advantageous due to the growing amount of data. In recent years, with the continued construction of digital library development, a large number of network databases, database mirrors, CD with books, online video and other new service product, the emergence of electronic resources directly lead to the growth of geometric data. The cloud computing has brought in plethora of new services, which offer space at no cost to store the files and documents. For example, Windows Sky Drive offers 25 GB to store files and share documents online. Similarly, Just cloud, Sugar Sync, Dropbox, Open drives, mozy, Carbonite, Box and many more initiatives offer storage space on the cloud to enable organisations and individuals to store and share their documents. Libraries and other organization can store and back up their large number data on remote servers (Iaas). Example, Rackspace, Microsoft Azure, Animoto, Jungle disk and Amazon's EC2 or S3 servers.

Searching Library Data : OCLC is one of the best

example for making use of cloud computing for sharing libraries data for years together. For instance, OCLC World Cat service is one of the popular service for searching library data now is available on the cloud. OCLC is offering various services pertain to circulation, cataloguing, acquisition and other library related services on cloud platform through the web share management system.

File Storage : To access any files on the internet, cloud computing present number of services such as Flicker, Dropbox, Jungle Disk, Google Doc, Sky Drive and so on. These services virtually share the files on the web and provide access to anywhere and anytime without any special software and hardware.

Search Services : Libraries have already migrated key services such as OpenURL providers, and federated and pre-indexed search engines on the cloud either by using commercial or open source solutions. For example, hosted Ex-Libris SFX Open-URL link resolver service offers libraries to linkup to the subscribed journal full-text articles.

Website hosting : Operating a web site that requires database access, supports considerable traffic, and possibly connects to enterprise systems requires complete control of one or more servers, to guarantee responsiveness to user requests. Servers supporting the web site must be hosted in a data center with access from the public internet. Traditionally, this has been achieved by renting space for physical servers in a hosting center operated by a network provider far from the enterprise's internal systems. With cloud computing, this can now be done by renting a virtual machine in a cloud hosting center. Google Sites serves as an example of a service for hosting websites outside of the library's servers and allowing for multiple editors to access the site from varied locations. (Kaushik & Kumar, 2013)

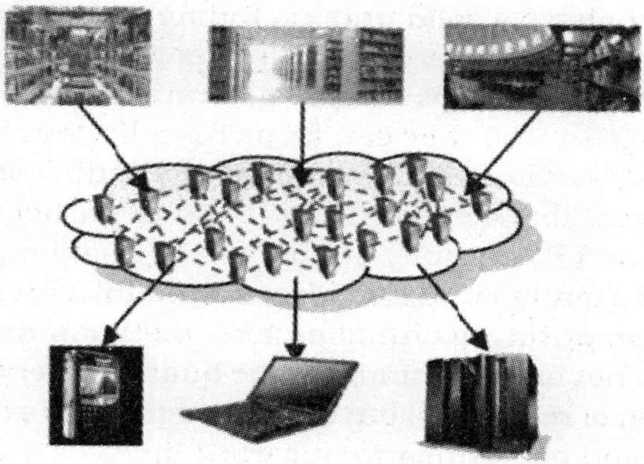

Fig.: Application of Cloud Computing in Library

Examples of Cloud libraries:

1. OCLC
2. Library of Congress (LC)
3. Exlibris
4. Polaris
5. Scribd
6. Discovery Service
7. Google Docs / Google Scholar
8. Worldcat
9. Encore

9. CONCLUSION

With the unlimited growth of electronic resources and technological developments, the demand of the users are multiplying day by day and becoming more challenging. In this purpose , the concept cloud computing have come to meet the demand of the users. Cloud computing becoming popular day by day because of its important features such as, cost effectiveness, efficiency, user-friendliness, flexibility, data security, scalability, world wide connectivity and automatic adaptation, etc.

To achieve cloud computing in libraries, it is essential for libraries to have a solid understanding and knowledge of this new technology landscape. The paper attempted how cloud computing helps in freeing libraries from managing technology so that they can focus on collection building, improved services and innovation. Cloud computing encourages libraries and their users to participate in a network and community of libraries by enabling them to reuse information and socialize around information. The Cloud computing techniques and methods applied to libraries, not only can improve the quality of services and utilization of resources, but also can make more extensive use of cloud computing to our work life.

Library staff should have proper knowledge regarding the cloud computing, to identify its potential advantages and disadvantages, and to explore the areas in which cloud computing can meet the needs of individual institutions. It is very difficult to ignore its advantages. This study provides cloud computing concepts and implications of cloud based applications in libraries in order to enhance their services in a more efficient manner. No doubt, libraries are moving towards cloud computing technology in present time and taking advantages of cloud based services especially in building digital libraries, social networking and information communication with manifold flexibilities but some issues related to security, privacy, trustworthiness and legal issues were still not fully resolved. Therefore it is time for libraries think seriously before clubbing libraries services with cloud based technologies and provide reliable and rapid services to their users. Another role of LIS professionals in this virtual era is to make cloud based services as a reliable medium to disseminate library services to their target users with ease of use and trustworthiness. Cloud computing can bring several benefits for libraries and give them a different future.

10. REFERENCES

1. Mahanta Prafulla Kumar. Application of Cloud Computing in Libraries.
2. Ogbu Richard Chukwhu And Lawal Ahmed. Cloud Computing And Its Applications In E- Library Services: Nigeria In Focus. *International Journal of Innovation, Management and Technology.* Oct 2013; 4 (5): 476-479.
3. Gosavi Nandkishor, Shinde Seetal S. And Dhakulkar Bhagyashree. Use Of Cloud Computing In Library And Information Science Field. *International Journal of Digital Library Services.* Sept 2012;.2 (3): 51-60.
4. Goyal Lakhmi Chand and Jatav Pradeep Kumar. Cloud Computing: An Overview And Its Impact On Libraries. *International Journal of Next Generation Computer Applications.* Sept 2012; 1 (1): 9-15.
5. Chand Subhash and Singh Nishi. Cloud Computing and Its Applications In Library Services. *Global Journal Of Multidisciplinary Studies.* April 2014; 3 (5): 31-50.
6. Kaushik A. and Kumar A. (2013). Application of Cloud Computing In Libraries. *International Journal of Information Dissemination and Technology,* 3(4), 270-273.
7. Suthar Ashok Kumar A. An Overview of Using Cloud Computing In Libraries. *Indian Journal of Applied Research.* June 2013; 3(6): 303-305.
8. Bhattacharjee Nilratan And Purkayastha Sriparna Das. Cloud Computing And Its Applications In Libraries. *E-Library Science Research Journal.* May 2013; 1(7): 1-6.

7

Cloud Computing: Libraries of the Future

Reena Rai
Yeshpal Singh

ABSTRACT

The paper present an overview of cloud computing and its possible applications that can be clubbed with library services on the web based environment. The libraries have been automated, networked and now moving towards paperless or virtual libraries. Cloud computing and Web collaboration are two major concepts that underlie new and innovative developments in libraries. Today, some libraries trust the cloud and creating services dependent on outside providers of computing software and services. Cloud computing has much offer to the library world. It changes the way of thinking. It is certain that cloud computing have a great impact on systems of librarianship.

Keywords : Cloud computing, virtualization, clouds models, clouds services, IaaS, PaaS, SaaS.

INTRODUCTION

During the first decade of the current millennium, the term "Cloud Computing" has become almost ubiquitous in certain circles. Gmail is in the cloud. Facebook is in the cloud. Remotely hosted integrated library systems (ILSs) are also in the cloud. The term "cloud" is on everyone's lips, yet depend on the community, the term may well mean different things both theory and in practice. While business may look to the cloud for low cost solutions to data storage and computing power problems? Cloud computing refers to the delivery of computing resources over the Internet. Instead of keeping data on your own hard drive or updating applications for your needs, you use a service over the Internet, at another location, to store your information or use its applications. Doing so may give rise to certain privacy implications.

CLOUD COMPUTING

The concept, cloud computing can be defined as simply the sharing and use of applications and resources of a network environment to get work done without concern about ownership and management of the network's resources and applications. With cloud computing, computer resources for getting work done and their data are no longer stored on one's personal computer, but are hosted elsewhere to be made accessible in any location and at any time.

In order to understand how the cloud can be used in this professional environment, it is necessary to first become familiar with the cloud's features and its potential applications in the library and information center industry.

Cloud Computing, also known as "The Cloud", is a highly scalable platform promising quick access to hardware and software over the internet, in addition to easy management and access by non-expert users. There are various types of "clouds".

Cloud Computing may be public, in the event that the owner is a provider maintaining the cloud for the entities that own the data: In this case, entities pay for the use and enjoyment of the resource on the internet.

CLOUD ARCHITECTURE

Cloud architecture the systems architecture of the software systems involved in the delivery of cloud computing, comprises hardware and software designed by a cloud architect who typically works for a cloud integrator. It typically involves multiple cloud components communicating with each other over application programming interfaces, usually web services.

Cloud architecture extends to the client, where web browsers and/or software applications access cloud applications. Cloud storage architecture is loosely coupled, where metadata operations are centralized enabling the data nodes to scale into the hundreds, each independently delivering data to applications or users.

TYPES OF CLOUD

Public cloud

Public cloud or external cloud describes cloud computing in the traditional mainstream. Public clouds are run by third parties, and applications from different customers are likely to be mixed together on the cloud's servers, storage systems, and networks. A public cloud provides services to multiple customers.

Hybrid cloud

Hybrid clouds combine both public and private cloud models. This is most often seen with the use of storage clouds to support Web 2.0 applications.

Private cloud

Private clouds are built for the exclusive use of one client, providing the utmost control over data, security, and quality of service. The company owns the infrastructure and has control over how applications are deployed on it. Private clouds can be built and managed by a company's own IT organization or by a cloud provider.

On-Premise Private Cloud

It is also known as internal clouds which are hosted within one's own data center. This provides a more standardized process and protection, but is limited in aspects of size and scalability. It department would also need to incur the capital and operational costs for the physical resources. This is best suited for applications which require complete control and configurability of the infrastructure and security.

Externally Hosted Private Cloud

This type of private cloud s hosted externally with a cloud provider, where the provider facilitates an exclusive cloud environment with full guarantee of privacy. This is best suited for enterprises that don't prefer a public cloud due to sharing of physical resources.

Categories

Cloud computing products and services can be classified into 4 major categories:

Application as a service (AaaS)

These are the first kind of cloud computing services that came into being. Under this, a service is made available to an end-user. The end-user is asked to create an account with the service provider and start using the application. One of first famous application was web-based email service by hotmail started in 1996. Scores of such services are available now on the web.

Platform as a Service (PaaS)

Cloud vendors are companies that offer cloud computing services and products. One of the services that they provide is called PaaS. Under this a computing platform such as operating system is provided to a customer or end user on a monthly rental basis. Some of the major cloud computing vendors are Amazon, Microsoft, and Google etc

Infrastructure as a service (IaaS)

The cloud computing vendors offer infrastructure as a service. One may avail hardware services such as processors, memory, networks etc on agreed basis for specific duration and price.

Software as a service (SaaS)

Software package such as CRM or CAD/CAM can be accessed under cloud computing scheme. Here a customer upon registration is allowed to use software accessible through Internet and use it for his or his business process. The related data and work may be stored on local machines or with the service providers. SaaS services may be available on rental basis or on per-use basis.

ADVANTAGES OF CLOUD COMPUTING

Cloud computing offers numerous advantages both to end users and businesses of all sizes. The obvious huge advantage is that supporting the infrastructure is not required or to have the knowledge necessary to develop and maintain the infrastructure, development environment or application, as were things up until recently. The burden has been lifted and someone else is taking care of all that. Business is now able to focus on their core business by outsourcing all the hassle of IT infrastructure.

COST EFFICIENCY

This is the biggest advantage of cloud computing, achieved by the elimination of the investment in stand-alone software or servers. By leveraging cloud's capabilities, companies can save on licensing fees and at the same time eliminate overhead charges such as the cost of data storage, software updates, management etc.

The cloud is in general available at much cheaper rates than traditional approaches and can significantly lower the overall IT expenses. At the same time, convenient and scalable charging models have emerged (such as one-time-payment and pay-as-you-go), making the cloud even more attractive.

EASY TO ACCESS

Public clouds offer services that are available wherever the end user might be located. This approach enables easy access to information and accommodates the needs of users in different time zones and geographic locations. As a side benefit, collaboration booms since it is now easier than ever to access, view and modify shared documents and files.

SECURITY: BACKUP AND RECOVERY

The process of backing up and recovering data is simplified and secured since those now reside on the cloud and not on a physical device. The various cloud providers offer reliable and flexible backup and recovery solutions. In some cases, the cloud itself is used solely as a backup repository of the data located in local computers.

USER FRIENDLY

The cloud is in general more efficient than the typical IT infrastructure and it takes fewer resources to compute, thus saving energy.

DATA REDUNDANCY

A cloud deployment is usually built on a robust architecture thus providing resiliency and redundancy to its users. The cloud offers automatic failover between hardware platforms out of the box, while disaster recovery services are also often included.

EASY TO ADOPT

A cloud system can be up and running in a very short period, making quick deployment a key benefit. On the same aspect, the introduction of a new user in the system happens instantaneously, eliminating waiting periods.

Sold on Demand

It is sold on demand typically by the minute or the hour.

Mobility

Users have the ability for the use to access data and applications from around the globe.

Virtualization

Each user has a single view for the available resources, independently of how they are arranged in term of physical devices.

Risk Reduction

User can use the cloud to test ideas and concept before making major investment in technology.

Increased Storage Capacity

The cloud can accommodate and store much more data compared to a personal computer and in a way offers almost unlimited storage capacity. It eliminates worries about running out of storage space and at the same time.

Device Diversity and Location Independence

Cloud computing services can be accessed via a plethora of electronic devices that are able to have access to the internet. These devices include not only the traditional PCs, but also smart phones, tablets etc. With the cloud, the "Bring your own device" (BYOD) policy can be easily adopted; permitting employees to bring personally owned mobile devices to their workplace.

Disadvantages of Cloud Computing

As made clear from the above, cloud computing is a tool that offers enormous benefits to its adopters.

However, being a tool, it also comes with its set of problems and inefficiencies. Let's address the most significant ones.

SECURITY AND PRIVACY IN THE CLOUD

Security is the biggest concern when it comes to cloud computing. By leveraging a remote cloud based infrastructure, a company essentially gives away private data and information, things that might be sensitive and confidential. It is then up to the cloud service provider to manage, protect and retain them, thus the provider's reliability is very critical.

DEPENDENCY ON SOURCE

One of the major disadvantages of cloud computing is the implicit dependency on the provider. This is what the industry calls "vendor lock-in" since it is difficult, and sometimes impossible, to migrate from a provider once you have rolled with him.

TECHNICAL PROBLEMS

Certainly the smaller business will enjoy not having to deal with the daily technical issues and will prefer handing those to an established IT company, however you should keep in mind that all systems might face dysfunctions from time to time. Failure is possible even to the best cloud service providers, as the past has shown.

INCREASED VULNERABILITY

Related to the security and privacy mentioned before, note that cloud based solutions are exposed on the public internet and are thus a more vulnerable target for malicious users and hackers. Nothing on the Internet is completely secured and even the biggest players suffer from serious attacks and security breaches. Due to the interdependency of the system, if there is a compromise one of the machines that data is stored, there might be a leakage of personal information to the world.

ROLE OF CLOUD COMPUTING IN LIBRARIES

The development of cloud computing provides an opportunity for library automation beyond computerizing manual functions. Modern library automation has now moved beyond this to the point where access to information now means that clients obtain resources and information in all formats wherever it was located, from anywhere, at any time, day or night.

Cloud computing is a completely new in technology and it is known as 3rd revolution after PC and Internet. Cloud computing is an enhancement of distributed computing, parallel computing, grid computing and distributed databases. Among these, grid and utility computing are known as predecessors of cloud computing. Cloud computing has large potential for libraries. Libraries may put more and more content into the loud. Using cloud computing user would be able to browse a physical shelf of books, CDs or DVDs or choose to take out an item or scan a bar code into his mobile device. All historical and rare documents would be scanned into a comprehensive, easily searchable database and would be accessible to any researcher. Many libraries already have online catalogues and share bibliographic data with OCLC. More frequent online catalogues are linked to consortium that share resources.

Data storage cloud is a main function of libraries, particularly those with digital collections storing large digital files can stress local server infrastructures. The files need to be backed up, maintained, and reproduced for patrons. This can strain the data integrity as well as hog bandwidth. Moving data to the cloud may be a leap of faith for some library professionals. A new technology and on the surface it is believed that library would have some control over this data or collections. However, with faster retrieval times for requests and local server space it could improve storage solutions for libraries. Cloud computing or IT infrastructure that exists remotely, often gives users increased capacity and less need for updates and maintenance, and has gained wider acceptance among librarians

ADVANTAGES OF CLOUD COMPUTING IN LIBRARIES

There are following main benefits of cloud computing for the smooth functioning of library is as:-

- To use the cloud computing technology in the field of libraries, the services can be made strong.
- Sharing of data base is possible.
- Cloud computing is very reliable, scalable and poses privacy concerns.
- Backup and recovery of data is much simpler than other traditional method of data storage in the libraries.
- Cloud computing is also helps in improving the utilization of the IT infrastructure to large extent.
- Information store in clouds gives the unlimited storage capacity.
- Cloud computing technology is user centric.
- It improves document format compatibility.
- It provides latest version availability.
- Take advantage of current and rapidly emerging technology to fully participate in the Web's information landscape.
- It increased visibility and accessibility of collections.
- It reduced duplication of effort from networked technical services and collection management.
- Streamlined workflows, optimized to fully benefit from network participation.
- Cooperative intelligence and improved service levels enabled by the large-scale aggregation of usage data.
- Make libraries greener by sharing computing power thus reducing carbon footprints.

EXAMPLES OF CLOUD LIBRARIES

1. OCLC
2. Library of Congress (LC)
3. Exlibris
4. Polaris
5. Scribd
6. Discovery Service
7. Google Docs / Google Scholar
8. Worldcat
9. Encore

CONCLUSIONS

The introducing chapter has discussed Cloud Computing's basic principles, reference framework and has surveyed the main computing paradigm's that gave birth to the cloud computing. The Cloud Computing paradigm is still evolving. New additions and refinements to the cloud models, characteristics and technologies occur on a daily basis. Cloud computing builds on decades of research in virtualization, distributed computing, utility computing, more recently networking, and web software services. It implies a service oriented architecture, reduced information technology overhead forth end-user, great flexibility, reduced total cost of ownership, on demand services and many other things. In today's global competitive market, companies must innovate and get the most from its resources to succeed. Cloud computing infrastructures are next generation platforms that can provide tremendous value to companies of any size. They can help companies achieve more efficient use of their IT hardware and software investments and provide a means to accelerate the adoption of innovations. Cloud computing is increase profitability by improving resource utilization. Cloud computing is enables innovation by alleviating the need of innovators to find resources to develop test and make their innovations available to the user community. In spite of some disadvantage, it is the most useful application in the information environment.

REFERENCES

1. Alex M. Andrew, (2012),"Cloud computing: views on Cybersyn", Kybernetes, Vol. 41 Iss 9 pp. 1396 – 1399. http://dx.doi.org/10.1108/03684921211275450.
2. Arto Ojala, Pasi Tyrväinen, (2011),"Value networks in cloud computing", Journal of Business Strategy, Vol. 32 Iss 6 pp. 40-49 http://dx.doi.org/10.1108/02756661111180122
3. Denis Galvin Mang Sun, (2012),"Avoiding the death zone: choosing and running a library project in the cloud", Library Hi Tech, Vol. 30 Iss 3 pp. 418 – 427. http://dx.doi.org/10.1108/07378831211266564.
4. Georgina D. Ekpenyong, (1997),"Automating a large library in Nigeria: the story so far", New Library World, Vol. 98 Iss 3 pp.106 – 110. http://dx.doi.org/10.1108/03074809710164604.
5. John-Oswald Amekuedee, (2005),"An evaluation of library automation in some Ghanaian university libraries", The Electronic Library, Vol. 23 Iss 4 pp. 442-452 http://dx.doi.org/10.1108/02640470510611508
6. Judith Mavodza, (2013),"The impact of cloud computing on the future of academic library practices and services", New Library World, Vol. 114 Iss 3/4 pp. 132-141 http://dx.doi.org/10.1108/03074801311304041
7. Mark-Shane E. Scale, (2009),"Cloud computing and collaboration", Library Hi Tech News, Vol. 26 Iss 9 pp.10-13 http://dx.doi.org/10.1108/07419050911010741
8. Michael Groenendyk, Riel Gallant, (2013),"3D printing and scanning at the Dalhousie University Libraries: a pilot project", Library Hi Tech, Vol. 31 Iss 1 pp. 34-41 http://dx.doi.org/10.1108/07378831311303912
9. Nuria Lloret Romero, (2012),""Cloud computing" in library automation: benefits and drawbacks", The Bottom Line, Vol. 25 Iss 3 pp. 110-114 http://dx.doi.org/10.1108/08880451211276566
10. Oghenevwogaga Benson Adogbeji, Esharenana E. Adomi, (2005),"Automating Library Operations at the Delta State

University Library, Nigeria", Library Hi Tech News, Vol. 22 Iss 5 pp. 13-18 http://dx.doi.org/10.1108/07419050510613800.

11. Pamela Cibbarelli, (1999),"Library automation: today's successes and concerns", The Electronic Library, Vol. 17 Iss 3 pp.155-157 http://dx.doi.org/10.1108/02640479910329743

12. Richard Levy, (2013),"Library in the Cloud with Diamonds: a critical evaluation of the future of library management systems", Library Hi Tech News, Vol. 30 Iss 3 pp. 9 – 13. http://dx.doi.org/10.1108/LHTN-11-2012-0071

13. Saim Ul Haq Quddusi, (2014),"Document management and cloud computing", The TQM Journal, Vol. 26 Iss 2 pp. 102-108 http://dx.doi.org/10.1108/TQM-06-2012-0038

14. Weiling Liu Huibin (Heather) Cai, (2013),"Embracing the shift to cloud computing: knowledge and skills for systems librarians", OCLC Systems & Services: International digital library perspectives, Vol. 29 Iss 1 pp.22 – 29.http://dx.doi.org/10.1108/10650751311294528

15. Yan Han, (2013),"IaaS cloud computing services for libraries: cloud storage and virtual machines", OCLC Systems & Services: International digital library perspectives, Vol. 29 Iss 2 pp. 87-100 http://dx.doi.org/10.1108/10650751311319296

16. Goldner,M.(2010), Winds of Change: Libraries and Cloud Computing. http://www.oclc.org/content/dam/oclc/events/2011/files/IFLA-winds-of-change-paper.pdf. (Retrieved on 30/05/2015)

17. Waters, John: Up, Up and Away. In: T.H.E. Journal 37:1 (January 2010) S. 22-4, 26-7.

8

Usage of Mobile Cloud Services in the Libraries

Amandeep Kaur

ABSTRACT

Mobile Cloud computing technology is using in libraries for providing services in a very qualitative and effective way. It provides a network for libraries to give better services to their users. This paper gives detailed information about the Mobile cloud library services in a very better way.

Keywords : Mobile Cloud Library, Cloud Computing, Services.

1. INTRODUCTION

In the information exploration era, ICT playing very important role in the libraries for storing, organizing, processing, delivering , disseminating library resources in a better way. Libraries are adopting new technologies for delivering goods services for their users. A large number of libraries are automated and providing electronic resources for their users with the use of ICT. Now e-resources, e-publication, Internet, web based tools are common in the field of library science. Mobile Cloud computing is latest technology in the field of library science. This technology is using for delivering a large number of service for the library users.

2. ARCHITECTURE OF MOBILE CLOUD COMPUTING

Mobile Cloud computing is a network of 'cloud servers' which is interconnected for running grid, it provides computing power per server. The following images describe the Mobile cloud computing functioning in the library.

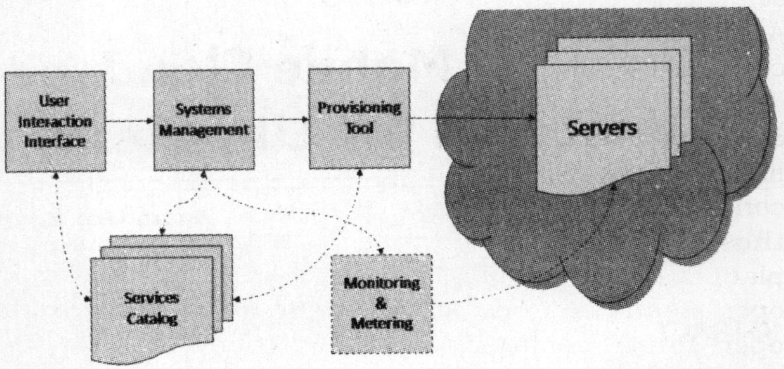

A front-end interface permits a user to select a service from a catalogue. This request is forward to the system which match the correct resource and after that users get provisioning service in the clouds. It includes:

1. **Users Interaction Interface:** Users send particular request in the cloud servers
2. **Service Catalogue:** it is a list of services which can be provided
3. **System Management:** it is a management who control all technological activities
4. **Provisioning Tool:** This tool deliver requested services from the cloud.
5. **Monitoring and Metering:** it tracks the usability of cloud for proper use of resources by the user
6. **Server:** it is part of management tools which deliver required information

3. MOBILE CLOUD SERVICES

In Cloud computing services are available like as IaaS, PaaS and SaaS and mobile technology is used for providing better services. Cloud services can be obtained as SaaS using mobile devices, if any vendor allows for a WAP subject for bearing the service via a web browser. Belonging to common mobile devices SaaS includes those services issued by vendors such as Google, Facebook, Apple, Amazon, etc. The growth of mobile application that calls for the use of cloud service in the basic structure degree is fixed in the set of tools allowed for each specific cloud vendor. The Apple, Google, Amazon cloud is the most prominent cloud providers that change the consumption of cloud services from a mobile handset, those solutions are formed with their own mobile platforms like Android, IOS, Etc. In place of conformity open standards in cloud computing technologies, many open source communities have growing libraries that enables the communication with product clouds. These libraries are unsatisfactory documented and in some cases are not adapted for an occasion for spreading within the mobile platform. These are the some library services

Jets3t : this is Java toolkit and application service, developed by James Murty for retrieving the simple storage service of Amazon . New version of Jets3t also enables accessing the Google storage services. It also allows for and support connecting S3 applying the android platform.

Amazon API : Amazon native APIs that integrated with the Eclipse environments for the growth of applications. That type of tools allows for connectivity with services such as EC2, EBS, etc. those sets of library services exactly the API for accessing S3 application integration of the Android operating system.

Jclouds : is also an open source library service, that directs to and affirm for accessing multiple clouds.

The new version of Jclouds supports the Amazon, vCloud, Azure etc. one drawback of Jclouds library services is not compatible with every mobile operating system is only used for the growth of complete web applications.

Typica : This library service basically uses computational of Amazon EC2 and Eucalyptus, and Typica library use Jets3t for developing rich application based on the uses of the cloud services.

4. MOBILE CLOUD COMPUTING BENEFITS

In order to benefit the most from Mobile cloud computing, developers must be able to refactor their applications so that they can best use the architectural and deployment paradigms that cloud computing supports. The benefits of deploying applications using Mobile cloud computing include reducing run time and response time, minimizing the risk of deploying physical infrastructure, lowering the cost of entry, and increasing the pace of innovation.

REDUCE RUN TIME AND RESPONSE TIME

For applications that use the cloud essentially for running batch jobs, cloud computing makes it straightforward to use 1000 servers to accomplish a task in 1/1000 the time that a single server would require. For applications that need to offer good response time to their customers, refactoring applications so that any CPU-intensive tasks are farmed out to 'worker' virtual machines can help to optimize response time while scaling on demand to meet customer demands.

MINIMIZE INFRASTRUCTURE RISK

IT organizations can use the cloud to reduce the risk inherent in purchasing physical servers. Will a new application be successful? If so, how many servers are needed and can they be deployed as quickly as the workload increases? If not, will a large investment in servers go to waste? If the application's success is short-lived, will the IT organization invest in a large amount of infrastructure that is idle most of the time? When pushing an application out to the cloud, scalability and the risk of purchasing too much or too little infrastructure becomes the cloud provider's issue. In a growing number of cases, the cloud provider has such a massive amount of infrastructure that it can absorb the growth and workload spikes of individual customers, reducing the financial risk they face. Another way in which cloud computing minimizes infrastructure risk is by enabling surge computing, where an enterprise data enter (perhaps one that implements a private cloud) augments its ability to handle workload spikes by a design that allows it to send overflow work to a public cloud. Application lifecycle management can be handled better in an environment where resources are no longer scarce, and where resources can be better matched to immediate needs, and at lower cost.

Lower cost of entry : There are a number of attributes of cloud computing that help to reduce the cost to enter new markets:

- Because infrastructure is rented, not purchased, the cost is controlled, and the capital investment can be zero. In addition to the lower costs of purchasing compute cycles and storage "by the sip," the massive scale of cloud providers helps to minimize cost, helping to further reduce the cost of entry.
- Applications are developed more by assembly than programming. This rapid application development is the norm, helping to reduce the time to market, potentially giving organizations deploying applications in a cloud environment a head start against the competition.

Increased pace of innovation : Cloud computing can be helpful to increase the pace of innovation. The low cost of entry to new markets helps to level the playing field, allowing start-up companies to deploy new products quickly and at low cost. This allows small companies to compete more effectively with traditional organizations whose deployment process in enterprise data enters can be significantly longer. Increased competition helps to increase the pace of innovation — and with many innovations being realized through the use of open source software, the entire industry serves to benefit from the increased pace of innovation that cloud computing promotes.

5. MOBILE CLOUD COMPUTING APPLICATION IN LIBRARIES

The mobile technology is very popular in the libraries because it is a portable device and users can access this device anywhere. In the library point of view users can use this device for access a large number of library resources. Mobile technology is using by the regular library users for accessing required information and its popularity is increasing day by day among their users.

Functions	*Description*
Processing	The digital libraries provide Facilities to transfer all kinds of informations to the user.
Centralization	Digital libraries also help to allocate all information on one platform for easy to retrieve data.
Data protection	The data and all programs of the libraries run and store under the cloud, this resource manages all information in the cloud computing environment.
Virtual platform	Virtualization is a one of the main requirements of the cloud computing environment. Cloud computing technologies include the virtualization, distributed, parallel, WEB X.0 and other technologies .
Data Setting	The cloud computing environment should allow

for a good data security mechanism . To protect the information all time through change the setting if user need.

---

6. ROLE OF MOBILE CLOUD COMPUTING IN LIBRARIES

Mobile Cloud computing is offers many interesting potentials for libraries which may reduce the cost of technology as well as increase capacity reliability and performance for some type of automation activities. Mobile Cloud computing has made strong inroads into other commercial sectors and is now beginning to find more application in library science. The Mobile cloud computing pushes hardware to more abstract levels. Most of us are acquainted with fast computing power being delivered from systems that we can see and touch. Digital Library is the most important academic and scientific research base, charges for providing information services for its users. In the past, most libraries insisted that their services are based on their own library resources. So librarians scarcely considered users' demands. But today, digital libraries have changed these views. And librarians usually need to collect as more information as they can accord users' requirements. Then they will analyze the information and sort out them.

7. CONCLUSION

After so many years, Mobile Cloud Computing today is the beginning of "network based computing" over Internet in force. It is the technology of the decade and is the enabling element of two totally new computing models, the Client-Cloud computing and the Terminal-Cloud computing. These new models would create whole generations of applications and business. Our prediction is that it is the beginning to the end of the dominance of desktop computing such as that with the Windows. It is also the beginning of a new Internet based service economy: the Internet centric, Web based, on demand, Mobile Cloud applications and computing economy.

REFERENCES

1. Arumugam, J. & Murugan, K. (2014). Emergence and architecture of mobile cloud library services. *CDICT*. Madurai, 202-207.
2. Bernard Golden. (2009) Computer World. [Online]. *http://www.computerworld.com/s/article/9126620/The_case_against_clo* ud_computing_part_one
3. Elastra. [Online]. http://www.elastra.com/
4. Hand, Eric. "Head in the Clouds."Nature. 25;449 (2007 Oct).
5. Parascale. [Online]. *http://www.parascale.com/*
6. Pollette, Chris. "How the Google- Apple Cloud Computer Will Work." *Howstuffworks.com*. 2 Mar. 2008<http://computer.howstuffworks.com/google-apple-cloud-computer.htm>.
7. Rajkumar Buyya and Chee Shin Yeo, "Cloud Computing and Emerging IT Platforms: Vision, Hype, and Reality for Delivering Computing as the 5th Utility," *Future Generation Computer*
8. Rochwerger B et al., "The RESERVOIR Model and Architecture for," *IBM Systems Journal*, pp. 599-616, 2009.
9. Wikipedia - Cloud Computing. [Online].http://en.wikipedia.org/wiki/Cloud_computing

9

Information Seeking Behavior of the Chemistry Major Students of Gurucharan College Silchar: A Survey

Subhajit Dutta

ABSTRACT

Information is basic necessity of everyday life. For anything and everything information is required. Information can be obtained and retrieved from various sources. Libraries perform as a centre to provide right information at the right time to the right user in a right way. This study was undertaken to determine information seeking behaviour and library use by the students of the Chemistry department at Gurucharan College, Silchar. This study attempts to know the student's behaviour to gather information from sources along with the statistic of the library resources and the infrastructure. This study examines some other aspects of library like user satisfaction, frequency of library visit, library collection etc. The study was conducted through survey by distributing questionnaire among 50 students. Some suggestions are also provided on the basis of the study to enhance library service satisfaction.

Key Words : Information Seeking Behaviour, Library Resources, Infrastructure, Chemistry.

1. INTRODUCTION

Bruce (2005) states that, "information plays a significant role in our daily professional and personal lives and we are constantly challenged to take charge of the information that we need for work, fun and everyday decisions and tasks." In the digital era, information-seeking behaviour has taken on even more importance worldwide.

During last two decades, the web technology, internet and Information communication technology (ICT) has changed the way people interact, communicate, share and seek information and acquire knowledge. Information is very important to every aspect of today's information society or human being. The process of information acquiring, using and implementing information are known as information seeking behaviour.

Information seeking behaviour is a broad term; which involves set of actions that an individual or a group takes to express their information need, seek information, evaluate and select information, and finally use this information to satisfy their information needs.

Libraries play an important role as in the case of academicians, researchers and students it is even more important because they all need right and update information for their research need. The library is the most widely-used source of information available to literate societies. Librarians must be aware of the kind of information being sought and how it can be obtained. Innovation of ICT has changed the concept of libraries from store house of books to gateway of information.

2. GURU CHARAN COLLEGE AND ITS LIBRARY: AN OVERVIEW

Gurucharan College, Silchar, abbreviated as G.C. College, was established on 15 July 1935. it is a full-fledged institution of higher education to the undergraduate level. It has attained a distinct identity of its own in the field of higher education in eastern India. Initially, the college had been affiliated to Calcutta University. In 1949, the college got affiliated to the Gauhati University. With the establishment of the Assam University (Central), Silchar, G.C. College has been affiliated to it since 1994. This college is having 3000 students enrolment and accredited by NAAC and graded B++. The institute enjoys the status of College with Potential for Excellence for its remarkable achievements in many fields of human endeavour.

The library of this college is known as B.C.Gupta Memorial Central Library established in the very same year of the establishment of the college. Library holdings 36000 print volumes including Text Book, Reference Book, Journals, Reports Manuscripts, Cartographs. Apart from these the library is holding 50,000 E-Books, 2700 Online Journals, 542 CD/DVDs etc.

Library is having Local Area Network with 27 computers with Server. Complete database of book s is available through OPAC. Automation is completed with SOUL software provided by INFLIBNET. The Library established its DIGITAL LIBRARY section connected with the library LAN and campus LAN. This is only college in Assam having a Digital Library section having its own digital server.

3. OBJECTIVES OF THE STUDY

This study has following objectives:

i. To find out awareness of the library services.

ii. To know the main purpose of information seeking behaviour.

iii. To find out the preferred source of information of the students.

iv. To find out the problems faced by the students while seeking information.

4. SCOPE AND LIMITATION OF THE STUDY

The scope of the study is confined to the students having Chemistry major in GuruCharan College only. This study will highlight the overall scenario of information need, problems to acquire information by the students of Chemistry department.

5. METHODOLOGY

In order to achieve the objective of the study, data collection method include survey method using questionnaire were used to collect information from the respected college and in addition observation of library and informal interviews are also used to collect additional information.

6. DATA ANALYSIS AND INTERPRIETATION

The respondents are students of Chemistry department of Gurucharan College. Data collected are scientifically analysed and interpreted to derive factual findings.

Although 50 respondents were invited to participate in the study and the response rate was 100%.

7. FREQUENCY OF LIBRARY VISIT

Survey respondents were asked whether they visit library daily/twice in a week/weekly/2/3 times in a month/monthly and occasionally. As shown in table 1, the majority of students 40% are visit the library occasionally and only 10% visit library weekly and twice in a week. No students use to visit library daily.

Table 1.

Frequency of library visit	*Number of respondent*	*Percentage*
Daily	0	0
Twice in a week	5	10%
Weekly	5	10%
2/3 times in a week	10	20%

Monthly	10	20%
Occasionally	20	40%
Total	50	100%

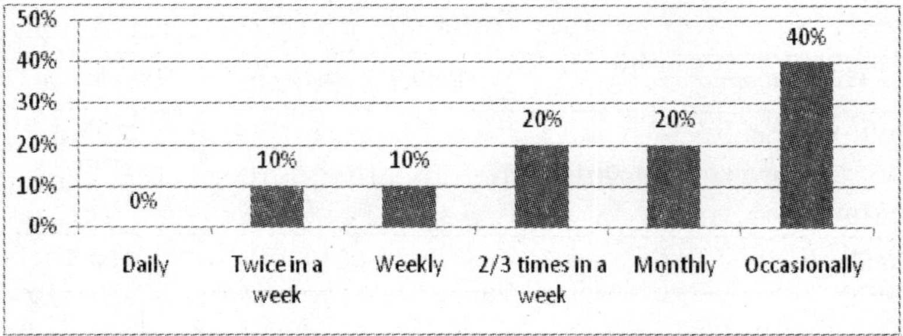

Fig. 1. Frequency of Library Visit of the Students

8. PURPOSE OF LIBRARY VISIT

Table 2 will indicates in response of purpose of library visit.

Table 2

Purpose of library visit	*Number of students*	*Percentage*
To Study	10	20%
Borrow Book	18	36%
Referring Book	15	30%
Internet Surfing	7	14%

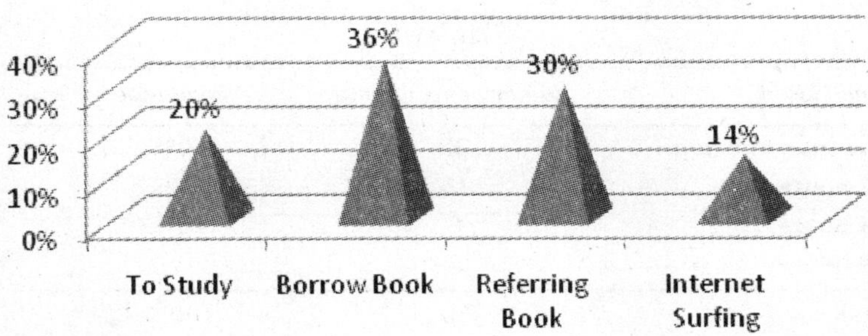

Fig. 2. Purpose of Library Visit

9. FORMAT OF INFORMATION SOURCES STUDENTS MOSTLY USE

Table 3 will indicate in which format students seek information for their use.

Table 3

Format of Information	*Number of Students*	*Percentage*
Print Material	35	70%
Electronic material (cd/dvd/PDF)	15	30%
Microfilms	0	0%
Total	50'	100%

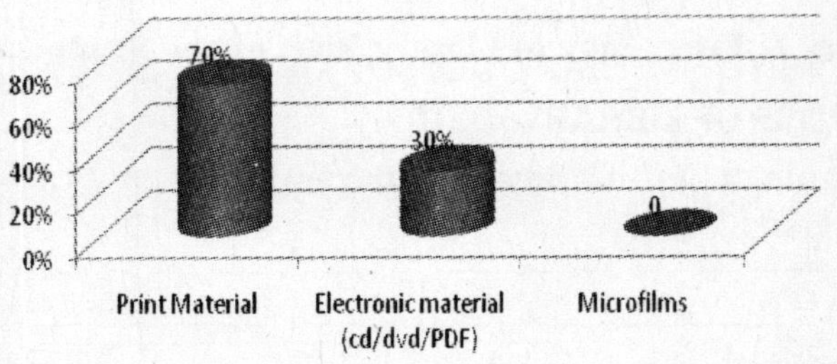

Fig. 3. Format of Information Sources students mostly use

10. TIME SPENT IN THE LIBRARY

Table 4 will indicate the percentage of total time spent in the library by users.

Table 4

Time Period	*Number of Students*	*Percentage*
Less than one hour	25	50%
1-2 hours	15	30%
2-4 hours	8	16%
4-6 hours	2	4%
Total	50	100%

11. CONSTRAINTS FOR MEETING INFORMATION NEED

This table will show that some constraints exist to meeting information needs to users in the library. Here respondents are allowed to give multiple answers.

Table 5

Constraints of Information	*No of Students Respondents*	*Percentage*
Poor Internet Facility	33	66%
Unavailability of Text Books	27	54%
Irregular Journal Subscribe	13	26%
Lack of technical support	28	56%
Inadequate Computer System in the Library	8	16%

12. RATING THE SATISFACTION OF LIBRARY SERVICE

Table 5 will represent the satisfaction level of students from the library service.

Table 6

Satisfaction Level	*No of Students*	*Percentage*
Beyond satisfaction	2	4%
Satisfied	29	58%
Less Satisfied	11	22%
Not Satisfied	8	16%

13. FINDINGS

The following are the findings which has found during the study.

i. Out of 50 students 0% student visits library daily and majority 40% of students visit library occasionally; this is every disappointing result.

ii. Majority of the students visit library only to borrow books

iii. Among 50 students 70% use only the print format document and 30% students use PDF or CD /DVD, none of them are aware about microfilms.

iv. Maximum of the students are satisfied from library service.

v. 50% students spent minimum time in the library which is less than one hour

vi. Maximum label of students are satisfied from library service.

vii. Poor internet facility and lack of technical support is the main constraints to access the information.

14. SUGGESTION

i. Students should be aware about the importance of library. Librarian and other library staffs should increase the habits of library visit of the students.

ii. Manpower development training program for the library staff is a must to provide the students proper technical support.

iii. Proper library orientation program should be there.

iv. Administration should provide more books and journals on Chemistry to the library.

v. Awareness should be there to make all the students aware about the service and materials and resources the library is having.

15. CONCLUSION

Information seeking behaviour depends upon the nature as well as needs of user. Library must understand the behaviour of seeking information of the students of different department. The core of the library profession remains the same but methods and tools for information delivery continue to grow and change dramatically. This study brings out that user education and orientation program to the students is must.

REFERENCES

1. Basimalla SR (2000). Communication patterns and information-seeking behaviour of health science researchers/

scientists: A study of ICMR institutes. Retrieved from *http://eprints.rclis.org/5662/1/ COMMUNICATION.pdf.*

2. Fatima N, Ahmad N. (2008). Information seeking behaviour of the students at Ajmal khan Tibbiya College, Aligarh Muslim University: Asurvey. Ann. Lib. Inf. stud., 55(6): 141-144.
3. Kakai, J.M., Ikoja-Odongo, R., & Kigongo-Bukenya, I.M.N. (2004). A study of the information seeking behaviour of undergraduate students of Makerere University, Uganda. *WorldLibraries14*(1) fromhttp://www.worlib.org/vol14no1/print/kakai_print.html
4. Retrieved from *http://www.gurucharancollege.ac.in/*
5. Retrieved from *http://en.wikipedia.org/wiki/Gurucharan_College*
6. Retrieved from http://en.wikipedia.org/wiki/Gurucharan_College

10

Information Seeking Behaviour of Newspaper Readers of Assam University Central Library: A Case Study

Tuhina Choudhury (Deb Roy)

ABSTRACT

The reading of newspaper as a habit is highly rewarding. Through reading newspapers we can be knowledgeable, well-informed, well-versed and alert about the affairs of the world. This paper attempts to find out the information seeking behavior of newspaper readers of Assam University Central Library. Survey method is used for the study. Questionnaire is used as the research tool. The sample of users is 200 library users, selected randomly within the library premises. The aim is to investigate the purpose of reading newspapers, the areas of interest of the users, the time spent in reading and constraints faced by the users in Newspaper readings. Recommendations are also made to improve Newspaper Reading Habits based on the findings of the survey.

Keywords : Assam University, Central Library, Newspaper reading habits, Information seeking behavior, Newspaper Readers.

INTRODUCTION

Newspapers are almost as essential as our daily morning tea or breakfast. Newspapers are the cheapest and a very rich source of latest news, information, views, comments, commodity, quotes, stock market positions, government policies, and programmes and much more. They bring the whole world at the readers' doorsteps and keep their knowledge updated and upgraded. They are practically an encyclopedia of day-to-day knowledge. They have leading articles, editorials, interviews, comments, and reviews, which are a good source of public enlightenment. The ads about vacancies, cultural activities, sales, marriages, hobbies, lost and found articles etc. are of great importance to the general public. Newspapers bring people closer and nearer to one another and serve a great social, cultural and national purpose. The news about games and sports, crimes, accidents, local issues, books, cinema, etc. is also of much value and significance. Newspapers can play the role of a medium for the readers and writers to articulate their thoughts and visions on various aspects. Thus reading newspapers is indispensable for young learners to be more responsible and enlightened citizens. But unfortunately, many students of our country do not have easy access to newspapers. To circulate up to date and crucial information modern societies rely on the media of which newspapers are an important constituent. Information is an indispensible resource for all human activities. Information has an important role in decision making, planning and every developmental activity. The technological progressions and modernizations that took place over the years have altered libraries from mere store house of printed materials in to gateways to the world of information. Libraries are no longer stagnant reservoirs of books or documents. ICT has brought radical changes in a way in which libraries gather, preserve and disseminate information. In a library or information centre, the users are the last link or the recipients of information in the communication cycle. Hence, understanding the user needs is a fundamental prerequisite for libraries which aim at satisfying the information needs of the users which vary from user to user (Durrance,1993). Information seeking behavior results from the recognition of some needs supposed by the users and may be defined as "the more common field of investigation, particularly concerned with the variety of methods people employ to discover"(Wilson,1999)

ASSAM UNIVERSITY LIBRARY: A BRIEF PROFILE

Assam University Library was started with the establishment of the University in the year 1994 as a central facility for meeting the information requirements of the academic community of the University. The Central Library of Assam University was shifted to its new permanent Central Library-cum-computer Centre building in 21st January 2006 and renamed as Rabindra Library. The new building has a total plinth area of 38,700 sq.ft. The main function of library includes collection and development of knowledge resources, technical processing, organization, retrieval and dissemination of information to the end users including the academic community of Barak Valley in particular and the entire North Eastern Region in general.(*www.aus.ac.in/library.html*)

The library has at present more than 1 lakh books and 1000+ nos. of PhD/MPhil/Master degree theses, dissertations and project reports received from the Examination Branch of Assam University. In addition to these the library has an archival collection contributed by eminent personalities, rare book section, gifted book collection and collection of 1000+ CDs received along with the books and journals. From 2000 onwards SOUL software was introduced in the library for digitizing the system. From 2003 onwards Assam University subscribes to Database services of DELNET which provides the facilities of accessing Digital Information Resources, Bibliographical and other Databases and Inter Library

Loan services of DELNET. Under UGC-INFONET e-journals Consortium, Assam University Library are also getting On-line access to 5000+ e-journals. Document Delivery Services are also being provided by Assam University. (Assam University Annual Reports,1994-2014). In 2014 KOHA software was introduced and as a result circulation section was digitized and OPAC facilities were made open to the users. Other sections are also being digitized using KOHA open source software.

REVIEW OF RELATED LITERATURE

Akanda & Haque (2013) in their study revealed that majority of the respondents preferred printed newspapers and also quite a large number preferred online newspaper reading. The major highlight of the study of Kumar,Singh & Siddiqui (2011) is that majority read newspapers to get information and improve their general knowledge and they preferred to read editorial sections followed by sports and politics.Panda & Swain (2011) in their paper attempted to make the user community aware of e-news and e-news services offered by different e-news channels all over the world. Majumder & Hasan (2013) also revealed in their study that print newspapers are more preferable than online newspapers. Krishnamurthy and Awari (2015) in their study too found that though majority of the respondents were tech savvy yet they preferred printed newspapers. Also education related news other than entertainment and sports were the more preferred section in the newspapers. Padmamma & Etal...(2002) in their paper identified the use of newspapers by the teachers in an undergraduate college environment.

SCOPE OF THE STUDY

The Scope of the study is limited to the users of Assam University Central Library. The users included undergraduate and postgraduate students, research scholars both M.Phil and PhD, faculty members and Staff of Assam University as a whole. The study is carried on the information seeking behavior of newspaper readers of the library. The total number of newspapers subscribed by the library is 18 which are listed below:

I. Local Dailies: i) Dainik Jugashankhya,ii) Samoyik Prasanga, iii)Anandabazar Patrika the trio being Bengali newspapers published from Silchar.

II. State Dailies: i) Asomiya Pratidin,ii) Amar Asom both being Assamese newspapers iii) The Assam Tribune,iv) The Sentinel-both English dailies v)Purbanchal Prahari-Hindi daily.

III. Kolkata Dailies-i)Bortoman, ii) Aajkal-both Bengali dailies.

IV. National Dailies:-i) The Telegraph ii) The Indian Express iii) The Times of India iv) The Hindu v) The Economic Times vi) The Business Standard-all being English dailies vii) Janasatta-Hindi daily.

V. Weekly- Employment News.

OBJECTIVES OF THE STUDY

i) To find out the purpose of reading newspapers by the users of the library.

ii) To find out the total time being spent for reading newspapers.

iii) To find out the information needs of newspaper readers of the Library.

iv) To find out the extent of preference of printed newspapers over e-newspapers.

v) To identify the factors affecting reading of newspapers.

vi) To provide possible recommendations to make newspaper reading more convenient.

METHODOLOGY

The study is conducted based on primary data through open and closed end questionnaires. A total of

200 questionnaires were distributed randomly among the library users in the library premises within a period of one month in the year 2015. Total no. of respondents were 200 resulting to a cent percent response rate.

ANALYSIS OF DATA AND INTERPRETATION

On the basis of filled up questionnaires the data has been analyzed and tabulated. The results are interpreted and shown in tabular and graphical representation. Percentage technique has been adopted for data analysis. As the questionnaires were distributed among the users within the library premises, the above table also depicts the percentage distribution of different categories of users visiting the library.

i) Category wise users and their responses

Out of 200 questionnaires distributed, 200 filled up questionnaires were received resulting to a 100% response rate. Among these 200 respondents total number of Faculty Members were 20, Ph. D Scholars 40, M.Phil Students 35, Undergraduate Students 55 and Post Graduate Students 50.

Table 1. User categories and percentage of their responses

Sl. No.	*Types of users*	*No. of responses received*	*Percentage distribution*
1.	Faculty Members	20	10%
2.	Ph.D Scholars	40	20%
4.	M.Phil Scholars	35	17.5%
5.	Undergraduate Students	55	27.5%
6.	Post Graduate Students	50	25%
	Total	200	100%

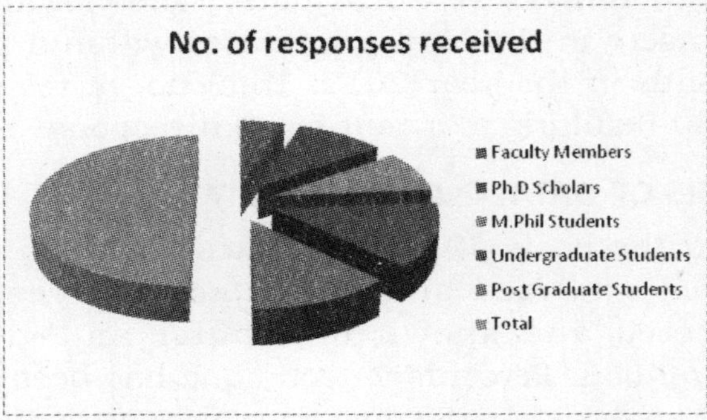

Fig.1. Showing user categories and percentage of responses

From the above table and figure it is clear that the least no. of users are the faculty members (10%) followed by MPhil Scholars (17.5%) and majority of the users are UG students (27.5%) followed by PG students (25%). There are no staff members among the 200 respondents

ii) Language wise Newspaper reading preferences

The following table shows users' language preferences of Newspapers. Assam University Library subscribes to Hindi, English , Bengali and Assamese language Newspapers.

Table 2. Language wise Newspaper reading preferences

Sl. No	*Types of users*	*Hindi*	*Bengali*	*English*	*Assamese*	*Total*
1	Faculty members	5	5	8	2	20
2	PhD Scholars	10	13	12	5	40
3	M Phil Students	6	12	13	4	35
4	Undergraduate	11	20	15	9	55
5	Post Graduate	10	20	12	8	50
	Total	42	70	60	28	200
	Average	21%	35%	30%	14%	100%

Source: Primary Data

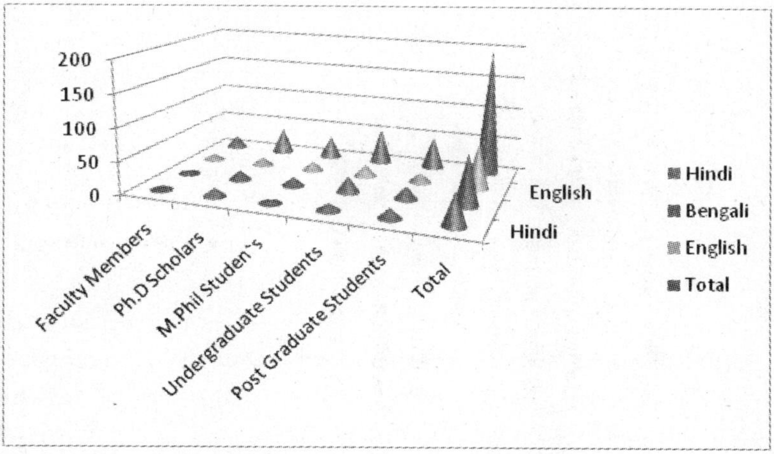

Fig. 2. Showing language wise newspaper reading preference

Out of the total 200 respondents, 21% preferred Hindi language newspapers, 35% preferred Bengali , 30% preferred English and 14 % preferred Assamese thus showing majority preference towards Bengali and English Newspapers.

iii) Purpose of reading Newspapers

While answering to the questions regarding purpose of reading Newspapers, the respondents opted for more than 1 options. The following table depicts the percentage of their responses.

Table 3. Purpose of reading Newspapers

Sl.No	*Purpose*	*No. of Respondents*	*% of Respondents*
1	Obtain General Knowledge	85	42.5%
2	Gather general information	76	38%
3	Gather up-to-date information	92	46%
4	Educational purpose	67	33.5%
5	Entertainment news	55	27.5%
6	Sports news	47	23.5%
7	Health related news	35	17.5%
8	Search for new jobs	56	28%
9	Regular habit	30	15%
10	Leisure activity	13	6.5%

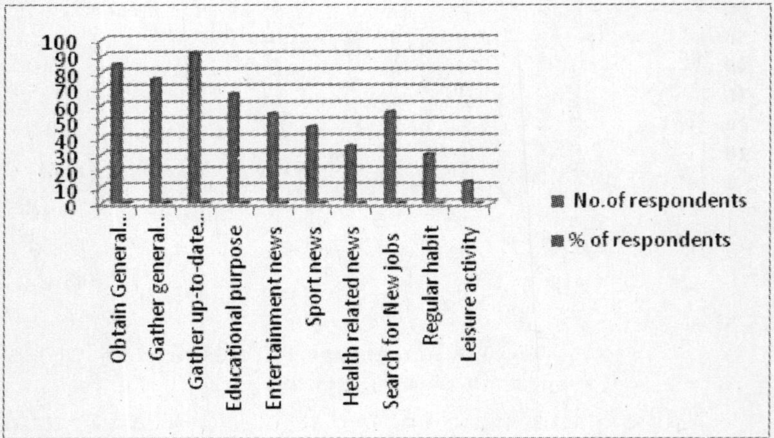

Fig. 3. Purpose of newspaper reading

The responses showed that the major purpose for reading newspapers are to gather up-to-date information (46%) followed by general knowledge (42.5%). Educational news (33.5%) and job hunting (28%) are also found to be important purposes for reading newspapers.

iv) Time spent in reading newspapers

Respondents are asked regarding total time spent on reading newspapers. Table 4 depicts the percentage of time spent in reading newspapers.

Table 4. Total time spent in reading newspapers

Time spent	*Faculty*	*PhD*	*Mphil*	*PG*	*UG*	*Average %*
Less than 1 hour	6	16	20	35	48	62.5%
1-2 hours	10	15	10	10	5	25%
More than 2 hours	4	9	5	5	2	12.5%
Total	20	40	35	50	55	100%

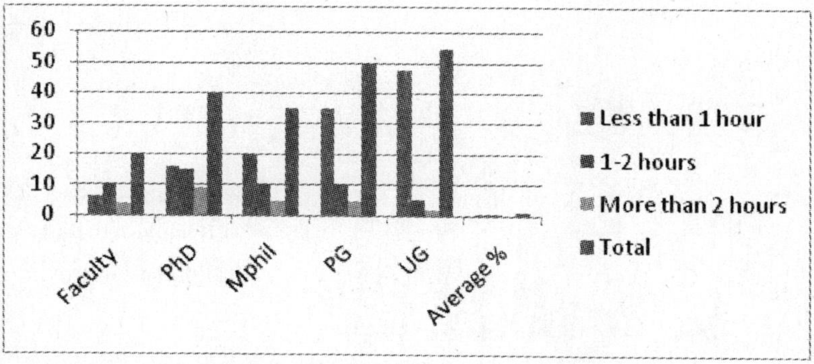

Fig. 4. Average percentage of total time spent in reading Newspapers

Table 5 and Fig. 5 showed that 62.5% of the total respondents spend less than 1 hour in reading newspapers while 25% spend 1-2 hours and 12.5% spend more than 2 hours. This of course includes the timing spent in going through e-newspapers.

v) Preference of medium of Newspapers

User's responses regarding choice of printed newspapers and internet versions were analysed as shown in the following Table.

Table 5. Preferences of printed and Internet versions of Newspapers

Preference	*Faculty*	*PhD*	*MPhil*	*PG*	*UG*	*Average %*
Printed version	14	25	19	30	37	62.5%
Internet version	6	15	16	20	18	37.5%
Total	20	40	35	50	55	100%

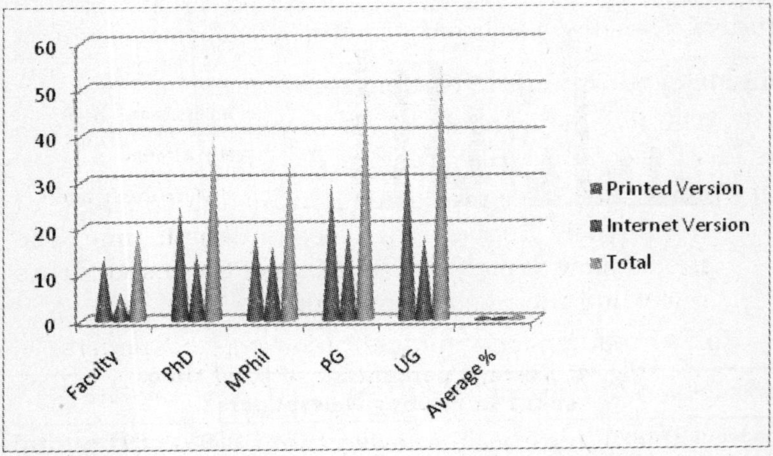

Fig. 5. Preferences of users for printed and Internet versions of newspapers

The above table and figure clearly depicts that 62.5% preferred printed version while 37.5% preferred Internet version which shows that maximum prefer printed version of newspapers.

vi) Place of preference for reading Newspapers

Regarding the place of preference for reading newspapers options like home, library, department, Hostel/mess etc. were provided. The responses were tabulated in the following table.

Table 6. Place of preference for reading newspapers

Preference	*Faculty*	*PhD*	*MPhil*	*PG*	*UG*	*Average %*
Home	15	7	9	18	26	37.5%
Library	0	20	16	20	18	37%
Department	5	8	5	0	0	9%
Hostel	0	5	5	12	11	16.5%
Total	20	40	35	50	55	100%

Table 6 clearly depicts that majority (37.5%) of the respondents prefer to read newspapers either print or e-versions from their home itself followed by (37%) from library. The least preferred place is the department (9%).

vii) Major constraints in reading Newspapers

The two major constraints for reading newspapers as identified by the researcher are:

I) Inadequate time and II)non-availability of newspapers at the right place and right time. The table below depicts the opinions of the respondents regarding the major constraints.

Table 7. Major constraints for reading newspapers

Major constraints	*Faculty*	*PhD*	*MPhil*	*PG*	*UG*	*Average %*
Inadequate time	8	17	20	44	50	69.5%
Non-availability of Newspapers at the right time	12	23	15	6	5	30.5%
Total	20	40	35	50	55	100%

It has been found that due to the geographical location of Assam University the national newspapers do not reach the university in time which is a major constraint in the part of the users. Analysis showed that 69.5% of the respondents face time constraint and 30.5% pointed to the fact that they do not get the right information at the right time through the newspapers and for which they have to depend on Internet sources.

FINDINGS AND SUGGESTION

i) The least no. of users are the faculty members (10%) followed by MPhil Scholars (17.5%) and majority of the users are UG students (27.5%) followed by PG students (25%). There are no staff members among the 200 respondents.

ii) Out of the total 200 respondents, majority (35%) preferred Bengali and (30%) English and least (14 %) preferred Assamese thus showing majority preference towards Bengali and English Newspapers.

iii) The major purpose for reading newspapers are to gather up-to-date information (46%) followed by general knowledge (42.5%). Educational news (33.5%) and job hunting (28%) are also found to be important purposes for reading newspapers.

iv) 62.5% of the total respondents spend less than 1 hour in reading newspapers while 25% spend 1-2 hours and 12.5% spend more than 2 hours. This of course includes the timing spent in going through e-newspapers.

v) 62.5% preferred printed version while 37.5% preferred Internet version which shows that maximum prefer printed version of newspapers.

vi) Majority (37.5%) of the respondents prefer to read newspapers either print or e-versions from their home itself followed by (37%) from library. The least preferred place is the department (9%).

SUGGESTIONS

i) Through user education programmes the users of the library should be encouraged to make use of the newspapers available in the library.

ii) The students must be made aware of the importance of reading newspapers regularly.

iii) Users should be made aware regarding the use of online newspapers. The news portals available online will help getting news instantly thus solving the problem of non availability of printed newspapers at the right time.

iv) The library should promote the use of such news portals among the library users by creating awareness through orientation programmes.

CONCLUSION

Reading is considered essential for the overall development of a human being. However, with the advent of modern digital technologies, especially the growing popularity of social networking on the web, mobile phones, televisions etc., and the reading habit is at its low ebb. Newspaper reading habit helps the readers to inculcate all round development in terms of knowledge, up-to-date information, language skills and many others.

The study revealed that user awareness programmes and orientation programmes should be organized by the library to create receptiveness and alertness about the various newsportals available online so that right information can reach the readers at the right time instead of depending on the printed versions which may not reach them in time due to geographical constraints.

REFERENCES

1. Akhanda, A.K.M Eamin Ali and Haque, A.(2013) Newspaper reading habits of university graduate students in Bangladesh: a case study, *International Journal of Research in Applied, Natural and Social Sciences*.1(*3*). Pp. 1-8.
2. Assam University. Annual Report.1994-2014.
3. Durrance, J.C. et al...(1993). *Serving job seekers and career changers: a planning manual for public librnries: part of public library development program*. Chicago: American Library Association.
4. Krishnamurthy, C and Awari, Veeresh H.(2015). Newspaper reading habits among postgraduate students of Karnatak University, Dharwad. *DESIDOC Journal of Library & Information Technology*,35(*1*). Pp.25-29.
5. Kumar, Devendra;Singh, Rajkumar and Siddiqui, Jamal Ahmad.(2011).Newspaper reading habits of University students: a case study of Chaudhary Charan Singh University, India. *Library Philosophy and Practice (e-journal)*. Paper 470.*http://digitalcommons.unl.edu/libphilprac/470.*
6. Majumder, Dipika and Hasan, Mehdi(2013). Newspaper reading habits of private university students: a case study

on World University of Bangladesh. *IOSR Journal of Business and Management.*12(*1*).Pp.87-91www.iosrjournals.org

7. Padmamma, S, Vijayakumar,M, Ishwari, J.S. and Walmiki, R.H (2002). Utilisation of Newspapers and magazines by the U.G. college teachers in Shimoga city: a case study. *Annals of Library and Information Studies,49(*3*);*Pp.89-98.

8. Panda,K.C. and Swain, Dilip K. (2011). E-newspapers and e-news services in the electronic age: an appraisal. *Annals of Library and Information Studies,* 58.Pp.55-62.

9. Wilson, T.D. (1999).Models in information behavior research, *Journal of Documentation,* 55*(3),* Pp.249-270.

11

Information Needs and Seeking Behaviour by the students in the University of Swaziland

Thiyam Satyabati Devi

ABSTRACT

The diversity in people account for how they seek information and this is what has encouraged this study. This paper investigated the Information needs and seeking behaviour by students in the University of Swaziland. The survey method was used and questionnaire administered to four hundred (400) students who come to the library. The data gathered from the questionnaire was analysed using the simple percentage. It was observed that majority of the students 71% sought information for writing an assignment. (55%) of the respondent expressed satisfaction with the library for being able to meet their information needs.

INTRODUCTION

Information is an essential need for all human endeavours in the present society. The increase in the amount, type, and format of information available on the Web has affected information-seeking behaviour (Fidel, et al., 1999). Current information is important to everyone.

The philosophical emphasis on direct, experiential acquisition of knowledge in the material, physical plane of existence is an important component of information seeking. Individuals have personal reasons for seeking certain forms of information (Leckie, Pettigrew, and Sylvain, 1996). Abels (2004) observes that from 1998-2000, both use of the Internet and expenditures for monographs increased.

The library is the most widely-used source of information available to literate societies. Librarians must be aware of the kind of information being sought and how it can be obtained. Because of the rapidly escalating cost of purchasing and archiving print journals and electronic media, the library has the duty to provide and maintain efficient services.

STATEMENT OF THE PROBLEM

The University Library is one of their major sources of information. Students at the University of Swaziland are also expected to extremely utilise it. However, noting from observation and from the studies conducted on library use in the University it was established that students do not use most of the library information resources. It was assumed that students could be experiencing technical problems in accessing information resources; coupled with lack of knowledge and awareness of the resources.

PURPOSE OF THE STUDY

Library information resources are expensive. The librarians needed to manage these resources and make them accessible. To attain cost effectiveness in the University library services and promotes the use of library information resources, this study sought to establish ways of improving the information–seeking behaviour of the students. To attain that goal, the study stipulated the following objectives:

1. To know the most preferred source of the information sought;
2. To discover the format that students use for information;
3. To find out the awareness and use of library resources by the students;
4. To know the use of Information resources & services.
5. To determine the factors that influence students' information-seeking behaviour;
6. To determine user satisfaction with the source and type of information obtained.

METHODOLOGY

The study used a questionnaire-based survey method, which was less time-consuming. The population of the study consisted of the 356 students who come to the library. The survey comprises of 9 questions personal information such as gender, Information sources used by the respondents, use of UNISWA library, adequacy of library collections, library use and computing skills of respondents, and the use of IT-based library sources and services in order to ensure reliability and effectiveness of the instrument. A total of 400 questionnaires are distributed and 356 filled-in-questionnaires were returned by the users with the overall response rate being 89%. The collected data were analysed, classified and tabulated by employing statistical methods.

DATA ANALYSIS

The analysis is based on the questionnaire collected from the students that comes to the library. The data collected are analyse and tabulated as follows:

Number of students

Table 1. Number of Students

Male	Female	Total
181	175	356
45%	44%	89%

Table 1 Indicate the response rate of the user. Out of the 400 questionnaire distributed 356 filled up questionnaire were return with an overall response rate of 89% of which 45% were male and 44% were female.

Awareness of e-resources

Table 2. Awareness of the E-resources

Yes		Total	No		Total	No response		Total
Male	Female		Male	Female		Male	Female	
170	157	327	7	9	16	5	8	13
42%	39%	82%	2%	2%	4%	1%	2%	3%

Table 2 shows the awareness of the E-resources subscribed by the library. Out of the 356 (89%) students respondent 82% of the students are aware of the E-resources. Only 4% of them are not aware. This shows that the students were well aware of the electronic resources available in the library. The students which are not aware and didn't response were the students mostly comprise of the students from IDE (Institute of distance education) who miss their information literacy class.

Satisfaction with the service available in the library

Table 3. Satisfaction with services

Yes		Total	No		Total	No response		Total
Male	Female		Male	Female		Male	Female	
117	103	220	57	62	119	8	9	19
29%	26%	55%	14%	16%	30%	2%	2%	4%

Table 3 depict the satisfaction of the services provided by the library. A total of 55% of the students were satisfied with the services but 30% of them are not satisfied. The comments that received from the students which are not satisfied with the services are mostly with the e-resources.

Frequency of visit

Table 4. Frequency of Visit

Frequency	*No. of respondent*		*Total*	*Percentage*		*Total*
	Male	*Female*		*Male*	*Female*	
Everyday	50	40	90	13%	10%	23%
2-3 times a week	96	85	181	24%	21%	45%
Weekly	30	45	75	8%	11%	19%
Monthly	5	5	11	1%	1%	2%

Table 4 shows the frequency of visit to the library. It has been observed from the above table that majority of the students 45% of them visited the library 2-3 times a week and 23% of them visited everyday followed by 19% weekly. And the least 2% monthly. It is not very encouraging to see the frequency of visit of the library.

Purpose of visit to the library

Table 5. Purpose of Visit

Purpose	*No. of respondent*		*Total*	*Percentage*		*Total*
	Male	*Female*		*Male*	*Female*	
To study	157	154	311	39%	39%	78%
To borrow books	121	106	227	30%	27%	57%
Browsing the shelves	16	27	43	4%	7%	11%
Used of reference materials	89	91	180	22%	23%	45%
Read the journals	40	27	67	10%	7%	17%
To collect course materials	35	39	74	9%	10%	19%
Know the latest arrival	19	9	28	5%	2%	7%
Read newspaper & magazines	65	44	109	16%	11%	27%
Browse e-resources	32	28	60	8%	7%	15%

Note: Multiple answers were permitted

From table 5 it is clear that the purpose of visit to the library is mainly for study purpose. Majority of the students 78% visit for study while 57% come to borrow books and 45% come to use the reference materials. It was surprising that only 7% of them come to know the latest arrival in the library.

Use of library Information Resources & Services

Table 6. Use of Information Resources & Services

Services	*No. of respondent*		*Total*	*Percentage*		*Total*
	Male	*Female*		*Male*	*Female*	
Issue / Return	65	74	139	16%	19%	35%
Reference service	88	98	186	22%	25%	47%
Books and journals	152	119	271	38%	30%	68%
Seminar/ conference	9	4	13	2%	1%	3%
Indexing & Abstracting	10	12	22	3%	3%	6%
Bibliography	31	33	64	8%	8%	16%
Newspaper	68	52	120	17%	13%	30%
Interlibrary loan	26	28	54	7%	7%	14%

Note: Multiple answers were permitted

Table 6 shows the use of library information resources and services. Majority of the students 68% of them come for books and journals while 47% for reference service and 35% for Issue/ return.

Purpose of seeking information

Table 7. Purpose of Seeking Information

Purpose	*No. of respondent*		*Total*	*Percentage*		*Total*
	Male	*Female*		*Male*	*Female*	
For carrier development	72	56	128	18%	14%	32%
To solve immediate practical problem	91	77	168	23%	19%	42%
To keep up to date	56	40	96	14%	10%	24%
To write an assignment	138	145	283	35%	36%	71%

Note : Multiple answers were permitted

The purpose of seeking information as shown in table 7 indicates that most of the students seeks information to write assignment which represent about 71%. 42% of them come to solve immediate practical problem followed by 32% for carrier development. The rest 24% come to keep up to date.

Preference

Table 8. Preference of Journals

E-journals		*Total*	*Print*		*Total*	*No response*		*Total*
Male	*Female*		*Male*	*Female*		*Male*	*Female*	
107	80	187	60	65	125	20	24	44
27%	20%	47%	15%	16%	31%	5%	6%	11%

Table 8 shows the preference of the journals whether print or electronic. 47% of them want the electronic journals while 31% of them still want to have the print. This shows that user still need time to get over the print journals.

Problem on use of e-resources

Table 9. Problem on use of e-resources

Yes		*Total*	*No*		*Total*	*No response*		*Total*
Male	*Female*		*Male*	*Female*		*Male*	*Female*	
43	55	98	132	113	245	8	5	13
11%	14%	25%	33%	28%	61%	2%	1%	3%

The students were asked to indicate whether they encounter problem while accessing the e-resources as shown in Table 9. Majority of the students 61% responded they don't faced any problem but 25% of them have some problems. The problems are mostly like difficult in accessing the information due to the lack of IT knowledge and skills.

5. RECOMMENDATIONS

The following recommendations are made while considering the comments from the students;

- Awareness programs must be organized for using the e-resources when new databases are added.
- Internet connectivity should be up and running in the library to enable students to make use of the available electronic databases.
- Library staff should be trained on interpersonal interaction for effective and efficient delivery of services.
- Lecturers should take the lead in initiating to use library to their student;
- Students should be guided to use the e-resources so that they do not depend mainly on lecturer notes;
- There should be sufficient number of computers to access the online resources.

6. CONCLUSION

Information seeking behaviour is influenced by a number of factors. The study is set to determine the information needs and seeking behaviour by the students at the University of Swaziland. All objectives are meeting and there was a good response in all the activities. But the frequency of visit of the library daily was not encouraging which stands only 23%. This shows that the library has needs to improve its services to attract the users. Librarians need to redesign the strategies to improve the provision of library services towards information skills development.

REFERENCES

1. Abels, E. (2004). Information seekers' perspectives on libraries and librarians. Advances in Librarianship vol.28, pp.151-170.
2. Beaulieu, M. (2003), "Approaches to user-based studies in information seeking and retrieval: a Sheffield perspective", Journal of Information Science, Vol. 29 No. 4, pp. 239-248.
3. Ford, Geoffrey. (1973), "Research in user behaviour in University Libraries. Journal of Documentation, Vol. 29 No. l, pp. 85-106.

4. Fidel, R. *et al.* (1999). A visit to the information mall: Web searching behavior of high school students. *Journal of American Society of Information Science,* 50(1), 24-37

5. Gelfand, J. (2005), "Library as changing place: viewpoints from university 5. undergraduates", Library Hi Tech News, Vol. 22 No. 4, pp. 10-12.

6. Kani-Zabihi, E., Ghinea, G. and Chen, S. (2005), "Digital libraries: what do users want?", Online Information Review, Vol. 30 No. 4, pp. 395-412.

7. Leckie, G.J., Pettigrew, K.E., & Sylvain, C. (1996). Modelling the information seeking of professional: A general model derived from research on engineers, health care professionals and lawyers. Library Quarterly, 66(2), 161- 193.

8. Lockyer, S., Creaser, C. and Davies, J.E. (2006), "Assessing the IBSS database from a novice user perspective", The Electronic Library, Vol. 24 No. 5, pp. 590-607.

9. Masterson, A.J. (1974) User of Libraries: A comparative Study. -Journal of Librarianship (London), 6(2), pp. 63-79.

10. Prabha, C., Silipigni Connaway, L., Olszewski, L. and Jenkins, L. (2007), "What is enough? Satisficing information needs", Journal of Documentation, Vol. 63 No. 1, pp. 74-89.

11. Rzasa, Philip V. and Moriarty, John H. (1970) The Types and Needs of Academic Library Users. A Case-study of 6,568 Responses. College and Research Libraries (Chicago), 31(6), pp. 403-409.

12. Sadler, E. and Given, L.M. (2007), "Affordance theory: a framework for graduate students' information behavior", Journal of Documentation, Vol. 63 No. 1, pp. 115-141.

13. University of Swaziland Library website: *http://www.library.uniswa.sz*

14. Wilson, T.D. (2006), "Revisiting user studies and information needs", Journal of Documentation, Vol. 62 No. 6, pp. 680-684.

15. Wilson, T.D. (1981) On user studies and information needs. *Journal of Librarianship,* 37(1), 3-15. *http://informationr.net/tdw/publ/papers/1981infoneeds.html* (Accessed on 25 October, 2012)

12

Online Reading Habit Among Science Students of Govt. P.G. College, Noida: A Case Study

Devendra Kumar

ABSTRACT

The study analyzed the online reading habit of B.Sc. 3rd year students of Govt. Post Graduate College, Noida. A total of 150 well structured questionnaires were distributed among B.Sc. 3rd year students of various departments in Faculty of Science. The 142 questionnaires were returned for analysis. The present study demonstrates and elaborates the various aspects of online reading habits of B.Sc. 3rd year students of natural science like purpose of use online reading, place where most frequently using online reading, frequency & time spent for online reading, awareness and use of online reading, problem faced during using online reading, search engines used by B.Sc. 3rd year students for online reading, opinion about online reading materials. Further an attempt has also been made to conclusion of the study. The statistical analysis of the data for the present study was done by applying simple percentage.

Key words : Online reading habits, B.Sc., Govt. Post Graduate College, Noida

INTRODUCTION

Online reading is a comprehensive term covering all the kinds of learning possible through the use of computers. Thus, it includes computer based learning materials, i.e. e-journals, e-books, multimedia, discussion forum, e-mail, blogs, chat, animations, simulations, games, virtual experiments of the foregoing and, learning through the resources available on the Internet. Online reading is a term that means something different to almost everyone who uses it. Some think only of web-based self-study while others realize online reading can encompass real-time learning and collaboration. Online reading is the unifying term to describe the fields of online learning web-based learning, learning and technology-delivered instructions. Online reading does not require physical classroom attendance. Via the Internet, the learning experience is delivered to the user personably and effectively. We are all familiar with classroom-based learning (c-learning) which is face-to-face group learning led by an instructor of subject matter expert. In Online reading environments learners interact with learning materials, their instructors and other learners from various locations and often at various times using network technologies. It has been said that there are two reasons why we learn; some learning essentially forced on us while the others is what we sit back and enjoy. Online reading has brought back the joy in learning through its innovative, interactive content and delivery. B.Sc. 3rd year students findings of reading habits varied on academic performance. Caverly and Peterson (2000) noted that research on the effect of technology on reading achievements demonstrated mixed results. On the one hand, Sheorey and Mokhtari (1994) indicated that there is no significant difference between high and low-proficient readers with regard to amount of time spent reading academic or nonacademic materials.

Smith and Robinson (1980) defined reading as "an active attempt on the part of reader to understand a writer's message". Reading is primarily an intellectual activity and its practice is influenced by many factors like home environment, subject background, age etc. Reading helps in the resolution of personal need and the attainment of mental maturity and independence of thoughts. Devrajan (1979) defined "reading is an art of interpreting printed and written words". It is a basic tool of education and one of the most important skills in everyday life.

Habit is a psychological aspect and is develop during a course of time as a part of personality of an individual. Rahman (1959) is in his report on "Reading for pleasure" mentioned that lack of appreciation and understanding of good books and failure to derive pleasure from a habit of reading underlines the problem of educational growth.

The four main information needs of B.Sc. 3rd year students are:

- Current information to keep up in a field
- Specific information which is often task related
- Retrospective information which forms the basis of projects
- Brush-up, often in related or peripheral areas to the research

OBJECTIVES OF THE STUDY

- To find out the various purposes of use online reading by B.Sc. 3rd year students.
- To find out the places where most frequently using online reading
- To find out the time spent for online reading
- To find out the awareness and uses various types of online reading materials.
- To know the problems faced by B.Sc. 3rd year students during using online reading.
- To find out the search engines used by the B.Sc. 3rd year students for online reading
- To indicates opinion about online reading materials

METHODOLOGY

The present study, questionnaire method was used for data collection that seeks to explore the online reading habit of natural science B.Sc. 3rd year students in Govt. Post Graduate College, Noida. The data collected are the situation of information about the views of B.Sc. 3rd year students of natural science. The questionnaire comprises 08 questions with an option to express any comments regarding online reading habit. 150 questionnaires were distributed among the natural science B.Sc. 3rd year students, convenience sampling method used for the data collection, 142 questionnaires were received back from the respondents.

Table 1. Sample Population

S. N.	*Department*	*Questionnaire distributed*	*Received questionnaires*	*%*
1.	B.Sc. 3rd	150	142	94

Table 2. Purpose of use online reading

S.N.	*Purpose*	*%*
1.	For study work	100
2.	To increase knowledge	91.54
3.	Update subject knowledge	94.36
4.	For recreation/message	74.64
5.	For entertainment	42.25

Table-2 shows that majority of B.Sc. 3rd year students use online reading for their course work (100%) followed by update subject knowledge (64.36%), to increase knowledge (91.54%). Nearly 75% B.Sc. 3rd year students for recreation/message and least number for entertainment.

Table 3. Place where most frequently using online reading

S.N.	*Place*	*%*
1.	College	97.18
2.	Home	36.61
3.	Other places i.e Cyber cafe	25.53

Table-3 revealed that majority of B.Sc. 3rd year students most frequently use online reading in their department/library followed by 36.61% B.Sc. 3rd year students at home. Least number of B.Sc. 3rd year students goes to other place (i.e. cyber café, etc) for use online reading (online resources).

Table 4. Frequency of online reading

S.N.	*Frequency*	*%*
1.	Daily	54.92
2.	2-3 times in a week	32.40
3.	weekly	12.68
4.	Occasionally	0
	Total	100

Table-4 shows that majority of B.Sc. 3rd year students (54.92%) uses online reading daily followed by 32.40% uses 2-3 times in a week. Whereas a very few B.Sc. 3rd year students uses weekly. However it is interesting to note that not a single B.Sc. 3rd year students reported that he/she uses their sources occasionally.

Table 5. Time spent for online reading

S. N.	*Time (in hour)*	*%*
1.	0-1	07.04
2.	1-2	73.23
3.	2-3	14.08
4.	4-above	5.63
	Total	100

Table-5 showed that majority of B.Sc. 3rd year students spent 1-2 hours for online reading and least number of B.Sc. 3rd year students spent less than 1 hour.

Table 6. Awareness and use of online reading

S. N.	*Resources*	*Awareness (%)*	*Use*
1.	News	100	92.95
2.	e-books	100	43.67
3.	e-journals	100	15
4.	e-mail	100	100
6.	Online databases	63.38	21.12
7.	Others online resources	43.66	43

Table-6 indicated that majority of science B.Sc. 3rd year students are aware about news, e-books, e-journals, e-mails, conference/seminar, etc., and least numbers of B.Sc. 3rd year students aware about online databases and others online resources. In case of use majority of B.Sc. 3rd year students use e-journals (15%) and e-mail (100%) followed by news (92.95%), and e-books (43.67%), a least number of B.Sc. 3rd year students uses online databases and other online resources.

Table 7. Problem faced during using online reading

S.N.	*Problems*	*Response*	*%*
1.	Speed of Internet	45	63.38
2.	Slow downloading	60	84.50
3.	Unawareness about the exact URLs	65	91.45
4.	Not access full text in many e-journals	71	100
5.	Printing facility	29	40.84

Table-7 showed that majority of B.Sc. 3rd year students not access full text in many e-journals (100%) followed by unaware uses about the exact URLs (91.45%) also slow downloading are a major problem faced by B.Sc. 3rd year students (84.50%) during online reading process.

Table 8. Search engines used by B.Sc. 3rd year students for online reading

S. N.	Search engines	%
1.	Google	100
2.	Yahoo	63.38
3.	Msn	29.57
4.	Others	7.04
	Total	100

Table-8 revealed that majority of B.Sc. 3rd year students used Google search engines (100%) for their online reading process followed by Yahoo (63.38%), MSN (29.58%), and others (7.04).

Table 9. Opinion about Online reading materials

S.N.	Opinion	%
1.	Excellent	7.04
2.	Good	38.03
3.	Average	40.85
4.	Not satisfactory	14.08
	Total	100

Table-9 indicated that majority of B.Sc. 3rd year students graded the online reading materials available online is average (40.85) and (38.03%) rated the good. Only (7.04%) rated the materials available are excellent.

CONCLUSION

Online reading materials are the most important for the research community. It is proceed that online materials saves time of the users. Lack of training among users and proper infrastructure in the library is a major de-motivating factor in the use of online reading. This study helps the librarian to know the importance of online reading and it helps them to improve the services related to online reading materials. The findings of this study lead us to conclude that B.Sc. 3rd year students need to improve their reading habits. It will be beneficial to have a record of their reading habits in order to make predictions about their academic success in the research. B.Sc. 3rd year students concur that generally their expectations of their reading ability, have not been met. B.Sc. 3rd year students should be encouraged to use the Internet as a tool to tap valuable online reading resources or participate in relevant discussion groups. This activity can assist in the promotion of autonomous learning and make B.Sc. 3rd year students more independent and resourceful.

REFERENCES

1. Caverly, D.C. & Peterson, C.L. (2000). Technology in college developmental reading. In R. Flippo & D. Caverly (Eds.): The Handbook of College Reading and Study Strategy Research. Mahwah, N.J.: Lawrence Erlbaum Associates.
2. Devrajan, G. (1979). Reading habits secondary school students in Trivendrum. *ALIS Bulletin*, 6: 93-94.
3. Sheorey, R. & Mokhtari, K. (1994). The reading habits of developmental college students at different levels of reading proficiency. Reading Improvement, 31(3): 156-166.
4. Smith, N. & Robinson, H. (1980). Reading instruction for Today's Children. Englewood Cliff, NJ. Prentice-Hall Inc.

13

Awareness and Use of UGC-Infonet Consortium by the Post-Graduate Students of Nagaland University and Mizoram University

Mhonbemo Ngullie
Lallaisangzuali

ABSTRACT

This paper focuses on the use of UGC-Infonet e-journals by the Post Graduate Students of Nagaland University (NU) and Mizoram University (MZU). The paper further tries to determine the awareness about the e-journal consortium, purpose of using the e-journals and the problems faced in using the e-journal consortium.

Keywords: *e-journals, UGC-Infonet e-journals, Nagaland University (NU), Mizoram University (MZU)*

1. INTRODUCTION

Owing to the emergence of information technology and its application in libraries, traditional print journals are being replaced by electronic journals with benefits for libraries and users apparent in many ways. Electronic journals consortiums are a boon to the libraries, as with this cooperation, the cost of basic journals can be shared; and library budgets can be utilized in the right positive way. Libraries are communal institutions whose aims are to provide information services to the people. Libraries play a very special role in the digital era. In the present era, computer and Internet plays an important role for the dynamic functioning of information technology. The growth of Internet technology is directly linked with the development of life and society. The major objectives of library consortia are to make best use of availability and accessibility of resources and services to a wider category of users with a very less budget.

2. UGC INFONET CONSORTIUM

The UGC-Infonet Digital Library Consortium was formally launched in December, 2003 by Honourable Dr. A P J Abdul Kalam, the President of India soon after providing the Internet connectivity to the universities in the year 2003 under the UGC-Infonet programme. The Consortium proved to be a recipe to university libraries which have been discontinuing subscription of scholarly journals because of "Serials Crisis". The term "serials crisis" refers to exponential and continuing increase in subscription cost of scholarly journals. The crisis is a result of rise in cost of journals much faster than the rate of inflation, increase in number of journals and the paucity of funds available to the libraries

The Consortium provides current as well as archival access to more than 7500+ core and peer-reviewed journals and 10 bibliographic databases from 26 publishers and aggregators in different disciplines. The programme has been implemented in phased manner. In the first phase that began in 2004, access to e-resources was provided to 50 universities who had Internet connectivity under the UGC-Infonet Connectivity programme of the UGC. In the second phase, 50 more universities were added to the programme in the year

2005. So far 209 Universities including 14 National Law schools and central universities that come under the purview of UGC, have been provided differential access to subscribed e-resources. These e-resources covers almost all subject disciplines including arts, humanities, social sciences, physical sciences, chemical Sciences, life sciences, computer sciences, mathematics and statistics, etc. The programme is wholly funded by the UGC and executed by the INFLIBNET (Information and Library Network) Centre, Gandhinagar.

3. EARLIER STUDIES

A number of surveys on the use of e-journals in academic libraries have been carried out during the last decade.

Chauhan and Prem Chand (2007) described the UGC-Infonet e-journals consortium initiative undertaken by the University Grants Commission (UGC) to facilitate free access to scholarly journals and databases in all fields and disciplines by the research and academic community across the country.

Madhusudhan (2008) revealed that e-journals perform an increasingly important role in research at the Department of Library and Information Science, University of Delhi where not only current e-journals are significant but electronic back runs are also required by the research scholars and students. There is an ever increasing demand for subscription of more e-journal titles in LIS.

Boncerino and Molteni (2007) indicated an increase in the use of electronic journals. This increase was attributed to user training, guidelines, manuals and tutorials prepared and delivered to users.

Ali and Nisha(2011) studied that seeks to examine the use of e-journals among research scholars at Central Science Library, University of Delhi. The survey reveals that majority of the research scholars are aware about the availability of e-journal consortia in the library and majority of them are using the e-journals to support their research work.

Mukherjee and Kumar (2010) conducted a study on the use of UGC-Infonet e-journals by research scholars of Banaras Hindu University (BHU). The study reveals that majority of the research scholars are satisfied with the existing model of UGC-Infonet consortium. However, the scholars are also of the opinion that further enhancement in terms of coverage is needed. The study also reveals that most of the important journals required by the scholars are not accessible in full-text format.

4. OBJECTIVES OF THE STUDY

The objectives of this study were to:

- Analyze the knowledge about UGC-Infonet e-journals among Post Graduate students of Nagaland University (NU) and Mizoram University (MZU).
- Find out the purpose of electronic journals usage by the Post Graduate students of Nagaland University and Mizoram University.
- Understand the barriers faced by the Post Graduate students while using e-journals.
- Suggest ways and means for the effective use of e-journals.

5. METHODOLOGY

The questionnaire method was used to collect the primary data, keeping in view the objectives of the study. The survey was designed to collect information about the use of e-journals for academic and research work by the Research Scholars of the two universities. A total of 300 questionnaires (150 each to the two universities) were randomly distributed among the Post Graduate Students. Of these 232 questionnaires were returned making the response rate 77.33%.

6. DATA ANALYSIS AND INTERPRETATION

The data collected were analyzed and interpreted and are presented in tables and figures.

6.1. Knowledge about UGC-Infonet Consortium

It is important to know whether the Post Graduate Students have knowledge about the existence of UGC-Infonet Consortium as it is very helpful for academic work. The PG Students were asked their knowledge about UGC-Infonet Consortium which is shown in Table 1.

Table 1. Knowledge about UGC-Infonet Consortia.

Knowledge	*University*		*Total*
	Nagaland University N=92	*Mizoram University N=140*	*N = 232*
Aware	64 (69.57%)	77 (55%)	141(60.78%)
Not Aware	28(30.43%)	63 (45%)	91(39.22%)
Total	92(100.0%)	140 (100.0%)	232(100.0%)

Table 1 shows the knowledge about the existence of UGC-Infonet Consortium by the Post Graduate Students of Nagaland University and Mizoram University. The analysis showed that out of the 92 PG Students of Nagaland University (NU), 69.57% were aware about UGC-Infonet Consortium. The remaining 30.43% were not aware about the existence of the Consortium.

Meanwhile, out of the 140 Post Graduate Students representing Mizoram University, 55% were aware about the existence of UGC-Infonet Consortium while 45% were not aware about the Consortium.

Out of the total respondents' i.e 232, 60.78% were aware about UGC-Infonet Consortium while the remaining 39.22% does not have knowledge about the Consortium.

6.2. Sources of knowledge of UGC-Infonet Consortium

Post Graduate Students were asked to identify their

sources of knowledge of UGC-Infonet Consortium which is shown in Table 2.

Table 2. Sources of knowledge of UGC-Infonet Consortium

Source of knowledge	*University*		*Total*
	Nagaland University N=92	*Mizoram University N=140*	*N=71*
No Response	11 (11.96%)	23 (16.43%)	34 (14.66%)
Library professionals	21 (22.83%)	30 (21.43%)	51(21.98%)
Teachers	11 (11.96%)	27 (19.29%)	38 (16.38%)
Friends	17 (18.48%)	13 (9.29%)	30 (12.93%)
University Website	5 (5.43%)	9 (6.43%)	14 (6.03%)
University Library	27 (29.35%)	38 (27.14%)	65 (28.02%)
Total	92 (100.0%)	140 (100.0%)	232(100.0%)

With regard to the sources of knowledge of UGC-Infonet Consortium, Table 2 reveals that 29.35% Post Graduate Students of NU and 27.14% Post Graduate Students of MZU stated that their sources of knowledge is the University Library.

On the other hand, it is interesting to note that 22.83% PG Students of NU and 21.43% PG Students of MZU stated that their sources of knowledge are the library professionals.

6.3. Purpose of using UGC-Infonet e-journals

Electronic journals have become an important part of library collection. The e- journals are used for various purposes of study. Even though the purposes are many, the value of UGC-Infonet Consortium to the Post Graduate Students can be ascertained by identifying their purpose of using the resources which is shown in Table 3.

Table 3. Purpose of using UGC-Infonet e-journals

Purpose	*University*		*Total*
	Nagaland Uni. N=92	*Mizoram Uni. N=140*	*N=232*
No Response	13 (14.13%)	15 (10.71 %)	28 (12.07 %)
For writing articles	4 (4.35%)	3 (2.14%)	7 (3.02 %)
To keep up-to-date	13 (14.13%)	53 (37.86%)	66 (28.45 %)
To prepare notes	50 (54.35 %)	65 (46.43 %)	115 (49.57 %)
For research purpose	12 (13.04 %)	4 (2.86 %)	16 (6.9 %)
Total	92(100.0 %)	140(100.0 %)	232 (100.0 %)

The Post Graduate Students' purpose of gathering information from UGC-Infonet e-journals can be observed from the following interpretation. 54.35% Post Graduate Students of NU and 46.43 % Post Graduate Students of MZU stated that they have used the UGC-Infonet Consortium journals to prepare notes.

14.13% Post Graduate Students of NU and 37.86% Post Graduate Students of MZU are using the Consortium to keep up-to-date.

6.4. Problems in accessing UGC-Infonet e-journals

It is interesting and challenging to know the problems faced while accessing the e-journals. Examination of the problem helps the library and information centres to increase the efficiency and effectiveness of its services. In order to understand the problems faced by the Post Graduate Students of NU and MZU, the problems are categorized into five different parts as shown in Table 4.

Table 4. Problems in accessing UGC-Infonet e-journals

Problems	*University*		*Total*
	Nagaland Uni. N=92	*Mizoram Univ. N=140*	*N=232*
No Response	14 (15.22%)	14(10%)	28(12.07%)
Limited access terminals	36 (39.13%)	12(8.57%)	48(20.69%)
Slow Internet connectivity	30(32.61%)	48(34.29%)	73(31.47%)

Insufficient time	5(5.43%)	43(30.71%)	53(22.84%)
Difficulty in finding relevant information	4(4.35%)	12 (8.57%)	16(6.90%)
Difficulty in accessing full-text	2(2.17%)	10(7.14%)	12(5.17%)
Retrieval problems	1(1.09%)	1(0.71%)	2 (0.86%)
Total	92(100.0%)	140(100.0%)	232(100.0%)

It can be seen from Table-4 that majority of the Post Graduate Students faced different kinds of problems. The most common problem faced by the Post Graduate Students of both the universities is slow Internet connectivity (32.61% and 34.29%). 39.13% Post Graduate Students of NU stated that Limited access Terminals is one of their problem, while the corresponding percentage is only 8.57% for the students of MZU.

7. SUGGESTIONS

- 39.22% of Post Graduate students are unaware about e-journals and the UGC-Infonet Consortium which are available for them. Nagaland University and Mizoram University Central Libraries should take action to promote awareness among Post Graduate Students about the UGC-Infonet Consortium for better utilization of the e-journals.
- Central Libraries of the two universities should conduct awareness programme with hands on training for the Post Graduate Students.
- Fast and continuous Internet connectivity is mandatory to increase access of the e-journals.
- More computer terminals should be provided for the users to access the e-journals.
- Library should conduct feedback/ user surveys to determine the needs of users from time to time.

CONCLUSION

UGC-Infonet e-journals are regarded as an important tool for conducting research. The study of the two universities reveals that Post Graduate Students need to enhance their skills and devote much of their time to make maximum use of the resources provided to them. To enhance the use of the e-journals, more awareness programmes need to be organized to acquaint them about the facilities and benefits which may be obtained from electronic format. A proper and well defined infrastructure remains to be an encouraging factor for the use of e-journals[4]. A more extensive study in this regard is needed to investigate how the students actually interact with the information, particularly electronic journals.

REFERENCES

1. Ali, P.M.Naushad & Nisha, Faizul (2011). Use of e-journals among research scholars at Central Science Library, University of Delhi. Collection Building, 30 (1), p53-60. Retrieved from *http://dx.doi.org/10.1108/01604951111105023* on 25th May 2012
2. Bal Ram & Karn, Bhaskar (2014). Study of UGC-Infonet e-resources Consortia in Universities of Eastern India. *International Journal of Computer Science and Information Technologies, 5* (6). P7977-7983
3. Boncerino, Gonzalez A. & Molteni, V.E. (2007). Electronic journals collection in Argentine private academic libraries. *The Electronic Library, 25* (1). Retrieved from *http://dx.doi.org/10.1108/02640470710729128* on 26th August 2013
4. Chauhan, Suresh K. & Chand, Prem (2007). UGC-Infonet: e-journals consortium and Indian academics: the right initiative at the right time. *Library Philosophy and Practice.* p.1-7. Retrieved from *http://digitalcommons.unl.edu/libphilprac/112* on 11th November 2012
5. Kaur, Baljinder & Verma, Rama (2009). Use and impact of electronic journals in the Indian Institute of Technology, Delhi, India. *The Electronic Library, 27* (4), p611-622. Retrieved from *http://dx.doi.org/10.1108/02640470910979570 on 26th August 2013*
6. Madhusudhan, M. (2008). Usage of UGC-Infonet e-journals by research scholars and students of the University of Delhi, Delhi: a study. *Library Hi Tech, 26* (3), p369-386. Retrieved

from *http://dx.doi.org/10.1108/07378830810903300* on 26th August 2013

7. Mukherjee, Bhaskar & Prashant Kumar (2010). Use of UGC-Infonet e-journals by research scholars of the Banaras Hindu University, Varanasi: a case study. *Annals of Library and Information Studies, 57*. p339-347

8. *www.inflibnet.ac.in/econ/about.php*. Accessed on 26th June 2015

14

IndCat! The Union Catalogue of Academic Libraries of India: A Case Study

Punit Kumar Singh
A. P. Singh

ABSTRACT

The Information and Library Network (INFLIBNET) Centre, an autonomous Inter-University Centre (IUC) of the University Grants Commission (UGC) located at the Infocity, Gandhinagar, acts as a nodal agency for networking of libraries and information centres in universities, institutions of higher learning and R & D institutions in India. "IndCat: Online Union Catalogue of Indian Universities" is the one of the initiatives taken by INFLIBNET. It contains bibliographic records of books, serials and theses contributed by participating universities in all disciplines. The purpose of this paper is describe concept of union catalogue; the efforts made by INFLIBNET to maintain the union catalogue database of books, serials, theses, and e-videos; and the present status of the IndCat database.

Keywords : Union Catalogue, Academic Libraries, IndCat

1. INTRODUCTION

Development in information communication technology, information technology and fast processing etc. are the driving force which leads the fast file transfer and data sharing over the network. The emphasis of these technologies have found over all the fields of library services viz. document delivery service, automated catalogue, circulation, inter library lending, resource sharing etc. Online shared cataloguing system is one of the parts of the resources sharing which become more practical, more economic, and faster due to these developments. The more number of catalogue records of library materials can be shared within large number of institutions not only at local level but also at national or international level. Collaborative cataloguing in academic libraries occurs at regional, national, and international level in different formats. The main reason of the collaboration is to share staff, resource, and materials to achieve optimum utility in less costs (Mugridge, 2013).

The Information and Library Network (INFLIBNET) Centre is established as a programme in 1991 in Gujrat University Campus, Ahmedabad. Later on in 1996, it is established by UGC as Inter University Centre (IUC) at Infocity, Gandhinagar. The centre is aimed to sharing of the infrastructure, services and resources for networking of libraries of universities and research institutions. INFLIBNET works collaboratively with Indian university libraries to shape the future of the academic libraries in the evolving information environment. The Centre has many major Activates such as UGC-Infonet: an Internet Connectivity Programme, UGC-Infonet Digital Library Consortium, Library Management Software, JCCC, etc. Apart from that the major activity of the centre is to create union databases of library resources such as books, serials, theses, etc. available in the Indian academic libraries. The INFLIBNET union database is a traditional union catalogue, in which records from multiple sources and formats are being converted into a single format (Chavda and Chandrakar, 2008).

2. UNION CATALOGUE

Union catalogue is the combination of the library catalogues of various libraries which is capable enough to provide the bibliographical details of the holdings of the each library. Union catalogue is seems to be a useful tool for implementation of resources sharing, inter library loan and document delivery services whether the collection is physical or virtual or both. A well-maintained union catalogue will serve as a discovery tool for end-users; therefore, maintaining the currency of union catalogues is essential. Since libraries are growing organisms, new documents are constantly being added. The visibility of such collections will improve if OPACs are built and made available for end-users independent of their geographical location. To further improve the visibility of the individual, distributed OPACs, an online union catalogue is a necessity (Alam and Pandey, 2010). There are many ways to develop union catalogue which can be summarized in two types:

1. CENTRALISED UNION CATALOGUES

It is the traditional way to develop union catalogue in which the centralised record of the library holdings is created at the central node and then made available to all the participating institutions either in physical catalogue card form or microfiche or any other format. Z39.50 cannot yet replace a well-managed centralized union catalogue, but it is also clear that in these days of funds shortages and essential resource sharing arrangements, a centralized catalogue is not always practical or available. In conclusion, there is room for both types of union catalogue in today's libraries, and the view that centralized catalogs are still the best way to support high volume searching against fixed collections that reflect explicit consortia or other resource-sharing arrangements (Sara, 1999). It has its own problems at local level due to the burden over the central node in processing of the records and inconveniencies.

2. DISTRIBUTED UNION CATALOGUES

Due to advent of the ICT, MARC and Z39.50 and other file exchange formats, it become possible to link the local catalogues through their respective servers to each other by doing the necessary processing works. In this model, each participating libraries creates its own catalogue of the holding and provide it to the central node to clamp these to union catalogue after authentication and duplicate check. It becomes the popular concept in creation the union catalogues now-a- days due to the production of the holdings records in real time. While the hybrid model of the both centralized and distributed union catalogues are also in the existence.

3. INDCAT

The Information and Library Network (INFLIBNET) Centre acts as a nodal agency for networking of libraries and information centres in universities, institutions of higher learning and R & D institutions in India. Major activities and services of the Centre are geared towards modernization of academic libraries and information centres, to promote information transfer and access, to support scholarship, learning and academic pursuits. The technology being a driving force in the contemporary education system, the Centre, on behalf of the UGC, has taken-up a number of initiatives for the benefit of the academic community. "IndCat: Online Union Catalogue of Indian Universities" is the one of the initiatives taken by INFLIBNET. It contains bibliographic records of books, serials and theses contributed by participating universities in all disciplines. It integrates a group of individual catalogues and provides locations. It serves as a document supply mechanism for different types of material owned by the participating libraries that is the key to resource sharing among member libraries. At the same time it functions as a central pool of data, which can be used for collection development and document supply. Overall, it represents the holdings of university libraries in India. In addition databases of research projects and experts in India are also being developed (Chand and Chauhan, 2008). Figure 1 represents the user interface of the IndCat database.

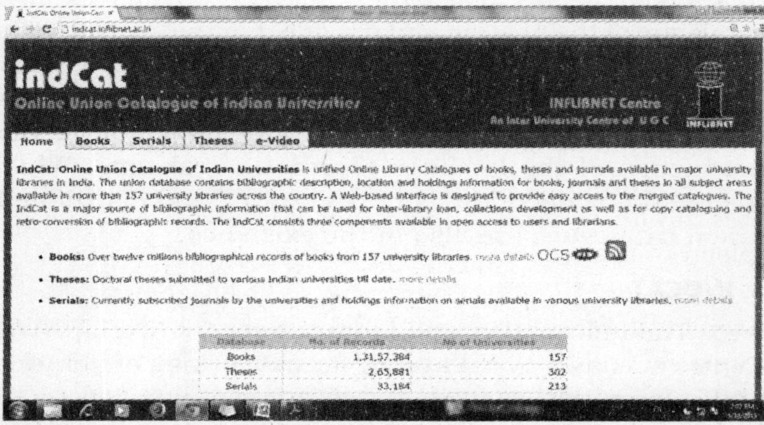

Fig. 1. IndCat database user interface

3.1. Workflow Process of IndCat

INFLIBNET is managing a central hub for maintaining union catalogues and in many ways a centralised catalogue is less likely to produce duplicate records. If duplicate records do occur during the searching this would not affect the success of the retrieval programme. The following process is done to build and maintain the IndCat database:

1. Collection of the Bibliographic Records : The bibliographic records from the different universities are received by the INFLIBNET centre. These records are the raw data in the different formats such as MS-Excel, MS-Access, Dbase / Foxpro, CDS/ISIS, WIN ISIS, MS-SQL Backup, CCF, MARC, Libsys, and SOUL 2.0 etc.

2. Conversion of the records in CCF format : These records in the different formats are needed to be converted into one format to maintain the uniformity in the records. Common Communication Format (CCF) is used to convert the records in one format with the help of tag mapping system of CDS/ISIS software.

3. Checking for authentication and Duplicate records : Authentication is the next process in which all records are undergo for duplicate check and for editing typographical errors in various fields such as place, publisher, edition, year of publication, etc with the help of Union Catalogue Management System (UCMS).

4. Merger of the records in the IndCat Database: After duplicate checking, the next step is the merger and upload of the records into the Indian catalogue.

The IndCat is the distributed online union catalogue in which the local catalogue of the particular institution is created first then it is uploaded to the union catalogue. It provides search facilities through author, title, subject, ISBN, place and publisher, and universities. It has also provision of advanced search and State-wise search.

3.2. Salient Features of the IndCat

IndCat provides the databases of union catalogues of the bibliographic records of books, theses, serials and e-Videos of the contributing universities of India. The salient features of the IndCat database is as follows:

1. Search within Universities : IndCat provides the search facility within the name of the University which is quite useful to the users to search the catalogue of its own university from anywhere under the name of author, title and subject.

2. State Wise Search : It provides the state wise search facility in which the bibliographic records of the participating universities of a particular state with location can be searched.

3. E-video Search : IndCat provides the video database search facility which is developed by INFLIBNET and Consortium for Education Communication (CEC) to promote the e-education with the help online video lectures. It provides more than 15,000 Courseware e-Contents for Undergraduate in 68 subjects under the 4 streams developed under NME-ICT project of CEC.

4. Special databases for Gujarat and NER :

GujCat **:** GujCat, subset of IndCat, is an Online Union Catalogue of books available in major college/institute/university libraries within Gujarat state. A separate dedicated web-based interface is designed to provide easy-access. GujCat is a major source of bibliographic information that can be used for inter-library loan, collection development as well as for copy cataloguing and retro-conversion of bibliographic records within Gujarat.

NERCat **:** It is an online union catalogue of books in universities in North-Eastern Region, is another subset of IndCat. NERCat is designed and implemented to restrict searching of bibliographic records to university libraries in North-eastern region so as to promote resource sharing amongst North-eastern universities. A separate dedicated web-based interface is designed to provide easy-access to the merged catalogues of university libraries in North-eastern region.

5. Online Copy Catalogue System (OCS) : The INFLIBNET has developed application software called "Online Copy-Catalogue System" (OCS) to promote co-operative cataloguing and avoid duplication of efforts. The interface called "Online Copy Catalogue System (OCS)" is a Window-based application that facilitates libraries to interact with the Union Catalogue of Books (IndCat) and catalogue their new acquisitions online.

3.4. Growth at a Glance

Development and maintenance of the union catalogue is a regular process which demands the steady and helpful efforts and collaboration between the parent institution and the contributing institutions. It is necessary to do update and to add new records in the databases at regular time interval.

3.4.1. Collection Status

Table 1 provides the number of bibliographic records in different databases contributed by participating universities till May 2015.

Table 1. Number of Records in IndCat

Database	*No. of Records*	*No of Universities*
Books	1,31,57,384	157
Theses	2,65,881	302
Serials	33,184	213
e-Videos	15,000	18

3.4.2. Growth of Book Data

The union catalogue of the books is started by INFLIBNET centre in 1999 with the 6.5 Lakh records of bibliographic details of books in which 2.7 Lakh records are unique. The figure 2 depicts the growth of the book database from 1999 to 2014. It is revealed that there is exponential growth in the book data during this period which means that the contributors are interested to share the bibliographical details of theses through IndCat.

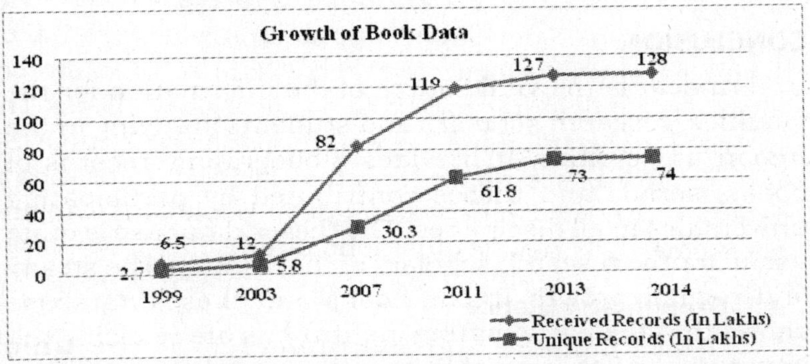

Fig. 2. Growth of book data from 1999 to 2014

3.4.3. Growth of Theses Data

The union catalogue of the theses is started by INFLIBNET centre in 1995 with 52000 records of 82 universities. During the period of 20 years, the theses database is steadily grown to more than 2.6 lakhs records as on 2014 from 298 universities. The figure 3 depicts the growth of the theses database from 2000 to 2014. It is revealed that the records in the theses database are doubled in the duration of 15 years. The growth in theses database is fast which means that the contributors are interested to share the bibliographical details of theses through IndCat and users have keen interest in search of the bibliographic details of theses through IndCat.

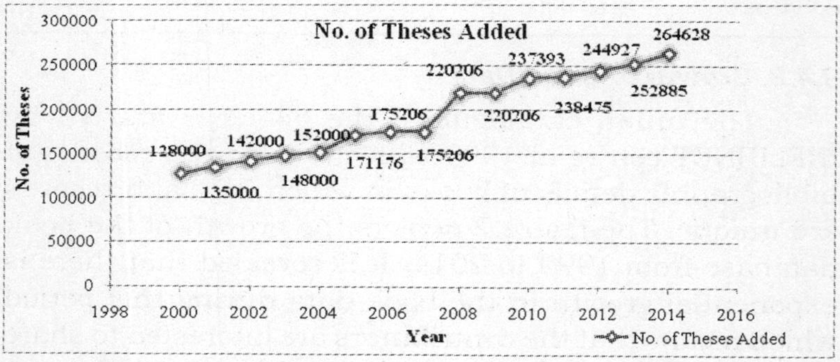

Fig. 3. No. of theses added from 2000 to 2014.

CONCLUSION

Indcat is the vital source of the information for the faculties, research scholars and students studying in the Indian universities. It provides bibliographic records of books, serials and theses contributed by participating universities in all disciplines. The theses database is quite useful for the research scholars of the country. The steady and regular growth in the books and theses database shows that the participating institutions are realizing the importance of sharing of the catalogues through IndCat. It is clear that the main aim of the creation of the union catalogue is to enhance the resource sharing and document delivery and interlibrary loan services among the participating libraries. It is quite helpful to provide the link of IndCat database on the library website of each participating institution in order to promote the use of the IndCat database by the end users.

REFERENCES

1. Alam, N. and Pandey, P. (2010), "SpaceCat: an online union catalogue for space science serials in India", Interlending & Document Supply, Vol. 38 No. 4, pp. 200–209.
2. Chand, P. and Chauhan, S. (2008), "The union catalogue of academic libraries in India: an initiative by INFLIBNET", Interlending & Document Supply, Vol. 36 No. 3, pp. 142 8.
3. Chavda, N. and Chandrakar, R. (2008), "Union Database of Theses at INFLIBNET Centre: An Overview", 6th Convention PLANNER - 2008, Nagaland University, Nagaland, November 06-07, 2008, pp. 466-473.
4. IndCat database. Retrieved from: http://indcat.inflibnet.ac.in/ (Accessed on: 12/05/2015)
5. INFLIBNET Centre. (2014). Annual Report April 1, 2013 to March 31, 2014. Gandhi Nagar: Author. pp. 12-24. (Accessed on: 12/05/2015, Retrieved from: http://ir.inflibnet.ac.in/bitstream/1944/1951/1/Annual%20Report%202013-2014.pdf)
6. Mugridge, R.L. (2013), "The value of collaboration and partnerships in cataloguing", Cataloguing and Classification Quarterly, Vol. 51 Nos 1/3, pp. 1-5.
7. Sara Gould, (1999),"From cards to clumps: a look at developments in the world of union catalogues", Interlending & Document Supply, Vol. 27 Iss 3. pp. 116 – 121.

FURTHER READINGS

1. Rekha Mittal, (2011),"The National Union Catalogue of Scientific Serials in India NUCSSI) on the web", Interlending & Document Supply, Vol. 39 Iss 1. pp. 53 – 60
2. Patti P.C. Cheung Maria L.C. Lau, (2014),"From union catalogue to fusion catalogue", Library Management, Vol. 35 Iss 1/2. pp. 88 – 101
3. George Macgregor Fraser Nicolaides, (2005),"Towards

improved performance and interoperability in distributed and physical union catalogues", Program, Vol. 39 Iss 3. pp. 227 – 247

4. Philip Hider, (2004),"The bibliographic advantages of a centralised union catalogue for ILL and resource sharing", Interlending & Document Supply, Vol. 32 Iss 1. pp. 17 - 29

15

Evernote : An Innovative Tool to Make Research Easier for Paperless Society

Manoj Kumar Pal

ABSTRACT

This paper supports the new techniques and software's of learning provided for research purpose to collect, create and organise various types of data. Through Evernote you can collect information according to your need, write without any distraction and present your ideas for betterment of the world. Here I am discussing about its need, usefulness, features, models and applications.

Keywords : Notes, Notebooks, Tags, Atlas, Trunk, Web clipper, Forms, OCR, Data security. Etc.

1. INTRODUCTION

We are using paper notebooks from last few decades. These paper notebooks have their own limitations. Sometimes you are making some important notes and you forget your notebook at home and you cannot perform any work without it. To solve such type of problems and many more, Evernote is created. Evernote is not single software it is a collection of software's and services designed for note taking and archiving. Evernote is cloud-based software for creating, organizing and storing various types of media. Whether it's a text document, a photo, an audio/video file or webpage, Evernote keeps all of your articles stored up in cloud through your very own personal Evernote account .

Evernote is designed as most useful software for personal and professional requirement. You can access files from anywhere from your any machine of office or home, nct only access you can email or save it very easily through Evernote. It automatically syncs everything up between your devices whenever you upload something new or make any changes to your notes or files.

Evernote is very easy to use. You can create a program list of the day in your computer and you will access it from your smart phone from anywhere. Just like if u want to go to super market simply you will make a list of things which you will want to buy and from market you will access it through your smart phone. This is mainly designed for research work and business purpose, by sharing files and collaborating on projects with colleagues.

2. HISTORY OF EVERNOTE

Evernote is an independent, private company founded by Stepan Pachikov in 2007. It is situated in Redwood City (California). It has approximate 100 million users worldwide. Phil Libin is the new CEO of Evernote and Linda Kozlowski is a new chief operating officer of Evernote who joined in June 2015.

3. ORGANS OF EVERNOTE

May be some people confused about the usefulness of Evernote, for your help I am going to define the best parts of Evernote. I think after that picture of Evernote is clear for its use and importance.

Notes : A "note" can be a piece of text, a full webpage, a snap, a voice/film clip, or a handwritten text. Notes have file attachments option also. It can be separate into folders/ subfolders, interpret, tagged and edit. It supports many Os like windows, Mac, Android, iOS, and also offers online sync and backup facility.—6

Notebooks : Notebooks are seems like folders. Where you will put and organize your notes and mange in groups for your better use.

Tags : It is just like a mark which is assign for searching. Tags are used for quickly locate one or many notes of a particular topic in your notebook. If you want to search simply type the term in the tag section of your note and you will found all the related topics of that term.

Atlas : If your device supports location tracking and atlas feature is enabled. It can automatically save the location where the note was created. It will help you if you going to travel, for that you will create notes and clipped places where you want to Visit. You will add hotel location and its contact no. and places to visit.

Trunk : It is a showcase of all apps and a product that makes your Evernote easier. Today in Evernote around 100 items listed across five categories: Hardware, Mobile, Desktop, Notebooks and Gear. In these 100 items, around 1/3 are completely new products and integrations.

Web Clipper : Web clipper is a bookmarking tool to help you save to webpage's for later access your web browser data and tab activity. You can add everything with Evernote account and you will able to browse by your own notes with the web clipper.

4. INFORMATION MODELS OF EVERNOTE

In this Information model you will see concepts and the relationships, rules, and operations of Evernote. It will show organized structure of information.

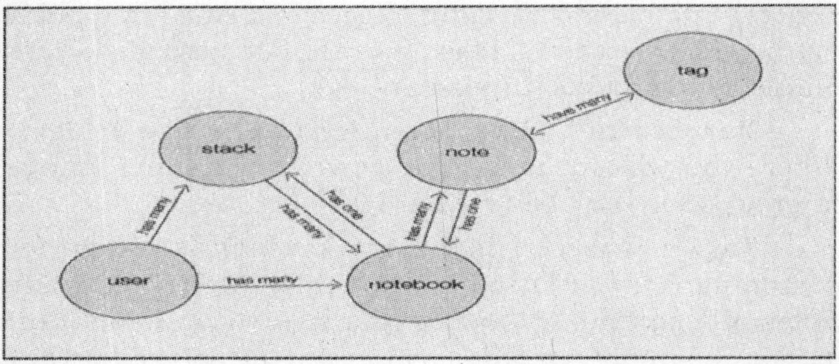

Information model for Evernote

A "note" can be a piece of text, a full webpage, a snap, a voice/film clip, or a handwritten note. Notes have file attachments option also. It can be sorted into folders, tagged, interpret and edit. Evernote supports many operating systems like windows, Mac, Android, iOS, and also offers online sync and backup facility.

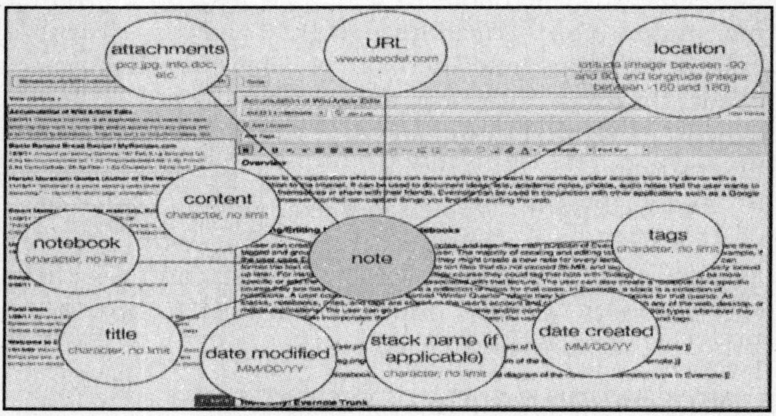

Information type model for notes in Evernote

This is an information type model of a user in Evernote with a screenshot of an example of a user's settings in Ever note's user interface

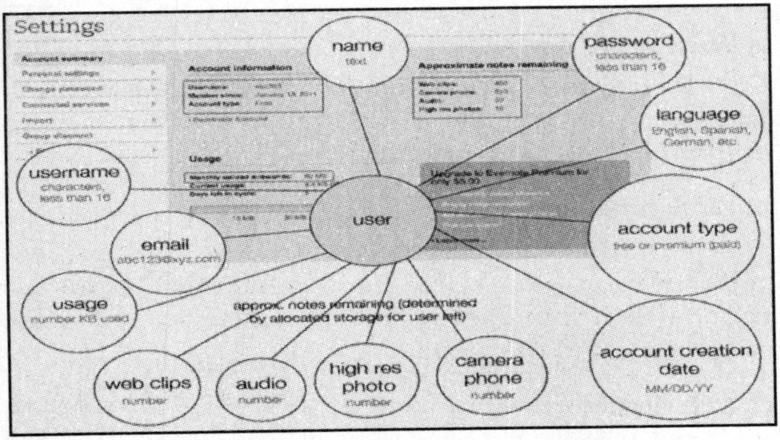

Information type model for users in Evernote

5. FREE EVERNOTE VS. PREMIUM EVERNOTE

Evernote is truly an amazing suite of software's, and you can do just fine with the free (Basic) version of Evernote. Basic version is also good and have maximum feature which is really need. It comes with almost functions discussed above sections.

In premium option they offers you more larger upload capacity rather than basic, It have better options to access history and share your notes between your colleagues. PDF search also possible, without any commercial advertise you will use another good services. Premium versions area complete business version for professionals who want to take collaboration to the higher level with the help of web technology.

Evernote is available in market according to level of requirement. It have three levels-Basic (free), Plus (24.99 $) and Premium (49.99 $). Evernote Basic, Plus and Premium have different-2 capacity and features. Basic (free) has only 60 MB/month uploading capacity in spite of that Evernote plus have 1GB monthly uploads and premium is unlimited uploads capacity.

6. FEATURES OF EVERNOTE

a) Write every day

Evernote is designed for new era of writing. Whatever you write stays with you everywhere you go from project plans to meeting notes.

b) Work together

It makes sharing of knowledge and project collaboration easier and more effective. It has no boundaries if your friends and colleagues are across the room or around the world.

c) Web clipper

Evernote Web Clipper is a plugin for Firefox and Chrome browser and is an accumulation of several features, the highlights of which are the Web Clipper, the Simultaneous Google Web Search, Related Notes and viewing all notes from the same web source. It is a web Clipper is the cluster of services at same place. Through web clipper you can Clip pages and save them in Evernote for research or reading in future. You can Share clipped pages instantly with Work chat.

Clip option

- Easily Save and organize web pages.
- Clip Para, article, text and images and paste it.
- Edit an article in one click for a better reading.
- Clip the main image with bookmark and a brief excerpt along with the URL.
- You will be able to view saved PDF online directly to your Evernote account.
- You can clip mail conversations along with any attachment.

Annotate option

- Annotate images or screenshots through arrows,

shapes, text and stamps.

- highlight anything to focus attention to any text in a screenshot.
- For getting feedback/collaboration, you can share any page through Chat.
- Post your clips to Facebook, Twitter etc. & you can share links of your clips.
- Email any clip/annotated page with friends/ colleagues.

Related results

- Whenever you search anything, Web Clipper displays related search result also.

Additional features

- Set reminders for clipped notes.
- Customize your workflow with additional settings & keyboard shortcuts on the options.

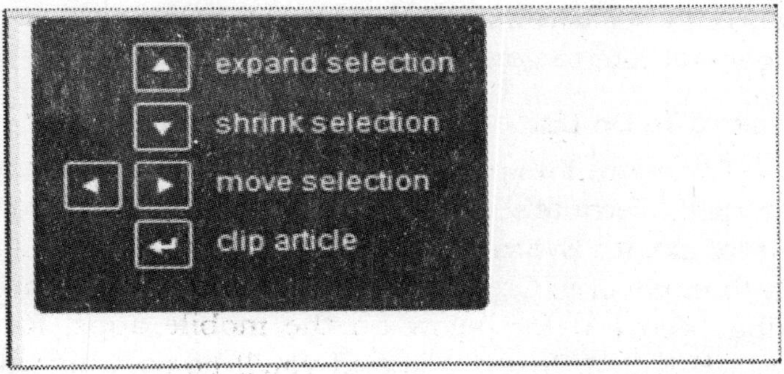

d) Find everything fast

Evernote's powerful search makes finding documents, text, and images lightning fast anytime, anywhere, and across all of your devices such as Phone, Laptop, Desktop etc.

e) Share your idea

Presentation mode gives meaning to meetings by

offering a more informal way to share ideas and seek input, no need to fuss with slides.

f) Sync with Evernote

With Evernote, your notes, web clips, files, and images are available whenever you need them on every device and computer you use.

g) Merge Several Notes into One

Sometimes you have multiple notes that just go better together. It's easy to merge them in the desktop versions (Windows, Mac, and Web) of Evernote. Simply select multiple notes and hold down the Shift key and click, you got a graphical version of them in a pile. There are many options just like email them or save/move them.

h) Add Reminders

Any note filed in Evernote can get a reminder. Click the alarm clock icon over the note in the Web or desktop interface, and you'll get a drop-down calendar, with options to set a reminder tomorrow, in a week, or any time you'd like to go back and reference it.

i) Make a To Do List

There are lots of online and mobile to-do list apps that kick Evernote's but, it's true. But if you're throwing your lot in with Evernote completely, it can't hurt to know how to make one. Create a new note and look on the text toolbar above it (or below on the mobile apps) for the Check Box tool. Insert one and you'll be on your way to creating a task list.

j) Integrate with Webmail

Powerbot is a service with a browser extension (for Chrome, Firefox, and Safari) that turns your Web-based email account on Gmail, Yahoo and Google Calendar also into an Evernote feeding powerhouse. Rather than just forwarding a message, you can click a button in your mail to send a message, an attachment, even an entire thread of emails to Evernote (or to Drop box or OneNote). Better yet, Powerbot also can access Evernote so you can attach an existing note to an outgoing message. For using Powerbot you will pay $1.99-a-month .

k) Blog by Notebook

Through Evernote you can share your notebook as a blog by using its one feature naming ***Postach.io***. It supports RSS feeds; tag facility for social networking sites i.e. Facebook and Twitter etc. Postach.io never deletes note or notebook or shows your account information publically. Your post will become visible on the blog once it's tagged as "published." It costs $9 a month or $90 a year.

l) OCR service

It is the electronic translation of data into an automatic machine-editable text. Mainly captured by a scanner, data entry through OCR is faster, more accurate and more efficient than keystroke data entry. Evernote has its own OCR service which means that it can read text, whether it's computer keyboard text, text in a PDF document, a photocopy of some text (say a page of a book) or even text in a photograph. If you are in a photo, standing in front of a plane that says "US Air Force" (for example), or any other identifying marks, Evernote's OCR function will read the words "US Air Force" (or whatever else it finds) and make those words searchable in your account.

m) E-mail service of Evernote

Evernote provides all users with their own unique email address. You can use this email address to automatically forward important emails, important files, photos, other attachments, and even email newsletters that you want to keep a hold of, but not have clog up your email quota.

Taken from makeuseof.com

n) Create Your Own Digital Scrapbook

Through Evernote you will be able to create up to 250 notebooks and organize your online digital life. Sub-categorize and tag each one so you can find them easily. Now when you want to put something quickly in a notebook, open that notebook up and drag your image or file directly into the notebook area.

o) Place Multiple Forms of Media Inside A Single Note

Through Note facility of Evernote, you can enter a picture/audio file, web links and more, all in the same place. This is very nice if you are planning a project or thinking something out.

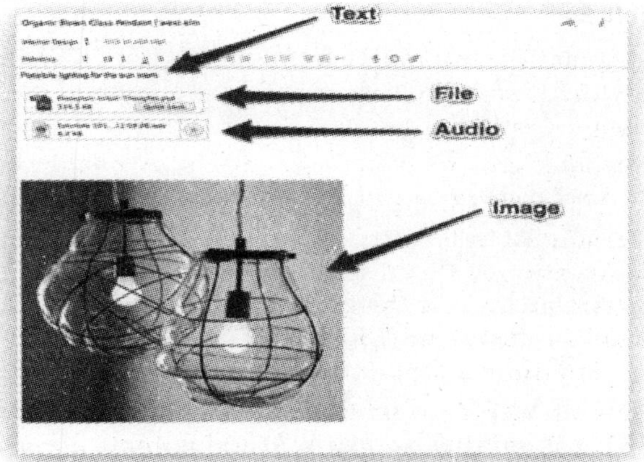

Keep all related ideas in one note.

Taken from makeuseof.com

i) Data security

If anyone will hack your password and the passwords were hashed and salted, which renders them completely inscrutable and unusable. This means that the passwords retrieved by the intruders were scrambled, preventing the intruder from accessing user accounts, including yours.

Content stored in Evernote was not stolen, as noted by the company: "In our security investigation, Evernote have found no evidence that any of the content you store in Evernote was accessed, changed or lost." So, any client-confidential data you added to Evernote was not compromised and it is safe for better use.

CONCLUSION

In this paper I've discussed how to use Evernote and its search function and web clipper. I think anyone can understand Evernote is an extremely versatile App and now you've got everything for getting started with Evernote. By using great functions of Evernote you will have to start saving whatever you have, and you'll never have to worry about forgetting things again.

REFERENCES

1. Evernote: The workspace for your life's work (2015). Available at *https://evernote.com/corp/ (Last Accessed on 25th June 2015).*
2. Evernote: choose your level (2015). Available at *https://evernote.com/pricing/* (Last Accessed on 25rd June 2015)
3. Evernote Architecture - 9 Million Users And 150 Million Requests A Day (2011). Available at http://highscalability.com/blog/2011/5/23/evernote-architecture-9-million-users-and-150-million-reques.html (Last Accessed on 23rd June 2015)
4. Evernote Web Clipper: Add-ons for Firefox - Mozilla Add-ons (2015) Available at https://addons.mozilla.org/en-us/firefox/addon/evernote-web-clipper/. (Last Accessed on 25th June 2015).
5. File:Information Type User.png (2015) Available at http://commons.wikimedia.org/wiki/File:Information_Type_User.png (Last Accessed on 23rd June 2015)
6. Griffith, Eric (2015). 30 Tips Every Evernote User Must Know. Available at http://www.pcmag.com/slideshow/story/323014/30-tips-every-evernote-user-must-know/2 (Last Accessed on 25th June 2015).
7. Moreau, Elise (2015). What is Evernote: introducing you to one of the best tools on the web for staying organised. Available at http://webtrends.about.com/od/Beginner-Cloud-Computing/a/What-Is-Evernote.htm (Last Accessed on 23rd June 2015).
8. O'Neil, Mark (2012). How to use Evernote: the unofficial manual. Available at http://www.makeuseof.com/tag/how-to-use-evernote-the-missing-manual-full-text/ (Last Accessed on 23rd June 2015).
9. Security overview | Evernote. (2015). Available at https://evernote.com/security/ (Last Accessed on 25rd June 2015).

16

Digital Management in Library Information System

Arun Kumar Sahu

ABSTRACT

Digital Libraries are emerging technologies for document management. It requires new methods of all aspects of data management. It is starting from the source through storage to delivery. Digital libraries have to use all modern network and servers technologies in order to supply services of a high quality. Its universal nature makes the digital library an excellent foundation for other services such as distance learning. It denotes the DL's interface functions, roles, skills and competencies for the management of digital information systems in the important areas of imaging technologies, optical character recognition, markup languages, cataloguing, metadata, multimedia indexing and database technology, user interface design, programming and Web technology.

Keywords : Information systems, Electronic publishing, Information superhighway, Digital libraries, Management

INTRODUCTION

An era of digital information, electronic technology, World Wide Web(WWW)'s growing popularity and the tremendous growth of CD-ROM products, digital libraries offer a huge range of information, everything from movies, speeches, images and photos to sounds, text and beyond. The amounts of online, CD-ROMs and other digital sources of information are exploding and infrastructure for accessing material improves almost daily. In building the next generation of digital libraries, artificial intelligence will play several important roles. The nature of digital libraries requires digital librarians for the locating of relevant information efficiently and cost effectively and disseminating it in a wide variety of a format of digital information system (DIS). The advent of digital libraries presents a plethora of challenges and opportunities to the digital personnel. Digitisation adds value and can make digital libraries truly useful and user friendly.

Digital library specialist is a Digital library and information professional who manages and organises the digital library, combines the functionality for information, elicitation, planning, data mining, knowledge mining, digital reference services, electronic information services, representation of information, extraction, and distribution of information, co-ordination, searching notably CD-ROMs, online, Internet-based WWW, multimedia access and retrieval. The ultimate goal of DL is faciliting access to information just-in-time to the critical wants of end users and additionally to facilitate electronic publishing. It also plays a distinctive and dynamic in easy accessing of computer held digital information including abstracts, audio-video clips, etc. A digital library may be considered to be any of these (1) machine-readable data files; (2) components of the emerging National Information Infrastructure; (3) various online databases and CD-ROM information products; (4) computer information storage devices on which information resides; (5) computerised networked library systems. A digital library maintains all or a substantial part of its collection in computer-processing form as an alternative, supplement or complement to the conventional printed and microfilm materials that currently dominate library collections. The component characteristics of digital libraries are the storage of information in digital form, direct usage of communication networks for accessing, obtaining information and copying by either downloading or online/offline printing from a master file. Its enable managing very large amounts of data, preserve unique collections, provide faster access to information, facilitate dealing with data from more than one location and enhance distributed learning environments. These also help to perform searches that are manually not feasible and offer to protect the content of the owner's information.

DIGITAL LIBRARY

Digital libraries are electronic libraries in which large numbers of geographically distributed users can access the contents of large and diverse repositories of electronic objects, networked text, images, maps, sounds, videos, catalogues of merchandise, scientific, business and government data sets. They also include hypertext, hypermedia and multimedia compositions.

A digital library is understood to have the information stored predominantly in an electronic or digital medium. The digital information collection may include digital books, digital scanned images, graphics, textual and numeric data, digitised films, and networked computers with a cable TV's capacity to transmit hundreds of programs. Services would be delivered by telecommunications networks, cable TV networks and the Internet and mobile communications. Infrastructure that provides band width on demand and information on demand services are called information superhighway. There will be two types of information services such as public services and commercial services. The use of existing telephone, fax, and analogue TV broadcast services will be supported in the initial information superhighway. In addition, new services such as videophone, multimedia electronic messaging, digital TV/

HDTV broadcast and movie and video on demand service will be provided.

ACADEMIC REPOSITORIES

Many academic libraries are actively involved in building institutional repositories of the institution's books, papers, theses and other works which can be digitised. Many of these repositories are made available to the general public with few restrictions with the goals of open access and the publication of research in commercial journals where the publishers often limit access rights. The Institutional and corporate repositories are sometimes referred to as digital libraries.

DIGITAL ARCHIVES

Physical archives differ from physical libraries in several ways. Traditionally archives are defined as:

1. Containing primary sources of information i.e. hard copy directly produced by an individual or organisation rather than the secondary sources found in a library like books, periodicals, etc.
2. Having their contents organised in groups rather than individual items.
3. Having unique contents.

The technology used to create digital libraries is even more revolutionary for archives since it breaks down the second and third of these general rules. In other words, "digital archives" or "online archives" will still generally contain primary sources but they are likely to be described individually rather than in addition to groups of collections, because they are digital their contents are easily reproducible and may indeed have been reproduced from elsewhere. The Oxford Text Archive is generally considered to be the oldest digital archive of academic physical primary source materials.

THE GOLDEN FUTURE

Large scale digitisation projects are underway at Google in the Million of Book Project and Internet Archive with continued improvements in book handling and presentation technologies such as optical character recognition and books and development of alternative depositories and business models. Digital libraries are rapidly growing in popularity. Libraries have ventured into audio and video collections. It has digital libraries such as the Internet Archive. Google Books project recently received a court victory on proceeding with their book-scanning project that was halted by the Authors' guild. This helped open the road for libraries to work with Google to better reach patrons who are accustomed to computerised information.

SEARCHING

Most digital libraries provide a search interface which allows resources to be found. These resources are typically deep web or invisible web resources since they frequently cannot be located by search engine crawlers. Some digital libraries create special pages or sitemaps to allow search engines to find all their resources. Digital libraries frequently use the Open Archives Initiative Protocol for Metadata Harvesting (OAI-PMH) to expose their metadata to other digital libraries and search engines like Google Scholar, Yahoo! and Scirus can also use OAI-PMH to find these deep web resources.

There are two general strategies for searching a federation of digital libraries:

1. Distributed searching
2. Searching previously harvested metadata

Distributed searching typically involves a client sending multiple search requests in parallel to a number of servers in the federation. The results are gathered, duplicates are eliminated or clustered, the remaining items are sorted and presented back to the client. Protocols like Z39.50 are frequently used in distributed searching. A benefit to this approach is that the resource-intensive tasks of indexing. Storage is left to the respective servers in the federation. A drawback to this approach like the search mechanism is limited by the different indexing and ranking capabilities of each database. Therefore, it making difficult to assemble a combined result consisting of the most relevant found items.

Searching over previously harvested metadata involves searching a locally stored index of information that has previously been collected from the libraries in the federation. When a search is performed, the search mechanism does not need to make connections with the digital libraries in searching. It has already a local representation of the information. This approach requires the creation of an indexing and harvesting mechanism which operates regularly, connecting to all the digital libraries and querying the whole collection in order to discover new and updated resources. OAI-PMH is frequently used by digital libraries for allowing metadata to be harvested. A benefit to this approach is that, the search mechanism has full control over indexing, ranking algorithms and possibly allowing more consistent results. A drawback is that, harvesting and indexing systems are more resource-intensive and expensive.

SOFTWARE

There are a number of software packages for use in general digital libraries. Notable ones is digital library software. Institutional repository software, which focuses primarily on ingest, preservation and access of locally produced documents. Particularly locally produced academic outputs can be found in Institutional repository software.

DIGITISATION

In the past few years, procedures for digitising books at high speed and comparatively low cost have improved considerably with the result that, it is now possible to digitise millions of books per year. Book-scanning project is also working with libraries to offer digitise books pushing forward on the digitise book realm.

ADVANTAGES

The advantages of digital libraries as a means of easily and rapidly accessing books, archives and images of various types are widely recognised by commercial interests and public bodies.

Traditional libraries are limited by storage space. Digital libraries have the potential to store much more information, because digital information requires very little physical space to contain it. Such as the cost of maintaining a digital library can be much lower than that of a traditional library. A physical library must spend large sums of money paying for staff, book maintenance, rent and additional books. Digital libraries may reduce or in some instances do away with these fees. Both types of library require cataloguing input to allow users to locate and retrieve material. Digital libraries may be more willing to adopt innovations in technology providing users with improvements in electronic and audio book technology as well as presenting new forms of communication such as wikis and blogs. Conventional libraries may consider that providing online access to their Online Public Access Catalogue (OPAC) is sufficient. An important advantage to digital conversion is increased accessibility to users. They also increase availability to individuals who may not be traditional patrons of a library due to geographic location or organisational affiliation. The main advantages of digital libraries are:

No physical boundary : The users of a digital library need not to go to the library physically. Hence people from all over the world can gain access to the same information, as long as an Internet connection is available.

Round the clock availability : A major advantage of digital libraries is that people can gain access 24/7 to the information.

Multiple access : The same resources can be used simultaneously by a number of institutions and patrons. This may not be the case for copyrighted material. A library may have a license for "lending out" only one copy at a time. This is achieved with a system of digital rights management where a resource can become inaccessible after expiration of the lending period or after the lender chooses to make it inaccessible or equivalent to returning the resource.

Information retrieval : The user is able to use any search term like word, phrase, title, name and subject to search the entire collection. Digital libraries can provide very user-friendly interfaces, giving click able access to its resources.

Preservation and conservation : Digitisation is not a long-term preservation solution for physical collections, but does succeed in providing access copies for materials that would otherwise fall to degradation from repeated use. Digitised collections and digital objects pose many preservation and conservation concerns that analog materials do not.

Space : Whereas traditional libraries are limited by storage space, digital libraries have the potential to store much more information, because digital information requires very little physical space to contain them and media storage technologies are more affordable than ever before.

Added value : Certain characteristics of objects, primarily the quality of images may be improved. Digitisation can enhance legibility and remove visible flaws such as stains and discoloration.

Easily accessible : It is easily accessible.

DIGITAL PRESERVATION

Digital preservation aims to ensure that digital media and information systems are still interpretable into the indefinite future. Each necessary component of this must be migrated, preserved or emulated. Typically lower levels of systems (floppy disks) are emulated, bit-streams (the actual files stored in the disks) are preserved and operating systems are emulated as a virtual machine. Only where the meaning and content of digital media and information systems are well understood is migration possible as is the case for office documents. However, the Wider Net Project of a organization has created an offline digital library in the e- Granary by reproducing materials on a 4 TB hard drive. Instead of a bit-stream environment, the digital library contains a built-in proxy server and search engine so the digital materials can be accessed using an Internet browser. Also, the materials are not preserved for the future. The e-Granary is intended for use in places or situations where Internet connectivity is very slow, non-existent, unreliable, unsuitable and too expensive.

COPYRIGHT AND LICENSING

Digital libraries are hampered by copyright law because of unlike with traditional printed works. The laws of digital copyright are still being formed. The republication of material on the web by libraries may require permission from rights holders and there is a conflict of interest between libraries and the publishers who may wish to create online versions of their acquired content for commercial purposes. It was estimated in 2010 that twenty three percent of books in existence were created before 1923 which is out of copyright. Only five percent were still in print after this date as of 2010. Thus, approximately seventy two percent of books were not available to the public.

There is a dilution of responsibility that occurs as a result of the distributed nature of digital resources. Complex intellectual property matters may become involved since digital material is not always owned by a library. Some digital libraries work to digitise out of copyright works and make them freely available to the public. An estimate of the number of distinct books still existent in library catalogues from 2000 BC to 1960 has been made.

The Fair Use Provisions (17 USC § 107) under the Copyright Act of 1976 provide specific guidelines under which circumstances libraries are allowed to copy digital resources. Four factors that constitute fair use are "Purpose of the use, Nature of the work, amount or substantiality used and Market impact."

Some digital libraries acquire a license to lend their resources. This may involve the restriction of lending out only one copy at a time for each license and applying a system of digital rights management for this purpose.

The Digital Millennium Copyright Act of 1998 was an act created in the United States to attempt to deal with the introduction of digital works. This Act incorporates two treaties from the year 1996. It criminalises the attempt to circumvent measures which limit access to copyrighted materials. It also criminalises the act of attempting to circumvent access control. This act provides an exemption for nonprofit libraries and archives which allows up to three copies to be made, one of which may be digital. However, this may not be made public or distributed on the web. Further, it allows libraries and archives to copy a work if its format becomes obsolete copyright issues persist. These proposals have been put forward suggesting that digital libraries be exempt from copyright law. Although this would be very beneficial to the public, it may have a negative economic effect and authors may be less inclined to create new works.

METADATA CREATION

In traditional libraries, the ability to find works of interest is directly related to how well they were catalogued. While cataloguing electronic works digitised from a library's existing holding may be as simple as copying or moving a record from the print to the electronic form, complex and born-digital works require substantially more effort. To handle the growing volume of electronic publications, new tools and technologies have to be designed to allow effective automated semantic classification and searching. While full text search can be used for some items, there are many common catalog searches which cannot be performed using full text, including:

- finding texts which are translations of other texts
- linking texts published under pseudonyms to the real authors
- differentiating non-fiction from parody

DISADVANTAGES

Digital libraries at least their digital collections, unfortunately also have brought their own problems and challenges in areas such as:

- Equity of access – the digital divide
- Interoperability between systems and software
- User authentication for access to collections
- Information organization
- Interface design
- Digital preservation
- Training and development

NATIONAL DIGITAL LIBRARY

Libraries are the storehouse of knowledge as they maintain the book and other knowledge resource available mostly in printed form. However, with the advent of digital technology and Internet connectivity, the library scenario is changing fast. Digital technology, Internet connectivity and physical content can be dovetailed resulting in Digital Library. Data available in physical form has been preserved digitally in Digital Library. Digital Libraries have the ability to enhance access to information and knowledge. They also Bridge barriers of time and space.

In the past initiatives have been taken by different Ministries / Departments / organisations for digitising and preserving data available in physical form. However, this activity has been restricted mostly in the area of the work and interest of the organisation. Department of Electronics and Information Technology (Doeit) too has in the past, supported projects in the area of Digital Library Initiatives. The initiatives have been essentially of two types:

- Setting up of Mega Centers and Scanning Centers in coordination with Indian Institute of Science, Bangalore and in collaboration with Carnegie Melon University, USA. Under the collaborative management, scanners for these centers were provided by Carnegie Melon University, USA, under its Million Book Universal Digital Library Programme. Indian Institute of Science, Bangalore is coordinating this Programme. Doeit provided financial support for computers, training, manpower, tariff etc.
- Digitisation with the full financial support from Department of Electronics and Information Technology

DIGITAL LIBRARY ACCESS TOOLS, POOLS AND SOURCES OF DIGITAL INFORMATION FOR THE DIGITAL LIBRARY

There are various tools available to use in digital information systems and they facilitate in accessing, searching, browsing, navigating, retrieving, indexing, storing, organising and dissemination of digitised information. The list given below is the digital information sources and pools and these are used as digital access tools which ultimately aim to facilitate universal access to all i.e. Online public access catalogues (OPACs), meta-databases (describe and provide link to other databases/ digital information sources), online databases (Knight-Rider, OCLC, MEDLINE). Internet-based tools i.e. e-mail networks, mailing lists, electronic conferences, World Wide Web, Website home pages, Wide Area Information Services (WAIS), Web browsers, Gopher systems, and Veronica Archie, FTP, Telnet, Usenet, Newsgroups, BBS, List servers, discussion groups, etc. and

- Digital networks/networking i.e. BLAISE, MEDLINE, NICNET, DELNETAGRIS, INIS and all sorts of networks.
- Hypertext/Hypermedia
- Multimedia (high bandwidth computer networks)
- Multimedia networking protocols
- Cellular and pager networks
- Electronic publishing tools
- Net-dwelling software agents
- Electronically fax/commercial vendors
- Telephone/TV

DIGITAL MANAGEMENT OF DIGITAL INFORMATION SYSTEMS AND DIGITAL LIBRARIES

(1) Internet and WWW

- Navigation, browsing, filtering;
- Retrieving, accessing, digital document analysis;
- Digital reference services, electronic information services;
- Searching network databases in a number of digital sources and Web sites;

- Creating home pages, content conversion, downloading techniques;
- Web publishing, electronic publishing;
- Archiving digital documents, locating digital sources;
- Digital preservation and storage;
- Electronic messaging, connectivity skills;
- Web authoring.

(2) Multimedia, digital technology and digital media processing:

- Multimedia indexing, image processing, object-oriented processing;
- Interactive digital communications and visualisation;
- Cataloguing and classification of digital documents, digital content;
- Searching and retrieval of text, images and other multimedia objects;
- Speech recognition, image visualization;
- Advanced processing capabilities exploiting digital medium;
- Conferencing techniques including teleconferencing, video conferencing.

(3) Digital information system, online and optical information

- Interfacing online and off-ramps, twists and turns of digital knowledge;
- Development of digital information sources;
- Digitisation of print collections;
- Competency to manage CD-ROM network station;
- Development of machine readable catalogue records;
- Design and development of databases;

- Design and development of software agents for digital libraries;
- Conversion of print media into digital media;
- Knowledge in digital knowledge structures.

COMPONENTS OF A DIGITAL INFORMATION SYSTEM

The components of a digital library may include:

I. Personal library system for the users;

II. Organizational library system for serving groups of individuals;

III. New users as well as existing local or distant database users;

IV. Database servers to handle remote requests; and

V. A variety of system functions to coordinate, manage the entry and retrieval of digital information.

CONCLUSION

There is need of greater use of information resources and information technology to support the vision, mission and objectives of the technologically oriented Library Information System. There is a tremendous demand in perfecting the library system which has to take into account information accessibility and flow. Thus application of state of the art ICT will enhance the quality of services offered. Therefore having a library computer information system will offer enhance services in the area of sharing information and communication besides easing access to information resources, courses and other services to users.

REFERENCES

1. Akst, D. (2003),"The Digital Library: Its Future Has Arrived"; Carnegie Reporter, 2(3), P.4-8
2. Breeding, Marshall (2002), "Preserving Digital Information"; Information Today Vol.19 (5)
3. Cain, Mark (2003), "Managing Technology: Being a Library

of Record in a Digital Age"; Journal of Academic Librarianship, Vol.29 (6)

4. Deschatelets, G. (1997), "Opening LIS curricula to the new world of electronic and strategic information"; FIS News Bulletin, Vol. 47(1), p. 13-20.

5. Edward A. Fox (1999), "The Digital Libraries Initiative - Update and Discussion"; Bulletin of the America Society of Information Science, Vol. 26(1)

6. European Commission (2006), "Steps up efforts to put Europe's memory on the Web via a European Digital Library"; Europa press release, March 2

7. Exit (1998), "Exit librarians, enter cybrarians"; Business Line, April 25, p. 20.

8. Gopinath, M.A.(1996), "Education for digital information system: a courseware", in Malwad, N.M., Rajasekahr, et al (1996), "Digital Libraries: Dynamic Storehouse of Digital Information"; papers presented at the SIS-96; 15th Annual Convention and Conference, Bangalore, January 18-20, New Age International Publishers, New Delhi, p. 210-15.

9. Gert, Janet (2000), "Selection for Preservation in the Digital Age"; Library Resources & Technical Services, Vol. 44(2), P.97-104.

10. Husler, R.P. (1996), "Digital library: content preservation in digital world"; DESIDOC Bulletin of Information Technology, Vol. 16 (1), p. 31-39.

11. Kelly, Kevin (2006), "Scan This Book!"; New York Times Magazine, Retrieved 2008

12. Koehler, AEC. (2006), "Some Thoughts on the Meaning of Open Access for University Library"; Technical Services Serials Review Vol. 32(1), p. 17

13. Kuny, T. and Cleveland, G. (1998), "The digital library: myths and challenges"; IFLA Journal, Vol. 24(2), p. 107-13.

14. Lankes, R.D. (1998), "AskA's lessons learned from K-12 digital reference services"; Reference & User Services Quarterly, Vol. 38(1), p. 63-71.

15. L. Candela, G., et al (2011)," The Digital Library Reference Model" April, 17

16. Ltaper, Thomas H. (2001), "Where Next? Long-Term Considerations for Digital Initiatives" Kentucky Libraries, Vol 65(2), P. 12-18.

17. Lu, G. (1996)," Communication and Computing for Distributed Multimedia Systems'; Artech House, Boston, p. 368-71.

18. Owen, J.M. (1999), "Knowledge management and the information professional: Information Services and Use", Vol. 19, p. 7-16.

19. P. Iglezakis, I., Synodinou, T. and Kapidakis, S. (ed.), "E-Publishing and Digital Libraries: Legal and Organizational Issues"; IGI Global, P. 1- 30.

20. Pomerantz, Jeffrey and Marchionini, Gary (2007), "The Digital Library as Place"; Journal of Documentation, Vol. 63(4), P. 505-533.

21. Pymm, Bob (2006), "Building Collections for All Time: The Issue of Significance"; Australian Academic & Research Libraries, Vol. 37(1), P. 61-73.

22. Sood, S.P. and Sreenivasulu, V. (1998), "Overhauling LISc curriculum with a slant to digital age: preparing databases"; Proceedings of 49th FID Conference towards the New Information Society of Tomorrow: Innovations, Challenges & Impact, INSDOC, New Delhi, October 1-17, FID Publication, No. 719, pp. III, P.134-41.

23. Sreenivasulu, V., Nirmala, N. and Deep, S. (1998), "User interfaces for a digital library to support construction of a virtual personal library"; Proceedings of Society for Information Science (SIS) library information centres and information professionals to the XXIst century, Proceedings of 49th FID Pre-Conference Education and Training, Jaipur, October 11-12, p. 112-18.

24. Sreenivasulu, V. (1998), "Computer information literacy: challenges for the modern information professional at the advent of the XXIst century"; Online CD-ROM Review, International Journal on Online, Optical and Networked Information, Vol. 22 (6), p. 395-397.

25. United States Copyright Office (1998), "The Digital Millennium Copyright Act of 1998"; U.S. Copyright Office Summary, P.2, 15.

26. Van Le, Christopher (2010), "Opening the Doors to Digital Libraries: A Proposal to Exempt Digital Libraries from the Copyright Act"; Case Western Reserve Journal of Law, Technology & the Internet, 1.2, spring, P.135

27. William, B.K. and Saffady, S. (1995), "Digital library concepts and technologies for the Management: an analysis of methods and costs"; Library Technology Reports, Vol. 31, May-June, p. 221.

28. William, B.K., Sawyer, S. and Hutchinson (1995), "Using Information Technology: A Practical Introduction to Computers and Communications"; Richard D. Irwin Inc, Chicago, IL, p. 579.

29. Wilson, T.D. (1995), "The role of the librarian in the 21st century:; keynote address for the Library Association Northern Branch Conference, Longhirst, Northumberland, 17 November, on Internet at http://www.shef.ac.uk/uni/academic/l-M/is/lecturer/ 21stcent.html

30. Yerkey, A.N. and Jorgensin, C. (1996), "A course in digital libraries"; DESIDOC Bulletin of Information Technology, Vol. 16(1), p. 31-9.

17

Preservation and Digitization of Library Material

Gurdev Singh

ABSTRACT

The present paper describes the methods, importance, need of digitization and preservation of library reading material. The paper describes various methods of digitization of documents in the library. The method of digitization is being used as preservation technique in modern libraries. This paper discusses briefly the techniques, process of digitization, problems and issues related to digitization.

Keywords : *Preservation, Digitization and Restoration*

INTRODUCTION

Libraries acquire reading material to meet the informational needs of its users. It is the responsibility of the library staff to keep these materials in good physical condition so that they are available for users at all times. Library is a central place where knowledge is preserved for future use. The climatic conditions of India are such that there are plenty of natural enemies. These enemies destroy the records of human knowledge available in the form of books and non-book materials in various libraries, archives etc. It is not very easy to preserve these materials. There are various methods available to preserve this reading material.

WHAT IS PRESERVATION?

Preservation encompasses activities intended to prevent, retard, or stop deterioration of materials or to retain the intellectual contents of materials no longer physically intact. Preservation—the protection of cultural property through activities that minimize chemical and physical deterioration and damage and that prevent loss of informational contents. Preservation includes selecting replacement copies, moving items to a protected area, and selected material for reformatting. It includes preservation of print as well as digital material. The primary goal of preservation is to prolong the existence of cultural property. It applies to the documents that are either in print form or "born digital" and stored on-line or on CD-ROM, diskettes or other physical carrier.

NEED OF PRESERVATION

Libraries acquire information resources to meet the needs of their community. More and more people use the collections as a result of increasing enrolments in higher education. There are shortages and decline in book budgets arising from the poor funding of the institutions as well as the high cost of books and other information resources. As a result, the libraries are left with damaged books and other reading material. The deterioration of information-bearing material has a long history. Unless something is done to stop the process, library collections deteriorate and will continue to deteriorate. Preservation and conservation of these materials is imperative. It is important to take adequate care of library resources. Limited funds, low-quality book production, and a high exchange rate are some reasons why preservation of library collections is essential. Library holdings may begin to deteriorate because of the organic materials from which they are made. The other factors include all of the conditions surrounding the processing, storage and use of the materials. Any loss to such materials is simply irreplaceable. Therefore, preserving this intellectual, cultural heritage becomes not only the academic commitment but also the moral responsibility of the librarians/information scientists, who are in charge of these responsibilities. Besides, proper dissemination of library material is possible if the documents are in good and usable condition. This demand for the proper preservation of library materials.

METHODS OF PRESERVATION

The process of preservation and digitization are generally used to safeguard the library material for further decay. It includes all the processes and actions taken to check the deterioration of documents. It also includes the methods to increase the life expectancy of undamaged or damaged of rare documents or archival material.

The following points should be taken care of while preservation of documents:

- Evaluation of heavily used, fragile materials and it should be decided what materials need to be preserved.
- Fragile materials are most often works printed on acidic paper and usually include most newspapers, clippings, some books etc. Damaged bindings with inside margins too narrow to rebind may also be considered fragile materials.
- Rare materials are usually works of which a limited number of copies were printed and/or the monetary value has escalated since their publication.
- Photographic prints, negatives and other digital material require special attention as they may be damaged by their emulsions, bases, mountings, display, or storage.

Choose Appropriate Preservation Techniques

Micro duplication, either as microfilm or microfiche,

generally is the least expensive method of preservation; however, the original may be damaged in micro-duplication and care should be taken. Electronic media reproduction may be useful and preferred for service copies of some materials.

Obtain Copyright Clearance

Under most circumstances it is necessary to obtain copyright clearance in order to duplicate local history and local genealogical materials in any form for library use or preservation. Some authors of local history and local genealogical materials may be willing to provide copyright clearance for the preservation of their work(s). Legal advice should be sought when questions arise.

FUNDING

1. Libraries should establish adequate funding for preservation and digitization of library material.
2. Grants should be available, particularly to libraries with long-range preservation. Additional consideration should also be given to requesting grants from local organizations, businesses houses and industries etc.

Microfilming

There is no doubt that microfilming is currently the most widely used format for preservation copying. Major libraries throughout the world are strongly committed to microfilming. Microfilming has a long history of use in libraries and considerable amount is known about it, including its longevity if stored under appropriate conditions. Microforms are produced in several formats, of these microform and microfiche are the most likely to be encountered in libraries. Libraries have traditionally produced or purchased 35 mm microfilm this size is best for the archival purposes and it allows larger size images with higher quality. Three types of microfilms are available; silver-gelatin, diazo, vesicular. Only silver-gelatin film which has been carefully processed to the appropriate standards should be used for archival master negatives which will be retained for long periods of time.

WHAT IS DIGITIZATION?

Digitization is the process of converting any item; it being in printed format, manuscript, image, sound, film and video recording-from one format (print or analog) into digital. "A strict definition might be the conversion of analog media to digital form (hence the fact that in many books "conversion" and "digitization" are synonyms). Basically it involves capturing an image of the physical object using various types of scanners and digital cameras and converting to digital format that can be stored electronically and accessed via computer. For building digital collection, digital libraries have to convert the existing print resources into electronic form. They can also acquire resources in electronic form or provide access to external resources. The creation of digital information from conventional is generally a two way format process. Thus, digitization means acquiring, converting, storing and retrieving the information in standardized and organized manner, with the help of modern technical gadgets such as computers, scanners, etc.

Why we need Digitization?

Through digitization there is unhindered access to contents over computer and communication network. Digitization may be considered as a means to enhance the life of material by preservation apart from the virtue of increased and easy access. The shrinking budget of the libraries, changing user needs and information seeking behavior ; remote preference increasing demand for digital resources and services are some of the factors responsible for the creation of digital collection and library.

Some of the reasons for digitization are:

1. Preservation of rare Documents : Book is one of the medium, which deals with comprehensive knowledge and information. Preserving the books and other rare material is a burning question, which the librarians of the past and present are facing. Therefore, it is urgently needed to find out some permanent solutions to preserve the library material in digital form. Most of the ancient manuscripts were written on bhuj patras. Ancient India was well developed in the subjects like, astronomy, mathematics, ayurveda, medicine, etc. Unfortunately many of these manuscripts were lost due to improper care. Some of them were destroyed due to water fungus, fire etc. and other natural calamities. These sources must be preserved in their original colors, texture, along with the text and graphics with the process of digitization.

2. Easy Transmission of Documents : Digitization is an important precursor to a variety of applications and projects. Specifically, it increases the ease and efficiency of transmitting documents. Images can be displayed on a computer screen; distributed to multiple destinations via e-mail; printed into any paper-based format; made available via a web portal or search database. Further, digitized files can be fully searched through character recognition.

3. Easy Handling of Rare Books : The handling and use of rare books, fragile books and non-book materials are not new problems to libraries. In recent years libraries are acquiring non-book materials and have been developing special collection at the accelerated rate. The rare and age-old collection of documents is deteriorating in many libraries because of excessive handling and exposure to non-archival conditions. Never the less, researchers and other users often seek access to the originals, or to reproduction of near original quality.

4. Easy Accessibility : In order to makes the library collection more accessible, conversion of its rare collection into digital form is essential. It has become widely known, even to those outside the computer field, that digital imaging technology can provide worldwide access to documents by many users simultaneously, as well as completely faithful reproduction, regardless of the number of copies produced. If the library collection were digitized, it would be possible for both local and distant researchers to use digital image in lieu of the originals. The collection covers rare books, maps, manuscripts, pamphlets, posters, newspapers, music, microfilms, archival material, slides and films, pictures, paintings, graphic materials, clipping files etc.

5. High Quality Reproduction : Digital technology has provided very high quality of reproduction of reality in terms of audio and video stimuli. It is also possible to have very compact storage capacity for a big volume of data and information. There is sudden change in the world of information because digital technology realizes quite high speed of communication and on-line access. The new technology is helping the library professionals to provide more accurate and better services to their users. Libraries are moving from experimental testing to planning large-scale preservation programmes using digital technology. Before building of database, we have to see why digital database is required?

6. Growth of Literature : There is a tremendous growth of literature, which includes printed, text and media. The high growth of information demand for the new techniques in processing and distribution of information and to access and process this enormous sea of information and serve it to the seekers is the greatest challenge of the information managers. To store such sea of information physically is very time consuming, complicated and difficult task with the emergence of digital library, storage and retrieval has become easier, comprehensive and affordable. The use of digitization can help in the preservation of original manuscripts and other such materials. It also has the potential to change the way scholars and activists utilize historical documents.

Benefits of digitization are many. Some of them are summarized below:

1. The use of digitization can help in the preservation of original manuscripts. It also has the potential of change the way scholars and activists utilize historical and rare documents.
2. Once the documents has been digitized, many benefits can be realized such as preservation of originals through reduced handling; unlimited data life span; wide availability of the public ease of access through digital libraries and online access; powerful search and browsing possibilities.
3. Today, access to most of such rare documents is quite difficult because of their wide spread distribution through the region. Many such documents are still not cataloged or replicated and simply remain unknown .This is primarily due to lack of interest, means and knowledge. Often stored in poor conditions, these precious articles, documents are prone to irreparable damage. Further, handling of originals establishes risk of permanent loss, because of no duplicates exists.

Digitization is the only solution to this problem. Digital technology has revolutionized the ability to create electronic replicas of print materials such as maps, rare books, manuscripts, photographs, sound records films etc., and institutions around the world. Many libraries around the world have digitized their collections.

PROCESS OF DIGITIZATION

It is to be decided whether it should be done:

1. In-house or
2. Through external agencies.

The conversion of the materials into digital form can be done either in-house or through some external agencies or commercial agencies. Digitization unit can be set up in-house. Using an external supplier to do some job such as scanning means that the equipments and expertise of the third party can be exploited. Both approaches have their merits but there are certain situations where the choice is more clear-cut. The reason for outsourcing may include where there is a large volume of work to be done in a short period of time or where the project has space, infrastructure or staffing constraints, which preclude the setting up of in-house facilities.

Before starting the process there are certain issues, which are to be discussed first:

1. Copyrighted material are digitized and made available online, only with written permission from the author and the publisher.
2. The rare and old books and other related material such as manuscripts, which are part of the Indian heritage, should be handling with care. Photograph technique is required.
3. Selection of documents to be digitized: The next step of digitization is to select the documents to be digitized. This is called target source. The images / contents of physical media such as periodical articles, books, rare manuscripts, research papers, newspapers, newspaper cuttings, images, sound, film and audio video cassettes, photographs etc. to be digitized is called target source. This is the material to be digitized.

STEPS INVOLVED IN DIGITIZATION

The following steps are involved in internal recourses:

1. Compiling a list of all the internal resources
2. Identifying suitable software for database creation.

3. Identifying suitable hardware and software (operating system and OCR)
4. Obtaining all the documents preferably in soft copy or hard copy(if soft copy is not available)
5. Input of the bibliographical data for each document submitted in a suitable software.
6. Editing the database: modification, addition and deletion.
7. Standardization of entry.
8. Digitization of documents (if soft copy is not available) using a good scanner.
9. OCR (ing) the scanned document—to convert the image fie into editable text.
10. Convert the OCR(ed) documents into pdf files.
11. Providing links to the full text document (pdf files) in the data base.
12. Indexing the full text using digital library software such as GSDL.
13. Testing.
14. Making it available on the library web server and the campus Internet for search, retrieval and browsing.

The following are various methods in the process of digitization:

1. Scanning.
2. Image enhancement.
3. Corrections.
4. File format.
5. Compression.
6. QC.
7. Indexing.
8. Storage /retrieval.

SCANNING PROCESS

Conversion of existing print and other reading material into digital format:

Nowadays, a part of conventional collection of a library is being converted into digital form. The process of conversion of paper document into digital format is mainly with the help of scanners. Printed text pictures and figures are transformed into computer accessible forms using a digital scanner or digital camera.

1. Scanning documents and making image file

Scanning is a typical part of digitization that requires hardware that so called scanner that can be used to take digital pictures of objects. The important step involved in the process of digitization is scanning, as explained above with the help of scanning. An image of the physical object is captured using a scanner or digital camera and converted to digital format that can be stored electronically and accessed via computer. The process involves conversion of paper documents into an electronic image using image scanner, fax card, digital camera, and other image capturing devices and also played for acquisition of images. Scanners can be simple desktop machines or very large and complex systems that process thousands of documents. The fragility, odd sizes, and bound volumes of some library materials pose greater difficulties for scanning. Now the new scanning systems are emerged which uses pattern recognition technologies. They are high productive scanners that suit to library applications.

Scanning is the easiest option to obtain the replica of original source document. An image of the physical object is captured using a scanner or digital camera and converted to digital format that can be stored electronically and accessed via computer. The process of scanning can be in a small scale or it may in a large scale. It can be done in-house by the staff or it can be done by the professional vendors. If the scanning is required in a large scale than commercial scanners are required.

SCANNING RESOLUTION

Resolution refers to the number of pixels that are used to describe a single image. Resolution affects the level of details that can depicted by the image file. The 300 dpi (dot per inch) on an average is good. The documents should not be scanned below 300 dpi resolution. With the resolution of 300 dots per inch (horizontal and vertically), good images can be made of most printed pages. If the resolution is increased to 600 dots per inch, or if eight levels of gray are coded, the clarity becomes excellent and halftone illustration can be represented.

(Scanning through digital camera)

Most scanning software generate default TIFF format which can be converted into PDF format using a number of softwares. The image can be browsed through a table of contents composed in HTML providing linked to scanned images. In this process the scanning of documents is an initial process. Basically, the resolution depends on the physical condition of the documents. The scanned images are typically stored in file formats like JPG, TIFF etc. The final output is converted to a light format like PDF, PDF format allow various security measures to be built into prevent a user from edition, downloading, or even printing.

2. Scanning and preparing full-text file

The scanned and processed images before being converted to PDF files, under the process to separate the text and media from the image files. Once the document has been digitally scanned, the images are available for rapid distribution, reproduction, and on-screen reading. Such document images are commonly stored in Portable Document Format (PDF), or Tagged Image File Format (TIFF). One can have additional benefits by using Optical Character Recognition (OCR) to convert images of book pages into machine –possible encoding of the document's text, dramatically reducing the storage needed for the book and allowing the text to be reformatted, searched, or used as input for text processing applications such as natural language processing.

METHODS OF SCANNING

There are three main ways that a large organization is relying on:

1. Outsourcing
2. Scanning in-house using commercial book scanners and
3. Scanning in-house using robotic scanning solution.

1. Outsourcing

Many organizations choose to scan in-house by using either overhead scanners which are time consuming , or digital cameras based scanning solutions which are substantially faster , and is a method employed by Internet Archives as well as well as Google.

Low budget scanning : The least expensive method to scan a book or magazine is to cut off the binding. This converts the book or magazine into a sheaf of loose-leaf papers, which can than be loaded into a standard automatic document feeder and scanned using inexpressive and common scanning technology. This is the traditional method, which includes cutting of the book's spine and scanning the pages in a scanner with automatic page feeder, with rebinding of the loose pages occurring afterwards. This is not a desirable solution for very old and rare books. It is a useful tool for books and magazines scanning where the book is not an expensive item and replacement of the scanned content is easy.

Scanning with help of commercial scanners : The commercial scanners are different from the other scanners. Commercial document scanners are not like normal scanners. These scanners are usually high quality digital cameras with light sources on either sides of the cameras mounted on some sort of frame to provide easy access for a person or machine to flip the pages of the document. Some models involve V shape book cradles, which provide support for book spines and also center book position automatically.

The advantage of this type of scanner is that it is very fast, compared to the productivity of overhead scanners. This type of camera based book scanner is much more cost effective.

(V-Shape cradle for scanning)

Robot Scanning : In recent years, software driven machines and robots have been developed to scan books without the need of dis-binding them in order to preserve both the contents of the document and a digital photo archive of its current state. This recent trend has been due in part to ever improving imaging technologies that allow a high quality digital archive image to be capture with little or no damage to rare or fragile documents in a reasonable short period of time. Some high end scanning system employ vacuum and air and static charges to turn pages while imaging is performed automatically, usually from a high resolution camera located over an adjustable v-shape cradle. Images are then shuttled from the imaging device into various editing suites which can further process the images for either an archival quality file such as TIFF or JPEG 2000, or a web friendly output such as JPEG or PDF.

The next step is the application of OCR software. This software is used for conversion of scanned text to machine-readable text that can be searched or indexed. A policy should be made not to make any correction for words not understood by the OCR software but retain the same in the image output because large numbers of documents may be produced by the conventional typing machine with a very small font.

DEVELOPING DIGITAL COLLECTION WITH OCR SOFTWARE

The OCR can be defined as "high speed process of reorganization and translating machine printed or hand printed words, letters, symbols, and numbers into computer processed information. OCR software is the system developed to scan a document, read and recognize the scanned image of the printed document and save the output on text files, or any other digital format that can be saved, printed, edited and reused. It is generally designed for features like speed, word accuracy and for producing a document that leads as close to the original as possible. The next process which is an important task is to rectify the errors and make text files error free with the help of Optical Character Recognition (OCR) process. This process also involves proof reading and checking quality of text files.

The data is directly machined readable while still being readable by people. The scanner and digital camera can be used for capturing of text and images. The scanned data can be stored in the form of CD, DVD, tape and hard disk. For text, this is scanned by using Optical Character Recognition(OCR) software, which recognizes the shapes of the letter of the alphabet and produces a file exactly the same as one produced by word processor used to type in the same text. OCR software is used for building bibliographic databases and full text retrieval system in the libraries and information centers. It is a method of direct entry of VCDs from hard copy. The software is consists of scanning the page into a bitmap image, recognizing the contents with it and translating it into a file that can be edited.

The OCR comprises of two steps in translating characters on a page into a digitized form:

1. Optical Scanning
2. Reorganization system

It is very much clear that no OCR software programme is hundred percent accurate. Accuracy, formatting, ability to handle columns and tables, image, quality, font and type size, preprocessing, templates, software compatibility are the main features of OCR software.

CRITERIA FOR SELECTING OCR SOFTWARE

The following criteria are for selection of OCR software can be used:

1. It should have ability to recognize a wide variety of typewritten and typed documents including books, magazines, reports newspapers etc.
2. It should able to maintain the layout of the original text.
3. It recognizes columns of text with a minimum of user intervention.

4. It provides on-line help while using the system.
5. It should come with engaging technical support from the manufacturer.
6. It should have ability to support different types of scanners like flat-bed, hand-held etc.
7. It should scan material at an efficient speed.

This process uses OCR software that takes a picture of the page and then turns it into digital text, which can be edited or fully indexed. Another method is Optical Character Recognition is the technique of converting scanned images of characters to their equivalent characters. The basic technique is for a computer programme to separate out the individual characters and then to compare each character to mathematical templates. When the individual words have been recognized, the next stage of conversion is to identify the structure of a document and to tag headings and other structural elements. An alternate method of conversion, widely used in practice, is to retype the document from scratch and add markup tags manually. This approach is often cheaper than a combination of automatic and human processing. It is usually carried out in the countries where labor cost is low.

Others Software Requirements

Other software you may need include:

Digitization software like Acrobat, Fine Reader, image editors, web server and browsers, word processing software including HTML/XML editors, and DBMS package. Many of these are available freely, both for windows and Linux operating system.

2. Compression : Scanned image required good amount of memory storage. In order to economies on storage space, images are to be to be stored in a compressed form. Cleaning job is required at this stage. Now the scanning of the documents to be done. A4 to A0 size maps are stored in hard disk.

3. PDF (Portable Data Format) conversion : The OCRed output is than converted to PDF file, sometimes through in-built technology of the OCR software or sometimes by separate software for PDF conversion. Interlinking of text pages, maps/ plates are done with the PDF file by book marking.

4. Checking : Before storing in the CD, checking of every stage is required by professional staff. Checking is required at the following stages:

1. Document identification stage
2. Post scanning stage
3. OCR checking and PDF conversion stage
4. Metadata creation and indexing stage.

The OCRed output is than converted to PDF file, sometimes through in-built technology of the OCR software or sometimes by separate software for PDF conversion. Interlinking of text pages, maps/ plates are done with the PDF file by book marking.

1. Standardizing the soft copy format (data from text, audio, video, etc.)
2. Editing, final formatting
3. Inputting documents into a document management system (Using/w like Data scan. Omni Docs)
4. Open database connectivity (Networks, Web)

5. Indexing and Processing:

Indexing : It is the second step after scanning is over. Indexing of documents converted into an image or text file is the second step in the process of document imaging. It is the second step after scanning is over. The processor indexing a text database. Scanned images are just like pictures describing. Animating system typically stored large amount of unstructured data in two file is traditional file that has a text description of the image along with key to second file. The second file contains document location. The user select a record from first file using a search algorithm. Once a user selects a record, the application key into the location index, find the document and display it. Digitized documents need to be processed using standards, protocols and indexing systems. Classification using library systems also hold much promise. Metadata application should be a major component of the digital information processing.

6. CD cutting(storage) : Scanned and checked records are then transferred to CDs with backup in duplicate. It includes transfer of scanned image from hard disk of scanning workstation to external storage device like CDs, DVDs etc.

7. Data Processing : Text in the convertible document may require conversion of diacritics or special characters; images may need enhancement, implications or compression. In many cases a simple conversion from print to digital is not enough.

8. Retrieval : In this process scanned images are retrieved through two files. One for text description and second for location of text or document

PROBLEMS AND ISSUES

Some of the problems related to digitization are:

- Information technologies become obsolete very quickly.
- Document and media formats continue to proliferate.
- Technology standards will not solve fundamental issues in the preservation of digital information.

The main constraints to proper preservation and conservation in libraries are lack of funds, lack of qualified conservation librarians, non-committal attitude of staff, and lack of adequate and dependable storage facilities. Very few librarians are conversant with preservation management, thus militating against any comprehensive preservation programme. There is need to improve of library materials in libraries; orientation for staff, everyday care, and staff trained in preservation and conservation.

Other aspects of this problem are non-technical issues such as management; funding, staffing, maintenance of digital documents and updated the development of policies for standard techniques and practices to prevent the loss of digital information. Generally, lack of policy, inadequately- trained staff in preservation and conservation, poor staff attitude towards preservation and conservation, and lack of funds are the problems of preservation of information-bearing materials in Indian libraries.

Media Problem

Advancement in the computer hardware, storage and software industries media obsolescence is a very common fact. When greater storage and processing capacities are available in market at lower cost, slowly old product's market will be surely down. So devices, processes and software for recording and storing information are being replaced with new products and methods on a regular three to five year cycles. Early attention to the difficulties in preserving information focused on the longevity of the physical media on which the information is stored. Even under the best storage conditions, however, digital media can be fragile and have limited shelf life. Moreover, new devices, processes and software are replacing the products and methods used to record, store, and retrieve information on breath taking cycles of 2 to 5 years.

The document created as digital form is equally vulnerable to technological obsolescence. For example, the short lifetime media are eight inch floppy disk, tape cartridges and reels. Hard sectored disks and seven track tapes those storage formats are inaccessible and more durable storage media are CD-ROM/DVD-ROM and optical WORM. There is lack of consideration of long term access requirements while creating digital information.

REFERENCES

1. Calmes, Alan.(1986).New Confidence in Microfilm. *Library Journal,* 38-42.
2. Chapman, Stephen. (2003). Digital Imaging and Preservation Microfilm: The Future of the Hybrid Approach for the Preservation of Brittle Books, July 23, 2003 from http://www.clir.org/pubs/archives/hybridintro.html#full
3. Conway Paul (1994). Digital preservation : paper and microfilm go electronic .Library Journal .119,1;42-45.
4. Guidelines for Control and Prevention of Termite Infestation in Archives and Libraries, (1991). New Delhi, National Archives Of India.
5. Harrod, Leonard Montague. (1977). The Librarians glossary. London, Clarion Books.
6. Harvey, Ross. (1993). Preservation in libraries : Principles, strategies, and practices for librarians. London, Bowker
7. Kathapalia, Yash Pal. (1973). Conservation and restoration of archive materials. Paris, UNESCO.
8. Mahapatra P.K and Chakrabarti B. (2003). Preservation in Libraries: perspectives principles and practice, New Delhi, ESS Publication.,
9. Prasad, Lalan Kumar. (1995). Protection of Documents from Photo Chemical Effects of Light-CCPI, vol- 28, New Delhi, p45-49
10. Rana, M. S. (1969). Mutilation of Books: A Case Study of Kirori Mal College Library. Library Herald, 154-167.
11. Repair and Preservation of Records. (1988). New Delhi, National Archives of India
12. Rothenberg, Jeff (1995). Ensuring the Longevity of Digital Documents. *Scientific American.* **272** (1): 42. doi:10.1038/scientificamerican,195-42.
13. Sunil A and Kumar P. (2009). Preservation of Library Materials: Problems and Perspective. DESIDOC Journal of Library and Information Technology. 29 (4): 37-40.

14. UNESCO (2000). Safeguarding our documentary heritage. Retrieved December 17, 2010 from http://webworld.unesco.org/.

15. Witten, Ian and Brainbridge, David. (2003). How to build a digital library. New York, Morgan Kaufmann.

18

Digital Preservation

Arpita Dutta

ABSTRACT

Digital preservation has become a common topic in digital library research and development. The rapid acceptance of digital technologies and the growth of digital libraries created three primary motivations for investments in digital preservation research and program development. In this paper, I will outline the main issues that digital preservation requirements raise for digital libraries, describe some of the current models for digital archiving, and discuss some of the outstanding issues for research and development. I will present a broad overview of the analysis of digital preservation. This paper examines factors that limit the ability of institutions to digitally preserve the cultural heritage of the modern era. The author takes a wide-ranging approach to shed light on limitations to the scope of digital preservation. The author finds that technological limitations to digital preservation have been addressed but still exist, and that non-technical aspect—access, selection, law, and finances—move into the foreground as technological limitations recede. The author proposes a nested model of constraints to the scope of digital preservation and concludes that costs are digital preservation's most pervasive limitation.

Keywords : Digital Preservation, Objectives, Polices, Strategies, Methods, Advantages, Disadvantages, and Challenges.

1. INTRODUCTION

Preservation generally means keeping an object safe

from harmful effects such as loss, damage, destruction and the like. In reaction of these challenges, there have been many advances and changes within the field of preservation. Digital technology and high speed networks are leading to sweeping changes throughout the society. In the past few years significant progress has been made to define the terms and outline a research agenda for preserving digital information that was either originally or transformed to digital form. Traditional source of information is increasing every day and the users expectations are to save the valuable information at safer place. To full fill the user's requirements for posterity, digital documents and resources should be managed and preserved at a tremendous rate. Digital technologies present a preservation solution for the documents in the libraries with increased access to digitized documents over the electronic networks. Digital technology as well as all others associated with Internet and web technologies is a continuous flux of change.

2. WHAT IS DIGITAL PRESERVATION?

Digital Preservation is the management and maintenance of digital objects (the files, or groups of files, that contain information in digital form) so they can be accessed and used by future users. It is important to start thinking about digital preservation early in the life cycle of a digital object because while traditional print objects may last relatively unharmed for decades untouched, this is not the case with digital objects, which have significantly shorter life spans. Therefore, by thinking about preserving the digital object early on, even when it is created, we save a great deal of time and stress later on when trying to retrieve the information an object holds before it is too late. In this sense, digital preservation, and especially early digital preservation, is important not only for personal data management but also large repositories that manage many objects. Though personal horror stories of lost data seem to be scattered and only happen from time to time, for larger repositories that contain many hundreds and thousands of digital objects, lost data can be a much bigger problem. Digital Preservation, after all, is frequently focused on long term use, which can be quite difficult to achieve considering how fragile digital objects can be.

Definition

Digital preservation is defined as the managed activities necessary: 1) For the long term maintenance of a byte stream (including metadata) sufficient to reproduce a suitable facsimile of the original document and 2) For the continued accessibility of the document contents through time and changing technology.

We will further define the digital object as the basic unit of both access and digital preservation and one that contains all of the relevant pieces of information required to reproduce the document including metadata, byte streams, and special scripts that govern dynamic behaviour. This data is encapsulated in the digital object and should be managed as a whole. If our archive is organized in such a way that bits and pieces of the object are scattered throughout the storage system, it becomes difficult, perhaps impossible, to keep track of all these pieces, and the digital archivist risks the possibility of not migrating all the relevant material as one unit.

A proposed definition of a reliable digital repository, also from the RLG report, is as follows:

"A reliable digital repository is one whose mission is to provide long-term access to managed digital resources; that accepts responsibility for the long-term maintenance of digital resources on behalf of its depositors and for the benefit of current and future users; that designs its system(s) in accordance with commonly accepted conventions and standards to ensure the ongoing management, access, and security of materials deposited within it; that establishes methodologies for system evaluation that meet community expectations of trustworthiness; that can be depended upon to carry out its long-term responsibilities to depositors and users openly and explicitly; and whose policies, practices, and performance can be audited and measured."

"Digital preservation is the set of process and activities that ensures long-term, sustained storage of, access to and interpretation of digital information, curation is an applied form of preservation that focuses on interpretation and is often (though not exclusively) used in relation to working with scientific datasets. The ultimate objective of all digital preservation activity, is to keep valuable and useful digital material (increasingly online) available for future generations of scholars, researchers and to the user groups."

Besser observes that "you cannot just lock it (digital content) away and it'll be OK, digital [archiving] requires ongoing management." "Today, preservation is an umbrella term for the many policies and options for action, including conservation treatments. Preservation is the acquisition, organization, and distribution of resources to prevent further deterioration or renew the usability of selected groups of materials."

3. OBJECTIVES OF DIGITAL PRESERVATION

The objectives of digital preservation are as follows:

1. To reduce the effect of deteriorating factors such as temperature, light, humidity, flood, fire, fungus, bacteria, insects, pollution, dust and the important factors called human.
2. Illustrate the combination of developments, events and decisions that led us to where we are today, in regard to technology that pertains to digital preservation.
3. Keep a place for new and emerging technology in

the context of digital preservation programs.

4. To maintain the historical value of information.
5. To make it easy to use & handle
6. To make information survive longer.
7. To provide worldwide accessibility.

4. Policies

Some general principles should be followed for qualifying this activity:

- A policy needs to convey the very philosophy of an organization concerning digital preservation; it should induce a common understanding of the objectives, of whether each collection item should be preserved with maximum effort possibly applying multiple preservation paths, or whether a certain pragmatism should be pursued;
- A digital policy should facilitate the sustainability of an institution's present and future digital holdings;
- A digital preservation policy has to demonstrate its benefits, its effectiveness;
- A digital policy should be connected and integrated with a risk assessment document;
- Every policy should be practicable, not definitive, capable of being put into practice by institutions with varying resources and needs, and, especially, flexible to adapt itself to changing administrative and technological circumstances;
- Any policy should be characterized by clarity, adequacy, transparency, efficiently, effectiveness and logical organization of contents;
- A digital preservation policy should be written in a simple and suitable language, without redundancies and, at the same time, without lowering the level of quality contained in its contents;

- Once a digital preservation policy is operative, it should be re-thought, reviewed or newly conceived on a regular basis to take into account changes in the organizational, legal and technical environment and to make rules and guidelines more precise and explicit where there is any ambiguity about implementation;
- A digital policy should offer achievable solutions, provide for the management training and, finally, be maintained through time.

5. DIGITAL PRESERVATION STRATEGIES

There are several strategies used to help preserve digital objects, such as emulation, migration and data redundancy.

Digitization requires certain technologies. These include storage technologies having a variety of devices to store & retrieve information in digital form such as magnetic tapes/cassettes, floppy discs, hard discs, DAT tape, CD-ROM smart cards. Processing technology for creating the system and application software that require for the performance of digital networks, communication technologies primarily to communicate information in digital form display technologies and various output devices.

There is no one single solution to the challenges of digital preservation. Digital preservation continues to present a complex challenge which is why there are so many different strategies and a number of different applications currently being undertaken by varying organisations around the world to address the digital preservation challenge.

The choice of which strategy to choose or if development of a new strategy is the best option is depend on the nature of the material to be preserved, the purpose of retention and the organisation. As stated there is no one single solution. Many organisations have chosen to design their own digital preservation strategy encompassing a number of the strategies because commercial products did not meet their needs.

As an introduction to digital preservation a list of some of the main digital preservation strategies available currently for addressing digital preservation.

i. Migration

Migration is the transfer of digital materials from one hardware or software type to another or from one generation of computer to another. Migration can also be the transfer to non digital media such as paper or microform, or the transfer to a more suitable medium for example floppy disc to CD-ROM. (National Library of Australia, 2008) Migration ensures the integrity of the object, preserving the essential characteristics of the data and retaining the ability to retrieve or view despite changes to technology.

With migration it is not always possible to make the 'copy' the same as the original whilst ensuring compatibility with the new technology. It is important that organisations if deciding to use migration determine what aspects to be migrated need to be preserved and determine if migration is appropriate.(Cornell University Library, 2007)

Another approach to migration includes migrating to standard formats. Standard formats are seen to be less volatile that other formats. However standards are also always in a state of flux and cannot be soley relied upon as a preservation strategy. Also although harder to achieve due to technology complexity using later versions of software which can decode earlier software versions or systems can work to simplify migration. (Cornell University Library, 2007)

Migration is a costly and time consuming process. Its use has also not been fully tested on complex file formats. Further investigation is required but migration offers a most promising approach. The Process of migration can also include refreshing. Refreshing is copying digital information from one long term storage media to another without changing the object or the bit stream. Refreshing ensures that the information is stored on a newer media before the old media becomes obsolete. An example of refreshing is an old CD RW to a newer CD RW. (Cornell University Library, 2007)

ii. Emulation

Emulation is duplicating the functions of one system using a different system so that the second system behaves and appears to be the first system and the original digital material is thought to still be available in its original form. (National Library of Australia, 2008 and Wikipedia, 2011) Emulation is a way to combat technological obsolescence as it provides a way of preserving the functionality of access to digital information which may be lost with the software or hardware when it becomes outdated.

The advantages of emulation are that the original data is not altered in anyway which helps to maintain the data and records integrity and functionality. It is also an efficient process in that once the data is emulated no further action is required, until it needs to be emulated again as a result of technology advances. (National Library of Australia, 2008)

Emulation involves the creation of emulators, which are programs that translate code and instructions from one computing environment to be correctly executed in the other. This strategy of emulation can be a costly and time consuming process. (Cornell University Library, 2007)

While emulation is a used method of preservation its practical benefits are again currently not widely demonstrated, but what testing has been done has been positive. More study will continue to be required and is currently being undertaken.

There are differing views on emulation as some experts think it will be a solution to digital preservation whereas others think it is only a small part of the overall strategy for digital preservation. (National Library of Australia, 2008)

iii. Encapsulation

Encapsulation is the grouping together of digital objects and metadata needed to provide access to the object. It lessens the chances that components needed to decode the object will be lost. It is seen as a solution to technological obsolescence for file formats because all the information to interpret the 'bits' is available.

It can be achieved by using physical or logical 'containers' or 'wrappers' to provide a relationship between the object and the supporting information. (National Library of Australia, 2008) The types of supporting information that should be included in the encapsulation include "the representation information used to interpret the bits appropriately for access; the provenance to describe the source of the object; the context to describe how the object relates to other information outside the container; reference to provide one or more identifiers to uniquely identify the object; and fixity to provide evidence that the object has not been altered" (National Library of Australia, 2008)

Encapsulation is an element of emulation and a number of methods are being developed using its theory, notably the universal preservation format. (National Library of Australia, 2008)

iv. Universal Virtual Computer (UVC)

Universal Virtual computer is a computer that creates a layer between the underlying computer platform and the underlying software. (National Library of Australia, 2008) It is a form of emulation and all files are backed up in a way that they can be accessed by the universal computer. To read the data in the future would only require a single layer between the UVC and the computer at the time. (Cornell University Library, 2007)

v. Normalisation

Normalisation involves the migration of digital records to standard formats. Normalisation is the most frequently used preservation strategy. What occurs is the data file format is detected and converted to an open format for preservation. Using this technique the records authenticity may be lost if during the conversion essential metadata is affected.

Normalising converts the record to an open standards based format that allows it to be documented and accessible. The normalised version of the digital record is also 'wrapped' in metadata. During the normalisation process some information may be lost, thus the new version is not considered an original copy.

vi. Bit Stream Preservation

Bit stream preservation is to be used as a foundation for other preservation strategies, it is no stand alone. Bit Stream preservation is storing the binary code of the digital object. The object will not be viewable without the original creation hardware and software, thus it needs to be used in conjunction with other preservation strategies to ensure accessibility. (New South Wales Government, n.d)

vii. Durable/Persistent media

Durable or persistent media is the use of media that is designed to be superior, for example using a gold CD because they are coated evenly and react slower to oxygen reducing CD rot and providing longevity. This technique reduced the need for regular refreshing and minimises loss from media deterioration. (Cornell University Library, 2007)

This technique does not combat media obsolescence or physical loss, it largely means that the short term preservation or storage techniques will last minimally longer. Many libraries hope to postpone have to complete migration or emulation by using formats thought to have a longer shelf life.

viii. Technology preservation

This involves preserving working replicas of key computer hardware with the programs that run it and on it. This is not a viable preservation option in the long run due to the costs associated with maintaining the aeging computers and the staff and training required to maintain and run the technology.

Development of different digital preservation strategies is currently being undertaken and should continue to be encouraged.

ix. Open Archival Information System (OAIS)

Open Archival Information System (OAIS) is the only official standard in digital preservation. A reference model is available that provides a model and framework for building and maintaining repositories for long term preservation and access to Digital material. (International Federation of Library Associations and Institutions, 2006)

6. INFRASTRUCTURE REQUIRED FOR DIGITAL PRESERVATION

The computer system having the multimedia facility integrates all the media components to a single platform and provides interactivity to the system.

The following IT components are suggested for the preservation of the collection:

1. Central processing unit with High-speed processor.
2. Large memory (RAM).
3. Hard disk with high volume.

4. Floppy drive.
5. CD drive (Read/Write)
6. Modem
7. Sound blaster card.
8. Key board having multimedia keys & mouse scroll
9. Color monitor
10. Color/B&W laser printer.
11. Better digitization tools (Scanner)
12. Digital Camera (still/move)
13. Video camera for capturing analog video and convert into digital
14. Graphic cards.

7. DIGITAL PRESERVATION METHODS

Many methods for preserving digital materials have been proposed to combat the approaching disintegration of information. Although each method approaches the problem from a distinct viewpoint, two themes reverberate throughout each scheme. The first is that archival methods should be reassessed periodically (i.e. at 5 year intervals). The second is that preservation metadata should be utilized to supply the maximum amount of information possible (i.e. provenance, hardware and software requirements, origin, authenticity, etc.).

Examination of the methods proposed uncovers another divide in the theories of digital preservation: Whether or not the aim is to preserve the content or the object (Morris, 2000). Change media, migration, mirroring, and emulation are concerned primarily with the preservation of the content of a digital resource, opting to keep the content accessible on current media, while technology preservation involves retention of the entire object and means to access. The plethora of archival theories is analogous to a reference librarian fulfilling a patron's request without conducting the reference

Table 1. Digital Preservation Methods

Method	*Description*	*Strengths*	*Limitations*
Change Media	Create hard copy of digital resource	Nullifies integrity concerns; long life expectancy	Does not accurately capture all ERs (i.e interactive media)
Emulation or Encapsulation	Use preservation metadata to detail hardware and software requirements of preserved data	Do not lose original functionality because future technology "mimics" old technology	Thousands of software applications are on the market with limited hardware options
Migration or Refreshing	Transfer preserved resources to new generation technology	Most common practice, nullifies life expectance concerns	Should undergo process every 5 years; lose some information during every migration
Mirroring or Redundancy	Keep an exact copy of an archive in geographically diverse locations	Can be used to back-up large databases	Maintenance costs
Technology Preservation	Preserving hardware and software used to create and access information (i.e. reel-to-reel film and eight-track tape machines)	May preserve data only and be assured to have the ability to read it	Costs and ability to maintain old technology decreases as rate of technological advances increases

interview. Though the answer found may be sufficient, complementing the search with relevant context would, in theory, elicit the optimal information best suited to the information need. Rothenberg (1999) and Woods (2002) concur and propose a strategy composed of complementary methods to resolve the unknowns in archiving online content.

Generally Digital Preservation process is being used as clarifying through following diagram and description:

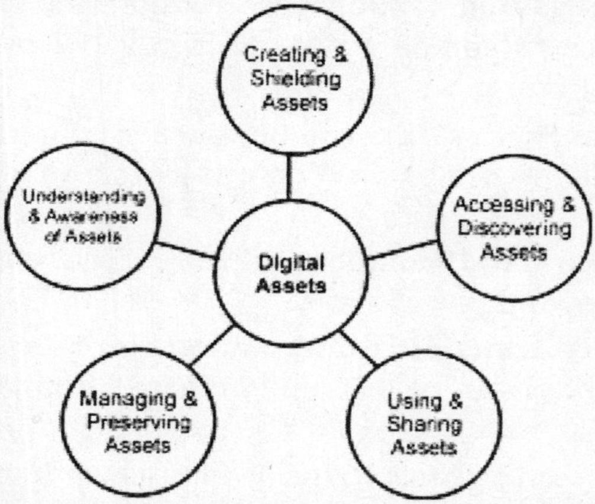

Fig. 1. Generally used Process for Digital Preservation

- *Creating and shielding assets* is first stair for the completion of digital preservation process. Digital content requires new expertise for its construction and use as well as needs the way to shield it from misuse.
- *Assessing and discovering assets* is essential to have an appropriate system to access and discover the digital content.
- *Using and sharing assets* is to allow users to use, recycle, and share the content as require.
- *Managing and preserving content* it is unavoidable to manage and preserve the digital assets for its continuation to existence and use for long period.

- *Understanding and awareness* of content if we want to make new resolution and investments in this area then first it is vital to understand and have sufficient knowledge about digital asset atmosphere as well as essential to know about its whole knowledge regarding choices, benefits, opportunities, limitations and challenges also.

8. ADVANTAGES

Space Saving : Such preservation occupies very limited space as compared to space covered by printed material in library.

Easy access : All information preserved in electronic form is easily accessible in different ways and with in no time.

Easy to handle : Information retrieval software is user friendly and easy to use.

Easy to transmit : Information stored on a CD or in the computer can be transmitted easily from one place to another by email.

Time saving task : Worldwide information can be retrieved within a few seconds.

Low cost : Very low cost is involved in developing an electronic document in comparison to printed document.

Less manpower involved : To generate electronic information, less manpower is involved.

9. DISADVANTAGES

Process of installation is complex and costly : In the initial stage, it is very complicated and long process. It involves preparing images, editing, proofing assigning keywords generating indexes converting into makeup language etc.

Lack of infrastructure : In developing countries like India, it is very tedious job to provide all infrastructure facilities at one platform as and when it is required.

Insufficient budget : The Indian labors are not financially strong. They have very limited budget and to procure the recommended system is not affordable.

Shortage of expertise in India : Lack of expertise in the field of multimedia is the greatest disadvantage.

10. CHALLENGES

Digital preservation has raised many challenges of a fundamentally different nature, which are divergent as compared to the problems of preserving traditional format materials. Some of them are in the areas of planning, resource allocation, and application of preservation methods and technologies necessary to ensure that digital information of continuing value remains accessible and usable. The challenges are as follows:

i. Durability : The durability of digital content has become problematic for a number of complex and interrelated reasons as most of the documents exist only in encoded form, specific software is required for handling them. The digital components like hardware and software are also often changing their versions or processing capacity. Other aspects of this problem are nontechnical issues such as management, funding, staffing, maintenance for digital documents and updating the development of policies for standard techniques and practices to prevent the loss of digital information, need to be well planned.

ii. Form of material : Digital materials have a very short life as compared to the traditional format. In this situation magnetic and optical media are qualitatively different as these are re-usable media.

iii. Media Problem : Due to advancement in the computer hardware, storage, and software industries, media obsolescence is a very common fact. When greater storage and processing capacities are available in the market at lower cost, slowly the market for the old product market goes down. The documents created in digital form are equally vulnerable to technological obsolescence. For example, the short-life time media are eight-inch floppy disks, tape cartridges and reels, hard-sectored disks and seven track tapes. Those storage formats are inaccessible and more durable storage media are CD-ROM/DVD-ROM and optical WORM.

iv. Software-dependent problem : The digital documents are generally dependent on application software to make them accessible and meaningful. But the problem is that software is also developing and changing versions. Every software has different kinds of encoding for which every computer needs some specific software to activate the digital documents. A bit stream can be made intelligible only by running the software that created it, or some closely related software that understands it.

v. Standards : The absence of established standards, protocols, and established methods for preserving digital information creates problems. The main objectives of digital libraries are to organize the information; maintain the intellectual property rights, and presentation, retrieval and visualization of digital materials. Digital preservation remains largely experimental and replete with the risks associated with unproven methods. Moreover, digital preservation requirements have not been factored into the architecture, resource allocation, or planning for digital libraries.

vi. Intellectual Property Rights : An intellectual property rights (IPR) is a big barrier for preserving the digital documents. Digitization of documents involves complex methods for resolving the legal and practical questions of migrating intellectual property that includes the creators and owners of intellectual property, managers of digital archives, and potential users of intellectual property.

There are many possible funding models for digital preservation, each with their own limitations. Creators and rights holders can preserve their own content but normally have little incentive to do so over the long-term, as demand for access slackens. Publicly funded agencies can preserve content, but they may lack a clear mandate for doing so, and they are chronically underfunded. Preservation may be voluntarily funded, as is the case for Wikipedia, although it is not clear if there is enough potential volunteer funding for more than a few preservation efforts. Fees may support preservation, either through charging users for access or by third-party organizations charging content owners for archival services; in such cases, however, fees may also discourage access or provision of content, respectively.

A Nested Model of Limitations

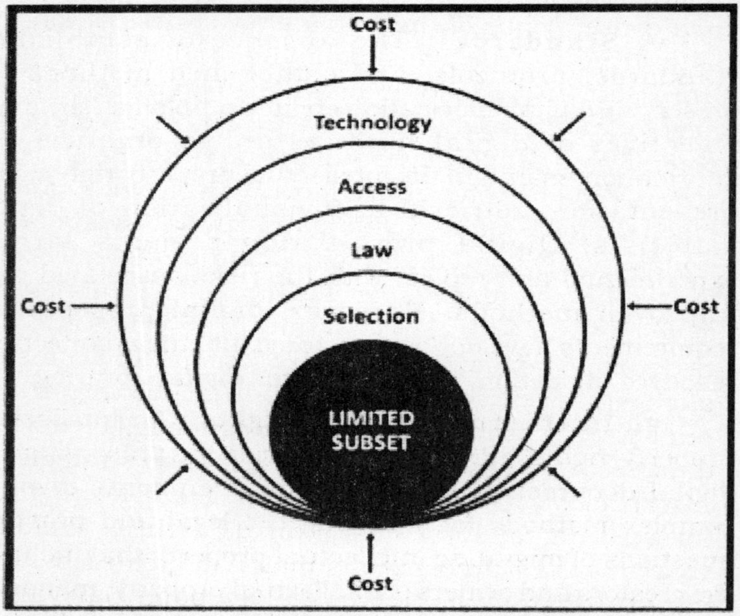

Fig. 2. Nested Model of Limitations

At the highest level, there are technical limitations

on how much digital information can be preserved at an acceptable quality. Within that constraint, only a limited portion of what could possibly be preserved can be accessed by archival institutions for digital preservation. Next, within that which is accessible, there are legal limitations on what may be archived. The subset defined by technological, access, and legal limitations still holds far more information than archival institutions are capable of archiving, therefore selection is required, entailing either the limited quality of automated gathering or the limited quantity of human-mediated appraisal. Finally, each of these constraints is in turn limited by financial considerations, so finances exert pressure at each level.

11. CONCLUSION

In conclusion, recent progress in digital preservation is a consequence of the growing awareness of longevity as a critical issue for sustainable and useable digital libraries, increased investments in research and development, and efforts to focus on discrete and potentially solvable aspects of the problem. As a result of these efforts, there are much improved models, mechanisms, tools, and organizational strategies for building and maintaining digital libraries that may persist for the long term. One particularly effective approach is to work with a specific community of providers and users to develop standards, acceptable formats for acquisition, storage, and dissemination. Yet, it is also important to remember how much digital information falls outside the domains where sound digital preservation strategies and methodologies are being developed. The collecting realm for most digital libraries and digital archives includes a vast array of heterogeneous material, created by a wide variety of producers but still of potential value to heterogeneous communities, including users far in the future whose interests, needs, and requirements are impossible to anticipate.

There are different schools of thought on digitization; some see it as the most important advancement in the topic of preservation, and others feel that while it has a place, it is not the even the best solution to keeping information safe. Despite these different attitudes, digitalization, and the subsequent preservation of the digitized files, is an important topic in the world of libraries, archives, and other information centers. As this is a dynamic topic that changes often according to new information and techniques, it is one that will need to be constantly readdressed. Librarians and archivists have two jobs when it comes to digital preservation; they have to keep up with existing practices, while still finding ways of making digitization happen. As well as this, it is important to focus on the future, anticipating what challenges could arise, and devising solutions. As with all topics surrounding the LIS field, it is important to remember not just the information that needs to be preserved, but also the needs of the information seekers. Librarians, archivists, and other information professionals must continually strive to ensure that users will be able to access the preserved information.

Storage systems should be capable of handling digital information in a wide variety of formats, including text, data, graphics, video & sound conversion from digital formats and migration to new generation of technology will be rapid, accurate and in expensive enough to permit very large scale transfer to heterogeneous materials storage space requirements will be minimal and not demand highly sensitive environmental control. To make digital preservation affordable to the widest possible range of organizations and individual's equipment, media & maintenance cost must be modest with enough coordination between library professionals and co-operation and support of higher or competent authority, the goal of preserving all of the important literature can be accomplished. It is also suggested that the libraries may consider developing a separate unit where the preservations work can be done regular basis.

REFERENCES

1. A. Smith, "Preservation in the future tense", Council of library and information resources Number 3. 1998. Retrieved on June 30, 2010 from *http://www. clir. org/ pubs /issues/ issues03.html*
2. Adrian Brown, Digital Preservation Guidance Note 3: Care, handling, and storage of removable media, June 2003.
3. Anderson, M.L. (2003). Electronic information and digitization: Preservation and security challenges. Journal of Library Administration, 38(3/4), 163-168.
4. Anderson, S. (2002). Digital preservation: The future of electronic resources. Alki, 18(2), 25-26.
5. Bearman, D. (1996). Preserving digital information: A review. Archives and Museum Informatics, 10(2), 148-153.
6. Borin, J. (2000). Site license initiatives in the United Kingdom: The PSLI and NESLI experience. Information Technology and Libraries, , 42-46.
7. Brian Cooper, Arturo Crespo, and Hector Garcia-Molina. Implementing a reliable digital object archive, 1999. Submitted for publication to ACM DL 2000
8. Bearman, D. (April 1999) Reality and Chimeras in the Preservation of Electronic Records, D-Lib Magazine, 5:4. Available: *http://www.dlib.org/dlib/april99/bearman/ 04bearman.html*
9. British Library. Digital Library System. *http://www.bl.uk/*
10. C.Berwick, "Digital art in all its forms is gaining prominence among artists, curators, and audiences." The New New Media Blitz, April 2001 Retrieved on July 02, 2010 from *http:// artnews.com/issues/article.asp?art_id=894*
11. Conway, Paul. 1996. Preservation in the Digital World. Washington, D.C.: Commission on Preservation and Access. Available at *http://www.clir.org/pubs/reports/conway2/ index.html.*
12. Day, M. (2003). Digital preservation and long-term access to the content of electronic serials. In W. Jones (Ed.), E-serials:

publishers, libraries, users, and standards. (2nd ed., pp. 167-195). New York: Haworth Information Press.

13. Francine Berman et al., Sustainable Economics for a Digital Planet: Ensuring Long-Term Access to Digital Information (Blue Ribbon Task Force on Sustainable Digital Preservation and Access, 2010), http://brtf.sdsc.edu/biblio/BRTF_Final_Report.pdf (accessed Apr. 23, 2011).

14. Falk, H. (2003). Digital archive developments. The Electronic Library, 21(4), 375-379.

15. Fleischhauer, C. (2003). Preservation, security, and digital content. Journal of Library Administration, 38(3/4), 141-147.

16. Gilliland-Swetland, A. J., (February 2000) Enduring Paradigm, New Opportunities: The Value of the Archival Perspective in the Digital Environment, Washington, DC CLIR. Available: *http://www.clir.org/pubs/abstract/pub89abst.html*

17. Granger, S. (September 2000) Emulation as a Digital Preservation Strategy. D-Lib Magazine6:10. Available: *http://www.dlib.org/dlib/october00/granger/10granger.html*

18. H. Besser "Digital Preservation Pioneer: Howard Besser", Pioneers of Digital Preservation, Library of congress website retrieved on June 30, 2010 from *http://www. Digital preservation.gov/partners/pioneers/detail_besser.html*

19. Hedstrom, M., (1997/98) "Digital Preservation: A Time Bomb for Digital Libraries,"Computers and the Humanities 31:3, 189-202.

20. Hedstrom, M. and Montgomery, S., Digital Preservation Needs and Requirements in RLG Member Institutions. A Study Commissioned by the Research Libraries Group, Mountain View, CA: RLG, December, 1998, also available: *http://www.rlg.org/preserv/digpres.html.*

21. Harris, L.E. (2002). Licensing Digital Content: A Practical Guide for Librarians. Chicago: American Library Association.

22. Hollaar, L.A. (2002). Legal Protection of Digital Information. Washington, D.C.: Bureau of National Affairs, Inc.

23. Hedstrom, M. (1998). Digital preservation: A time bomb for digital libraries. Computers and the Humanities, 31, 189-202.

24. Hunter, K. (2000). Digital archiving. Serials Review, 26(3), 62-64. 58

25. Kenney, A. R., and Reiger, O. (2000) Moving Theory Into Practice. Digital Imaging for Libraries and Archives. Mountain View, CA.: Research Libraries Group, Inc.

26. Lawrence, G.W., Kehoe, W.R., Rieger, O.Y., Walters, W. H., and Kenney, A. R. (June 2000)Risk Management of Digital Information: A File Format Investigation. Washington. DC: CLIR. Available: *http://www.clir.org/pubs/abstract/pub93abst.html*

27. LOCKSS. Lots of Copies Keep Stuff Safe. *http://lockss.stanford.edu/*

28. Lorie, R. A. (October 23, 2000) Long Term Preservation of Digital Information. IBM Almaden Research Center. Available: *http://www.almaden.ibm.com/u/gladney/Lorie.pdf*

29. Marcum, D.B. (1996). The preservation of digital information. Journal of Academic Librarianship, 22(6), 451-454.

30. Muir, A. (2003). Copyright and licensing for digital preservation. Library & Information Update, 2(6), 34-36. 59

31. M.Hedstrom, "Digital Preservation: Problems and Prospects", Journal of Digital Libraries No 20, March 2001 retrieved on June 30, 2010 from *http:// www. dl. ulis. ac. jp/ Dljournal / No_20/ 1-hedstrom/ 1-hedstrom.html.*

32. M. Hedstrom, "Digital preservation: a time bomb for Digital Libraries". Computers andthe Humanities, Vol. 31, No. 3, 1998, pp. 189-202.

33. M. Winget, "Digital Preservation of New media art through exploration of established symbolic representation systems." ACM/IEEE Joint conference on Digital Libraries'2005 Doctoral Consortium. Denver, Colorado, June 7-11, 2005.

34. M. Winget, "Like a Wave upon the Sand: Digital Preservation of Variable Media Art" retrieved on July 02, 2010 from *www.ischool.utexas .edu/~megan/research/WingetDigPres.pdf*

35. National Library of Wales, Digital Preservation policy and strategy: http://www. llgc. org. uk/ fileadmin/documents/pdf/digital_preservation_policy_and_strategy_S.pdf

36. NEDLIB, Networked European Depository Library *http://www.kb.nl/coop/nedlib/*

37. Open Archives Initiative. *http://www.openarchives.org/*

38. P. Conway, "Preservation in the Digital World" 1996, retrieved

on June 30, 2010 from *http://www.clir.org/pubs/reports/conway2/*.

39. Preserving Digital Information: Report of the Task Force on Archiving of Digital Information. (May 1, 1996) Commissioned by the Commission on Preservation and Access and the Research Libraries Group, Inc., Washington DC: Commission on Preservation and Access. Available: *http://www.clir.org/pubs/abstract/pub63.html*

40. Ross, S. and Gow, A. (1999) Digital Archaeology: Rescuing Neglected and Damaged Data Resources, London: Library Information and Technology Centre. Available: *http://www.ukoln.ac.uk/services/elib/papers/supporting/#blric*

41. Rothenberg, J. (September 1999) Avoiding Technological Quicksand: Finding a Viable Technical Foundation for Digital Preservation. Washington, DC: CLIR. Available: *http://www.clir.org/pubs/abstract/pub77.html*

42. S. Kataria and J. Anbu k., 2010 "How safe is our digital tomorrow? Role of libraries and information centers in digital preservation" Proceedings of ICSIT 2010

43. T. Hendly, "comparison of methods and costs of digital preservation" British library research and innovation report. 106, 1998.

44. The Library of Congress, for instance, only began digital preservation in 2000 (www.digitalpreservation.gov/partners/pioneers/index.html [accessed Apr. 24, 2011]).

45. UK Data Archive Preservation Policy – large data archive with an example of a good policy where the contractor is providing a preservation service: http://www.data-archive.ac.uk/media/54776/ukda062-dps_preservation policy.pdf

46. U.S. Library of Congress. Digital Information Infrastructure and Preservation Program. *http://www.loc.gov/today/pr/2001/01-006.html*

47. Wheatley, P. and Holdsworth, D. (2001) Emulation, Preservation and Abstraction. Draft paper for public comment. Available: *http://129.11.152.25/CAMiLEON/dh/ep5.html*

19

Media Literacy: Skills and the Challenges of New Information and Communication Technologies

Sudhir Kumar Jena

ABSTRACT

In this electronic and digital era, the concept of media literacy is being extended from its traditional focus on print and audiovisual media to encompass the internet and other new media. The present article addresses three central questions currently facing the public, policy-makers and academy: What is media literacy? What are its concepts and principles? And what are the uses of literacy? The article begins with a definition: media literacy is the ability to access, analyse, evaluate and create messages across a variety of contexts. Having the three questions addressed the article brings out the purpose and skills required for media literacy and identifies some outstanding issues for new media literacy crucial to any policy of promoting media literacy among the population and programmes that will help the population navigate the media, especially the internet, safely and responsibly.

Keywords : Media Literacy, ICT, Internet, skilled based approach, representation of knowledge.

INTRODUCTION

Today's information and entertainment technologies communicate to us through a powerful combination of words, images, and sounds. As such, we need to develop a wider set of literacy skills helping us to both comprehend the messages we receive and effectively utilize these tools to design and distribute our own messages. Being literate in a media age requires critical thinking skills that empower us as we make decisions, whether in the classroom, the living room, the workplace, the boardroom, or the voting booth.

Media literacy is the ability to understand how mass media work, how they produce meanings, how they are organized, and how to use them wisely. The media literate person can describe the role media play in his or her life. The media literate person understands the basic conventions of various media, and enjoys their use in a deliberately conscious way. The media literate person understands the impact of music and special effects in heightening the drama of a television program or film...this recognition does not lessen the enjoyment of the action, but prevents the viewer from being unduly credulous or becoming unnecessarily frightened. The media literate person is in control of his or her media experiences.

The following definition of media literacy came out of the Trent Think Tank, a 1989 symposium for media educators from around the world sponsored by the Canadian Association for Media Literacy: "The goal of the media literacy curriculum must be to develop a literate person who is able to read, analyze, evaluate, and produce communications in a variety of media (print, TV, computers, the arts, etc.)."

Most often, "the media" are lumped together as a single entity. But "the media" are actually many forms of communication...including newspapers, magazines, and billboards, radio, television, videocassettes, video games, and computer games. Since the students participating in VidKids are primarily engaged in television viewing (most of them are too young to read newspapers and magazines), our activities focus on video and TV.

WHAT IS MEDIA LITERACY?

Media Literacy is ability to ACCESS, ANALYZE, EVALUATE, and COMMUNICATE information in a variety of forms-is interdisciplinary by nature. Media literacy represents a necessary, inevitable, and realistic response to the complex, ever-changing electronic environment and communication cornucopia that surround us.

These four components - access, analysis, evaluation and content creation - together constitute a skills-based approach to media literacy. Each component supports the others as part of a non-linear, dynamic learning process: learning to create content helps one to analyze that produced professionally by others; skills in analysis and evaluation open the doors to new uses of the internet, expanding access, and so forth.

For the moment, let us agree that this is a useful definition - though I argue later that these are necessary but not sufficient components for literacy - and ask, how far is it possible or desirable to adapt what we know of print and audiovisual media literacy in order to map a research agenda for new forms of literacy, in today's changing media environment?

According to Ontario Ministry of Education's *Media Literacy Resource Guide*: "Media literacy is concerned with helping students develop an informed and critical understanding of the nature of mass media, the techniques used by them, and the impact of these techniques. More specifically, it is education that aims to increase the students' understanding and enjoyment of how the media work, how they produce meaning, how they are organized, and how they construct reality. Media Literacy also aims to provide students with the ability to create media products."

SIX CORE PRINCIPLES OF MEDIA LITERACY EDUCATION (CPMLE):

The National Association of Media Literacy Education (NAMLE) also advocates six core Principles through their project.

i) Media Literacy Education requires active inquiry and critical thinking about the messages we receive and create.

ii) Media Literacy Education expands the concept of literacy (i.e., reading and writing) to include all forms of media.

iii) Media Literacy Education builds and reinforces skills for learners of all ages. Like print literacy, those skills necessitate integrated, interactive, and repeated practice.

iv) Media Literacy Education develops informed, reflective, and engaged participants essential for a democratic society.

v) Media Literacy Education recognizes that media are a part of culture and function as agents of socialization.

vi) Media Literacy Education affirms that people use their individual skills, beliefs, and experiences to construct their own meanings from media messages.

PURPOSE OF MEDIA LITERACY

"The purpose of media literacy education is to develop the habits of inquiry and skills of expression needed to be critical thinkers, effective communicators and active citizens in today's world." No matter what the next new gadget is, students will need to be able to analyze the content to which it provides access, reflect on the meaning of that content for themselves and others, and evaluate its utility for accomplishing their own communication tasks. The essence of inquiry-based Media Literacy education is asking questions. Lots of questions. All the time. About everything, but especially about media. That is what National Association of Media Literacy Education (NAMLE) means by "habits of inquiry."

SKILLS FOR MEDIA LITERACY

- Understand how media messages create meaning
- Identify who created a particular media message
- Recognize what the media maker wants us to believe or do
- Name the "tools of persuasion" used
- Recognize bias, spin, misinformation and lies
- Discover the part of the story that's not being told
- Evaluate media messages based on our own experiences, beliefs and values
- Create and distribute our own media messages
- Become advocates for change in our media system

Media literacy education helps to develop critical thinking and active participation in our media culture. The goal is to give youth and adults' greater freedom by empowering them to access, analyze, evaluate, and create media.

In Educational Institution : Educational standards in many states in language arts, social studies, health and other Subjects -include the skills of accessing, analyzing and evaluating information found in media. These are media literacy skills, though the standards may not use that term. Teachers know that Students like to examine and talk about their own media, and they've found that media literacy is an engaging way to explore a wide array of topics and issues.

In the community : Researchers and practitioners recognize that media literacy education is an important tool in addressing alcohol, tobacco and other drug use;

obesity and eating disorders; bullying and violence; gender identity and sexuality; racism and other forms of discrimination and oppression; and life skills. Media litercy skills can empower people and communities usually shut out of the media system to tell their own stories, share their perspectives, and work for justice.

In public life : Media literacy helps us understand how media create cultures, and how the "media monopoly" - the handful of giant corporations that control most of our media - affects our politics and our society. Media literacy encourages and empowers youth and adults to change our media system, and to create new, more just and more accessible media networks.

MEDIA LITERACY CONCEPTS

The study and practice of media literacy is based on a number of fundamental concepts about media messages, our media system, and the role of media literacy in bringing about change. Understanding these concepts is an essential first step in media literacy education. We've organized Media Literacy Concepts into three levels: Basic, Intermediate and Advanced. Basic concepts focus on how media affect us. Intermediate concepts examine more closely how we create meaning from media messages. Advanced concepts examine the interaction of media and society, and the role of media literacy in bringing about change.

Basic Concepts

Media construct our culture : Our society and culture – even our perception of reality-is shaped by the information and images we receive via the media. A few generations ago, our culture's storytellers were people – family, friends, and others in our community. For many people today, the most powerful storytellers are television, movies, music, video games, and the Internet.

Media messages affect our thoughts, attitudes and actions : We don't like to admit it, but all of us are affected by advertising, news, movies, pop music, video games, and other forms of media. That's why media are such a powerful cultural force, and why the media industry is such big business.

Media use "the language of persuasion" : All media messages try to persuade us to believe or do something. News, documentary films, and nonfiction books all claim to be telling the truth. Advertising tries to get us to buy products. Novels and TV dramas go to great lengths to appear realistic. To do this, they use specific techniques (like flattery, repetition, fear, and humor) we call "the language of persuasion."

Media construct fantasy worlds : While fantasy can be pleasurable and entertaining, it can also be harmful. Movies, TV shows, and music videos sometimes inspire people to do things that are unwise, anti-social, or even dangerous. At other times, media can inspire our imagination. Advertising constructs a fantasy world where all problems can be solved with a purchase. Media literacy helps people to recognize fantasy and constructively integrate it with reality.

No one tells the whole story : Every media maker has a point of view. Every good story highlights some information and leaves out the rest. Often, the effect of a media message comes not only from what is said, but from what part of the story is not told.

Media messages contain "texts" and "subtexts": The text is the actual words, pictures and/or sounds in a media message. The subtext is the hidden and underlying meaning of the message.

Media messages reflect the values and viewpoints of media makers : Everyone has a point of view. Our values and viewpoints influence our choice of words, sounds and images we use to communicate through media. This is true for all media makers, from a preschooler's crayon drawing to a media conglomerate's TV news broadcast.

Individuals construct their own meanings from media : Although media makers attempt to convey specific messages, people receive and interpret them differently, based on their own prior knowledge and experience, their values, and their beliefs. This means that people can create different subtexts from the same piece of media. All meanings and interpretations are valid and should be respected.

Media messages can be decoded : By "deconstructing" media, we can figure out who created the message, and why. We can identify the techniques of persuasion being used and recognize how media makers are trying to influence us. We notice what parts of the story are not being told, and how we can become better informed.

Media literate youth and adults are active consumers of media : Many forms of media like television – seek to create passive, impulsive consumers. Media literacy helps people consume media with a critical eye, evaluating sources, intended purposes, persuasion techniques, and deeper meanings.

Intermediate Concepts

The human brain processes images differently than words : Images are processed in the "reptilian" part of the brain, where strong emotions and instincts are also located. Written and spoken language is processed in another part of the brain, the neocortex, where reason lies. This is why TV commercials are often more powerful than print ads.

We process time-based media differently than static media : The information and images in TV shows, movies, video games, and music often bypass the analytic brain and trigger emotions and memory in the unconscious and reactive parts of the brain. Only a small proportion surfaces in consciousness. When we read a newspaper, magazine, book or website, we have the opportunity to stop and think, re-read something, and integrate the information rationally.

Media are most powerful when they operate on an emotional level : Most fiction engages our hearts as well as our minds. Advertisements take this further, and seek to transfer feelings from an emotionally-charged symbol (family, sex, the flag) to a product.

Media messages can be manipulated to enhance emotional impact : Movies and TV shows use a variety of filmic techniques (like camera angles, framing, reaction shots, quick cuts, special effects, lighting tricks, music, and sound effects) to reinforce the messages in the script. Dramatic graphic design can do the same for magazine ads or websites.

Media effects are subtle : Few people believe everything they see and hear in the media. Few people rush out to the store immediately after seeing an ad. Playing a violent video game won't automatically turn you into a murderer. The effects of media are more subtle than this, but because we are so immersed in the media environment, the effects are still significant.

Media effects are complex : Media messages directly influence us as individuals, but they also affect our families and friends, our communities, and our society. So some media effects are indirect. We must consider both direct and indirect effects to understand media's true influence.

Media convey ideological and value messages: Ideology and values are usually conveyed in the subtext. Two examples include news reports (besides covering an issue or event, news reports often reinforce assumptions about power and authority) and advertisements (besides selling particular products, advertisements almost always promote the values of a consumer society).

We all create media : May be you don't have the skills and resources to make a blockbuster movie or publish a daily newspaper. But just about anyone can snap a photo, write a letter or sing a song. And new technology has allowed millions of people to make media-email, websites, videos, newsletters, and more — easily and cheaply. Creating your own media messages is an important part of media literacy.

Advanced Concepts

Our media system reflects the power dynamics in our society : People and institutions with money, privilege, influence, and power can more easily create media messages and distribute them to large numbers of people. People without this access are often shut out of the media system.

Most media are controlled by commercial interests : In the United States, the marketplace largely determines what we see on television, what we hear on the radio, what we read in newspapers or magazines. As we use media, we should always be alert to the self-interest of corporate media makers. Are they concerned about your health? Do they care if you're smart or well informed? Are they interested in creating active participants in our society and culture, or merely passive consumers of their products, services, and ideas?

Media monopolies reduce opportunities to participate in decision making : When a few huge media corporations control access to information, they have the power to make some information widely available and privilege those perspectives that serve their interests, while marginalizing or even censoring other information and perspectives. This affects our ability to make good decisions about our own lives, and reduces opportunities to participate in making decisions about our government and society.

Changing the media system is a justice issue : Our media system produces lots of negative, demeaning imagery, values and ideas. It renders many people invisible. It provides too little funding and too few outlets for people without money, privilege, influence, and power to tell their stories.

We can change our media system : More and more people are realizing how important it is to have a media system that is open to new people and new perspectives, that elevates human values over commercial values, and that serves human needs in the 21st century. All over the world, people are taking action to reform our media system and create new alternatives.

Media literate youth and adults are media activists : As we learn how to access, analyze and interpret media messages, and as we create our own media, we recognize the limitations and problems of our current media system. Media literacy is a great foundation for advocacy and activism for a better media system.

A NEW ROLE FOR LIBRARY PROFESSIONALS

Library media professionals are logical coordinators for inquiry-based media literacy education efforts. To call attention to that role, I propose a new job title. Imagine that every school had a "Chief Inquiry Officer." The primary responsibility of the people working in the library would be to promote active inquiry in every facet of school life. Media literacy is an expansion of traditional literacy, and books are media (yes, just like electronic or screen-based technologies, books are media). The Chief Inquiry Officer's hunt for opportunities to integrate inquiry might begin by looking at instruction involving books and reading. When students come to story time knowing that they will be asked, "What in the story (or in your experience) makes you think that?" they understand that they will be expected to give evidence based answers, or in more developmentally appropriate terms, to name the specific clues they are using to form their ideas. Like the anticipation of the question from Santa, this expectation changes the way that children look and listen, drawing their attention to important details in the media document. Ask the question enough times and children will begin to ask themselves and one another.

MEDIA INVENTORY

One simple way library media specialists can recognize and respond to media in the lives of our students is to survey their media tastes, habits, and preferences. This simple instrument can often generate rich quantitative and qualitative data as students reflect on and describe the type of media they are exposed to each day, their personal program and media preferences, as well as the crucial context in which they are exposed to these messages (alone in their bedroom, viewing with siblings, with or without parental supervision etc.). Among other potentially valuable outcomes of such a survey is the insight it gives us into their favorite media and genres (film, TV, music, graphic novels, magazines, video games) and the opportunity to help them further examine and expand these interests.

BEYOND A SKILLS-BASED APPROACH

Thus far it has developed a skills-based approach to new media literacies that applies across all media, relying on media-neutral terms. This has the advantages of generality and historical continuity, focusing on interpretative skills long valued in Western culture. In a media environment characterized by rapid change, a pan-media definition of literacy is surely practical. But problematically, this also implies that the ability to access, analyze, evaluate and create communication content is common across the book, television, the internet. If, instead, it seems that new media, especially online media, represent a radically new information and communication environment, then an account of a literate engagement with this environment must encompass the technological interface as well as the user's skills. In other words, to focus solely on questions of skill or ability neglects the textually and technology that mediates communication. In consequence, it unwittingly supports a Universalist, cognitive framework, thereby neglecting in turn the historical and cultural contingency of both media and the social knowledge processes that interpret them. Visualize someone reading a book, watching television, playing a computer game, searching the World Wide Web – evidently there is not only skill involved but also an interpretative relationship with a complex, symbolically-encoded, technologically mediated text. I suggest that, as people engage with a diversity of ICTs, we must develop an account of literacies in the plural, defined through their relations with different media rather than defined independently of them. In the language of audience research, the conceptual shift is from an exclusive focus on the viewer to a focus on the interaction between text and reader or between inscribed and actual viewer/user.

INDIVIDUAL AND INSTITUTIONAL USES OF LITERACY

As we move into an information society, is media literacy increasingly part of citizenship, a key means, a right even, by which citizens participate in society? Or is literacy primarily a means of realizing ideals of self-actualization, cultural expression and aesthetic creativity? Will these goals be subordinated to the use of media literacy to achieve the competitive cultural and economic advantages vital in a globalized, information society? This seems plausible insofar as media literacy, in the UK at least, is part of a package of measures to lighten top-down media regulation by devolving responsibility for media use from the state to individuals, a move which can be interpreted either as 'empowering' or, more critically, as part of a Foucauldian shift from centralized government to individual governance (Foucault, 1991).

Perhaps even these economic goals will be undermined by the reproduction of the divisive standards and values of the established cultural elite? Of the research task developed in this paper, namely to extend our understanding of access, analysis, critical evaluation and content creation from familiar to new media, interestingly it is the latter two which have proved more contentious; yet these are the most crucial to the democratic agenda. Only if these are firmly foregrounded in a definition of media literacy will people be positioned not merely as selective, receptive and accepting but also as participating, critical; in short, not merely as consumers but also as citizens.

CONCLUSION

Media Literacy gives individuals power over their culture and thus enables people to create their own meanings and identities and to shape and transform the material and social conditions of their culture and society. Many critical educators have been promoting these goals, including Len Masterman, who proposed that media education aim at critical autonomy, empowering students to be independently critical. Robert Ferguson (2001) suggested that our relationships with media are not autonomous; rather, they depend on taking positions related to social contexts. Since we are always taking sides, Ferguson called for critical solidarity, which he described as "a means by which we acknowledge the social dimensions of our thinking and analysis. It is also a means through which we may develop our skills of analysis and relative autonomy". Media literacy offers an excellent framework to teach critical solidarity and the skills that can challenge the social construction of ICT, from hypertext to video games. Schools must change the way they teach, by instructing students to become empowered to analyze and use media to express their opinions in critical solidarity with the world around them.

The basis of media literacy is that all messages are constructed, and when education begins with this understanding of the social construction of knowledge the literacy process can expand critical inquiry into multiple forms of ICT, including television programmes, Internet, advertising, artificial intelligence, biotechnology, and books. Carmen Luke (2000) wrote "unless educators take a lead in developing appropriate pedagogies for these new electronic media and forms of communication, corporate experts will be the ones to determine how people will learn, what they learn, and what constitutes literacy". Media literacy offers the tools and framework to help students become subjects in the process of deconstructing injustices, expressing their own voices, and struggling to create a better society.

REFERENCES

1. Ang, I. (2002). On the politics of empirical audience research. In M. G. Durham & D. M. Kellner (Eds.), Media and cultural studies key works (pp. 177_/197). Malden: Blackwell.
2. Aufderheide, P. (Ed.) (1993). Media Literacy: A report of the national leadership conference on media literacy. Aspen, CO.: Aspen Institute.
3. Bagdikian, B. H. (2004). The new media monopoly. Boston: Beacon Press.
4. Barthes, R. (1998). Mythologies . New York: Hill and Wang.
5. Buckingham, D. (2000). After the Death of Childhood: Growing Up in the Age of Electronic Media. Cambridge: Polity Press.
6. Castells, M. (2002). The Internet Galaxy: Reflections on the internet, business, and society. Oxford: Oxford University Press.
7. Dewey, J. (1997). Democracy and education. New York: Free Press. (Original work published 1916).
8. Facer, K., Sutherland, R., Furlong, R., and Furlong, J. (2001). What's the Point of Using Computers? The Development of Young People's Computer Expertise in the Home. New Media and Society.

9. Fleming, D. (1993). Media teaching. Oxford: Basil Blackwell.

10. Fornas, J., Klein, K., Ladendorf, M., Sunden, J., and Sveningsson, M. (2002). *Digital* Borderlands: Cultural studies of identity and interactivity on the internet. NY: Peter Lang.

11. "Great transitions: Preparing Adolescents for a New Century." Carnegie Council on Adolescent Development. New York: 1995.

12. Hartley, J. (2002). Communication, Cultural and Media Studies: The key concepts. London: Routledge.

13. Iser, W. (1980). Interaction between text and reader. In S. R. Suleiman & I. Crosman (Eds.), The Reader in the Text: Essays on audience and interpretation. Princeton: Princeton University Press.

14. Kubey, R. (Ed.). (1997) (Ed.). Media Literacy in the Information Age. NJ, New Brunswick: Transaction Publishers.

15. Luke, C. (1994). Feminist pedagogy and critical media literacy. Journal of Communication Inquiry.

16. Rice, R. (2002). Primary Issues in Internet use: Access, Civic and Community Involvement, and Social Interaction and Expression. In L. L. Lievrouw, S (Ed.), Handbook of New Media: Social Shaping and Consequences of ICTs. London.

17. Singer, D. G., and Singer, J. L. (Eds.) (2001). Handbook of Children and the Media. Thousand Oaks, Cal.: Sage.

18. Street, B. (1995). Social Literacies: Critical approaches to literacy in development, ethnography and education. London: Longman.

19. Tyner, K. (1998). Literacy in a Digital World. Mahwah NJ: Lawrence Erlbaum Associates.

20. Warnick, B. (2002). Critical Literacy in a Digital Era: Technology, rhetoric, and the public Interest. Mahway, New Jersey: Lawrence Erlbaum Associates.

20

Review of Information Literacy with Reference to India

Saikat Soren

ABSTRACT

Tremendous developments in information and communication technology have forced us to be proficient in information literacy. Information literacy is absolute necessity to tap the enormous amount of information generated every moment for the development of any nation. The paper analyzes the objective, standard and need for information literacy internationally and particularly in Indian context for life long learning.

Keywords: Information, Information literacy, Information literate, Information literacy standards

INTRODUCTION

With rapid development in information technology new information is being generated all the time. In recent times information results in generation of wealth. A nation is considered rich because it has access to accurate and up-to-date information, which in turn results in generation of more information. Expenditure on Research and Development has become a major criterion for measurement of development of a particular country.

Developed countries across the globe spend huge amount on R&D as compared to the developing nations. It is a massive challenge at all levels to utilize the generated information effectively. Some nations are overburdened with excess information while others are starved of quality information. As a result, it is necessary to develop the skills to use the information in a proper way so that it enhances the overall development of a nation. This type of learning outcome is referred to as 'information literacy'.

The demand for information has increased tremendously from common man to subject specialists in recent decades. Almost everyone needs information for some purpose or the other. Therefore knowledge about information itself becomes very crucial in the present context. The word "information" is derived from the Latin words "Forma" and "Formatio", which convey more or less the same meaning. In fact information is the act of informing the fact. Therefore the concept of information is taken to the meaning as a collection of facts or other data. It is also an assemblage of data in a comprehensible form recorded on paper or some other medium, and capable of communication.

The first public use of the term 'Information Literacy" occurred in 1974 when Paul Zurkowski, president of the Information Industry Association, introduced the concept of "Information Literacy" in a proposal submitted to the National Commission on Libraries and Information Science (NCLIS). The word "Literacy" has been linked with cultural literacy, information literacy, library literacy and technological literacy and recently with digital literacy and multimedia literacy also. Information literacy is the ability to identify, evaluate organize and use the information judiciously. The American Library Association defines Information Literacy as "a set of abilities requiring individuals to recognize when information is in need and have the ability to locate, evaluate and use effectively the needed information". ALA also states that" Information

Literacy is a survival skill in the information age". Information literacy forms the basis for lifelong learning. It is common to all disciplines, to all learning environment, and to all levels of education. The Chartered Institute of Library and Information Professionals, defines "Information literacy is knowing when information is needed and have the ability to locate, evaluate, and use effectively the needed information." (American Library Association. Presidential Committee on Information Literacy. Final Report. The American Association of School Librarians (AASL), a precursor in the Information Literacy field, and the Association for Educational Communications and Technologies state that "information literacy is the ability to find and use information- is the keystone of lifelong learning." (Byerly/Brodie,1999). Users "should have both information gathering strategies and the critical thinking skills to select, discard, synthesize, and present information in new ways to solve real life problems". (Byerly/Brodie,1999). The Association of College and Research Libraries defines "information literacy" as the set of skills needed to find, retrieve, analyze and use information. In other words, information literacy is the ability to access, organize and use information in order to learn, problem-solve and make decision in formal and informal learning contexts, at work, at home and in educational settings.

The world economy and education scene depends entirely on the information it receives. Information is an important input to technological and scientific change as well. Information posses challenges to students, workers and citizens in all walks of life. Information literacy requirements can be divided in five stages starting from childhood, student life, young age, working professionals and post retirement age. Though information requirement is different at different stages of life yet the need and importance of information remains the same. People have to validate and access its reliability and accuracy in this age of information overload. Mere ability of surfing the internet does not make oneself information literate. Literacy has often been seen as a prerequisite for economic growth, social mobility and political stability. Ill-literacy by contrast, has frequently been related to increased poverty, higher crime rates, unemployment, political volatility and economic stagnation.

The need for information literacy is felt due to enormous increase in information resulting both in printed and electronic form. The tendency of humans to be satisfied with easily accessible information regardless of its authentication created a way for information literacy. Information literacy instructions has originated from "bibliographic instruction" or "user education" and has become a vital part of academic and other types of libraries. Information literacy can be of immense help dealing with misinformation, inaccurate information, partial information, complex information and most importantly fabricated information which are common on the internet. Librarians play a vital role in training their clients to independently find, retrieve, analyze and use information effectively and efficiently. The ALA 1998 states "To be information literate, a person must be able to recognize when information is needed and have the ability to locate, evaluate, and use effectively the needed information. The information literate persons are those who have learned how to learn".

An information literate person is one who has the following attributes:

- Has the ability to recognize accurate and complete information which can be used for quality decision making.
- Capability to stress on the need for accurate and timely information.
- Capability to formulate questions based on information needs.

- Ability to locate potential sources of information.
- Ability to formulate successful search strategies.
- Access sources of information including computer based and other technologies.
- Analytical mind to evaluate information.
- Capacity to organize information for practical applications.
- Integrates new information into an existing body of knowledge, and use information in critical thinking and problem solving.
- Ability to determine the extent of information needed.
- Capability to incorporate selected information into one's knowledge base; and
- Ability to use information effectively to accomplish specific purpose.

NEED FOR INFORMATION LITERACY

Information literacy is a key component of and contributor to lifelong learning. Since higher education institutions vary widely in mission and student body. Information Literacy Programs are to be designed, tailored to meet specific needs of the user rather than a prescribed set of criteria. All the academic institutions are witnessing a rapid growth in computer networking and the use of computerized databases to access information in their libraries. In fact, most academic libraries today are "hybrid libraries", adding the new e-library features to their traditional library services. Information literacy is therefore essential for users to cope with new online services and provide a competitive advantage to themselves and the wider society. Information literacy programs need to be implemented from the very school level to college and university level gradually thereby advocating lifelong learning. Without training it is difficult to use electronic information sources effectively. It is necessary to have requisite skills to obtain relevant information quickly and effectively from electronic sources and become what is referred to as information literate.

OBJECTIVES OF INFORMATION LITERACY

- Determine student's information literacy skills in order to provide more appropriate service.
- To acquaint the users with the academic power of Internet and Intranet.
- To acquaint users with the use of various search techniques enabling them to retrieve relevant information.
- To be able to evaluate, organize, interpret and communicate information at all formats.
- To establish a direct interaction between users and library professionals.
- To enable learners develop systematic method of searching for information related to their area of interests.
- To acquaint users with the availability with the wide range of information sources to meet their specific needs.
- The users would develop database searching techniques for accessing both web-based and other non-print databases.
- They would be able to use current awareness methods to keep up-to-date with the published literature.
- They would be able to use national and international academic networks for getting information.
- They would be able use discussion forums, list servers, online chat services and blogs for obtaining and disseminating information.
- They would be able to use local library network for obtaining documents through inter-library loan and

document delivery services.

- They would be able to compare and critically evaluate information obtained from various sources.
- They would be able to cite bibliographic references in their academic projects, papers, articles, reports or thesis; and
- They would be able to construct a personal bibliographic system.

Various standards have been advocated for Information literacy to be globally accepted. Some of these are discussed below:

ACRL (AMERICAN COLLEGE AND RESEARCH LIBRARIES) INFORMATION LITERACY STANDARDS

Standard One

The information literate student determines the nature and extent of the information needed.

Performance Indicators

- The information literate student defines and articulates the need for information.
- The information literate student identifies a variety of types and formats of potential sources for information.
- The information literate student considers the costs and benefits of acquiring the needed information.
- The information literate student revaluates the nature and extent of the information need.

Standard Two

The information literate student accesses needed information effectively and efficiently.

Performance Indicators

- The information literate student selects the most appropriate investigative methods or information retrieval systems for accessing needed information.

- The information literate student constructs and implements effectively designed search strategies.
- The information literate student retrieves information online or in person using a variety of methods.
- The information literate student refines the search strategy if necessary.
- The information literate student extracts records and manages the information and its sources.

Standard Three

The information literate student evaluates information and its sources and incorporates selected information into his or her knowledge base and value system.

Performance Indicators

- The information literate student summarizes the main ideas to be extracted from the information gathered.
- The information literate student articulates and applies initial criteria for evaluating both the information and its sources.
- The information literate student synthesizes main ideas to construct new concepts.
- The information literate student compares new knowledge with prior knowledge to determine the value-added, contradictions, or other unique characteristics of the information.
- The information literate student determines whether the new knowledge has an impact on the individual's value system and takes steps to reconcile differences.
- The information literate student validates understanding and interpretation of the information

through discourse with other individuals, subject area experts, and or practitioners.

- The information literate student determines whether the initial query should be revised.

Standard Four

The information literate student, individually or as a member of a group, uses information effectively to accomplish a specific purpose.

Performance Indicators

- The information literate student applies new and prior information to the planning and creation of a particular product or performance.
- The information literate student revises the development process for the product or performance.
- The information literate student communicates the product or performance effectively to others.

Standard Five

The information literate student understands many of the economic legal and social issues surrounding the access and use of information ethically and legally.

Performance Indicators

- The information literate student understands many of the ethical, legal and socioeconomic issues surrounding information and information technology.
- The information literate student follows laws, regulations, institutional policies, and etiquette related to the access and use of information resources.
- The information literate student acknowledges the use of information sources in communicating the product or performance.

STANDARDS IFLA INFORMATION LITERACY

The IFLA standards are grouped under the three basic Information Literacy components.

1. *Access* : The users access information effectively and efficiently.
   - Decides to do something to find the information.
   - Express and defines the information need.
   - Initiates the search process.
   - Location of information.
   - Identifies and evaluates potential sources of information.
   - Develops search strategies.
   - Access the selected information sources.
   - Selects and retrieves the located information.
2. *Evaluation* : The user evaluates information critically and competently assessment of information.
   - Analyses and examines, extracting information.
   - Generalizes and interprets information.
   - Selects and synthesizes information.
   - Evaluates accuracy and relevance of the retrieved information.

   Organization of information
   - Arrange and categorize information.
   - Groups and organizes retrieved information.
   - Determines the best and most useful information.
3. *Use* : The user uses information accurately and creatively.

   Use of information
   - Finds new ways to communicate, present and use information.
   - Applies the retrieved information.

- Learn for personal knowledge.
- Present the information product.

Communicate and ethical use of information.

- Understands ethical use of information.
- Respects legal use of information.
- Communicate the learning product with acknowledgement of intellectual property.
- Uses the relevant acknowledgement style standards.

Library and information professionals aim to ensure all persons throughout the world to have the same opportunity to participate in the information society without any regard to physical, mental, regional, social or cultural barriers. Information literacy include computer literacy, digital literacy, hyper literacy, information technology literacy, interactive literacy, internet literacy, library literacy, media literacy, network literacy, oral literacy and also virtual literacy. All these literacy need to be developed and maintained throughout life by library professionals. Information literacy recognizes that the library professionals, educators and users need to work at their ability to be information literate over a lifetime.

OTHER "LITERACY" CONCEPTS RELATED TO INFORMATION

Information literacy is linked with other types of related literacy, but it should be differentiated from them, especially from information technology, media literacy, digital literacy, network or Internet Literacy.

Basic Literacy

From the perspective of education, "basic literacy" means the traditional literacy of learning how to read, to write, and to perform numeric calculations and operations. Basic literacy is generally confined within the basic and secondary formal education setting in public or private schools, but sometimes it also learned at home or community centers.

Visual Literacy

Visual literacy is defined as the ability "to understand and use images, including the ability to think, learn, and express oneself in terms of images".(Braden & Hortin, 1982, 41) Visual literacy may be divided into three categories.

- Visual learning
- Visual thinking, and
- Visual communication (Randhawa & Coffman, 1978)

Visual learning refers to the "the acquisition and construction of knowledge as a result of interaction with visual phenomenon" (Moore & Dwyer: 1994: 107). Visual thinking involves the ability to "organize mental images around shapes, lines, colors, textures and compositions" (Wileman: 1980: 13). Visual communication is defined as "using visual symbols to express ideas and convey meaning".(Moore & Dwyer: 1994: 109). Visual thinking and visual learning are coming to a person more easily than visual communication.

Computer Literacy

The knowledge and skills necessary to understand information and communication technology, including hardware, the software, system, networks (both local area networks and the Internet), and all the other components of computer and telecommunication systems.

Network Literacy

Network Literacy is closely related with the term "Computer Literacy". A person who wants to locate, search and access information from the World Wide web must be network literate. McClure states that a network literate person is one who:

- "Has an awareness of the range and use of global networked information resources and services.
- Has an understanding of the system by which

networked information is generated, managed and made available.

- Can retrieve specific types of information from the network using a range of information discovery tools.
- Can manipulate networked information by combining it with other resources, enhancing it, or otherwise increasing the value of information for particular situations.
- Can use networked information to analyze and resolve both work and personal related decisions and obtain services that will enhance their overall quality of life.
- Has an understanding of the role and uses of networked information in problem solving in performing basic life activities". (McClure: 1993: 160)

Media Literacy

The knowledge and skills necessary to understand all the mediums and formats in which data, information and knowledge are created, stored, communicated and presented, i.e. print, newspapers and journals, magazines, radio, television broadcasts, cable, CD-ROM, DVD, mobile telephones, PDF text formats, & JPEG format for photo and graphics.

NEED FOR INFORMATION LITERACY IN INDIA

- To develop information literacy skills in learners.
- To become independent learners without depending solely on institutions to guide them locating sources of information
- To make the common people part of IT revolution and help them reap benefits of the initiatives of the Govt. of India.
- The young population's likings of the World Wide Web are to be used fully to promote information literacy.

- To provide knowledge and motivate people acquire IT ability; and
- Help librarians develop, assess and improve their information literacy programs.

INFORMATION LITERACY: INDIAN SCENARIO

Analyzing the present educational system and financial constraints in higher education in our country, it is felt that highest importance be given to information literacy programs. With developments in ICT India cannot lag behind the world and hence to tap unlimited potential of the technologies, the Govt. of India has taken a few initiatives to aid its people bear the fruits of life long learning through its programs and agencies. A few of these are discussed hereunder.

The Government of India has established National Knowledge Commission in June 2005 with the following objectives:

- To prepare the education system to meet the knowledge challenges of the 21st centaury and to increase India's competitive advantage in the field of knowledge.
- Promote creation of knowledge in Science and Technology laboratories.
- Improve the management of institutions engaged in intellectual property rights.
- Promote knowledge applications in agriculture and industry.
- Promotes the use of knowledge capabilities in making government an effective, transparent and accountable service provider to the citizen and promote widespread sharing of knowledge to maximize public benefit.

The National Knowledge Commission (NKC) has five distinct focus areas:

- *Access to knowledge*: Providing access to knowledge resources through strengthening library and information infrastructure and networks, promoting and adopting open access literature, open courseware and open source software.
- *Knowledge Concepts* : Nurturing intellectual capabilities and enhancing professional skills, including information handling skills of youth.
- *Knowledge Creation* : Making self-sufficiency in knowledge creation; strengthening indigenous research capabilities in science, technology and medicine areas: generating knowledge for social development.
- *Knowledge Application*: Deriving maximum benefits from intellectual assets, applying knowledge in fields like agriculture, industry, health, education, etc. and
- *Knowledge services* : Making governance and government functionaries more accountable, transparent, efficient and sensitive to the cause of common man.

UGC-INFONET

The University Grants Commission (UGC) has initiated a program called The UGC-Infonet E-Journals Consortium to provide online access to electronic journals and databases in all disciplines to the universities in India. The program aims at increasing accessibility of electronic resources to the universities. Its prime objective is to mitigate the severe shortage of periodicals faced by the university libraries.

The salient features of UGC- Infonet are as follows:

- Scalable Architecture to grow from Universities to affiliated Colleges.
- Nation-wide Terrestrial Backbone using Fiber Optics links.

- Integrated Satellite WAN supporting broadband and SCPC VSAT technology.
- Comprehensive Network Management Systems for overall monitoring of the network, down to each and every device.
- Linkage with other academic and research networks all over the world.
- Data security and virus protection using firewalls and Intrusion Detection Systems.
- Dedicated Data Centre for Web hosting, e-journals and Mail Boxes.
- Mirror sites spread all over the country for content hosting.
- Broadband Multimedia and Video Channels for Distance Learning.

INFLIBNET

It is another program of the UGC started in the year 1996 with the aim of linking all universities, colleges, R&D laboratories, institutes of national importance, etc. in the country through their libraries by computer networks. The objective is to make all the available bibliographic and non-bibliographic information resources in the country accessible and usable to any user from any place in the country. The INFLIBNET is a cooperative venture where all its participants join hands to derive mutual benefit of resource sharing. It tries to avoid unnecessary duplication of costly journals, indexing and abstracting periodicals and other documents. The main objective of the INFLIBNET Centre is to provide information services to academic and research community in the country. For this the Centre has subscribed to some important databases and e-journals to cater to the needs of academic community. This centre catalogues the Internet resources and provides online access to e-resources. The Centre also enables access to full Text journals and e-books through N-LIST program. This centre provides CD-ROM based bibliographical information services, content page service STN International, Database Service, document delivery service. It promotes SOUL, organizes Internet resources and also organizes workshops for the librarians in both basic and advanced level there by enabling life long learning.

CONCLUSION

Information literacy is the only answer to the information overload faced by the entire world. In a developing country like India capability to locate, identify, evaluate and use accurate and appropriate information within legal boundaries from the jungle of information is the key to the success. Therefore study of information literacy is of highest importance in the present context.

REFERENCES

1. Anderson, Gregory L. On My Mind: The Joy of Information Literacy. American Library Association. American Libraries, Vol. 32, No. 8 (Sep., 2001), p.43. (Available at *http://www.jstor.org/stable/25646033*). Accessed on 15/04/2015

2. Bhatt, (R. K.). Information Literacy Models and Competencies. Development Initiatives in India. Branding and Marketing and Strategic Direction, Best Practices and Performance Evaluation of Special Library Services, 2011.(Available at *units.sla.org/chapter/cas/R%20K%20Bhatt.doc*). Accessed on 20/04/2015

3. B. K. Vishala and Bhandi, M. K. 4th International Convention. CALIBER-2006, Gulbarga,2-4February, 2006. (Available at *ir.inflibnet.ac.in/bitstream/1944/565/1/22%28cal%2006%29.pdf*). Accessed on 18/04/2015

4. Das, Anup Kumar. Library Advocacy in India in the Light of Education for Sustainable Development-Perspectives of an Emerging Economy. World Library and Information Congress: 76th IFLA General Conference and Assembly. 10-15 August 2010, Gothenberg, Sweden. (Available at *http://*

www.ifla.org/en/ifla76.) Accessed on 23/04/2015)

5. Gedam, Pranall B.& Agashe, Ajay T. Information Literacy Competencies and Programmes in India. (Available at *crl.du.ac.in/ical09/papers/index_files/ical-88_100_227_2_RV.pdf*). Accessed on 17/04/2015

6. Ghosh, S. B. and Das, Anup Kumar. Information Literacy Initiatives in India with Special Reference to Emerging Knowledge Economy. Published in the proceedings of the International Conference on Information Literacy (ICIL 2006), June 14-15, 2006; Kuala Lumpur, Malaysia. Hosted by Faculty of Information Management, Universiti Teknologi MARA with the Librarians Association of Malaysia. (Available at *conference.ifla.org/past-wlic/2010/87-das-en.pdf*). Accessed on 20/04/2015

7. Information Literacy Competency Standards for Higher Education by the Association of College and Research libraries (ACRL). Chicago, Illinois, 2000. (Available at *http://www.ala.org/arcl/standards/informationliteracy competency.*) Accessed on 23/04/2015)

8. Julien, Heidi. Education for Information Literacy Instruction: A Global Perspective. Journal of Education for Library and Information Science, Vol. 46, No. 3 (Summer 2005), pp. 210-16. Association for Library and Information Science Education (ALISE). Available at (*http://www.jastor.org/stable/40323845*). Accessed on 15/04/2014

9. Lau, JesuAs. Guidelines on Information Literacy for Lifelong Learning. IFLA.(Available *at www.ifla.org/files/assets/information-literacy/publications/ifla-guidelines-en.pdf*) Accessed on 17/04/2015

10. Marcum, James W. Rethinking Information Literacy. The Library Quarterly, Vol. 72. No 1 (Jan., 2002), pp.1-26. The University of Chicago Press. Available at (*http://www.jstor.org/stable/4309580*). Accessed on 15/04/2015

11. Mestre, Lori S. et al. Learning objects as Tools for teaching Information Literacy Outline: a survey of librarian usage. College and research Libraries. (Available at *citeseerx.ist.psu.edu/viewdoc/download?doi=10.1.1222.9041&rep=rep1&type=pdf*). Accessed on 23/04/2015

12. Roberts, Peter. Knowledge, Information and Literacy. International review of Education. Springer. Available at (*http://www.jstor.org/stable/3445260*). Accessed on 15/04/2015

13. Singh, Neena. Information literacy in India and Germany-university libraries as activators of lifelong learning.(Available at *eprints.rclis.org/3858/1/Singh_Klingenberg_Information-literacy-in-India-and-Germany.pdf*). Accessed on 17/04/2015

14. The SCONUL Seven Pillars of Information Literacy: Core Model for Higher Education. SCONUL Working Group on Information Literacy. April 2011. (Available at *http://www.sconul.ac.uk/groups/information_literacy/seven_pillars.html*). Accessed on 23/04/2015)

15. Zurkowski, P G. The information service environment relationships and priorities. 1974. National Commission on Libraries and Information Services, Washington DC.(Available at *files.eric.ed.gov/fulltext/ED100391.pdf*). Accessed on 16/04/2015